HEAVENWARD

A child's book of the Catholic Religion

by

E. T. W. BRANSCOMBE

Author of "Young Children to Christ"

Illustrated by
CLARE DAWSON

ST. AUGUSTINE ACADEMY PRESS
HOMER GLEN, ILLINOIS

This book was originally published in 1941
by Pax House.

This facsimile edition reprinted in 2019
by St. Augustine Academy Press
based on the 1958 edition by Dacre Press.

ISBN: 978-1-64051-105-7

TO EVERY CHILD WHO READS THIS BOOK

My dear Child,

I expect that you have at some time been on a journey—perhaps a long journey. If you have, it has been necessary to find out the best possible way, so that you didn't spend a long time going in the wrong direction and then had to waste time getting back on to the right road. This book may, I hope, help you to choose the right road and keep to it on the most important journey of all.

With love from

THE PRIEST WHO WROTE THIS BOOK.

TABLE OF HEADINGS

GOD AND ME

THERE was once a time when nobody had ever thought of you! I wonder how old you are—nine?—ten?—eleven?—or perhaps you are nearly twelve? Well, twelve years ago nobody had ever imagined that YOU could be YOU! Isn't it funny to think that there ever was a time when we were not alive, at school, playing our games and going out with our friends?

But SOMEONE did know about us, and thought about us as well, long, long before we came into the world. That SOME-ONE was GOD. God knew all about us, just as He knows all about us now. And

ME·12 YEARS AGO

ME·9, 10, OR 11 YEARS AGO

at last, in HIS OWN GOOD TIME God made us, with a tiny body and, most important of all, a *Soul* which cannot die; and He gave us as a Special Present to our mothers and fathers to look after for Him.

So we started to be tiny babies.

If any one were to ask you, 'Who made you?' you will know what to answer, won't you?

GOD MADE ME.

ABOUT GROWING UP

I do not expect that you can remember being a tiny baby—people can't as a rule, but we do know that we do not stay 'little babies' for always. It would be rather funny 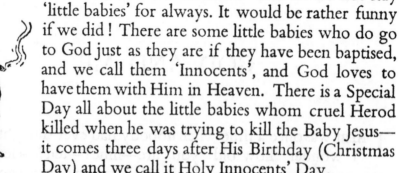 if we did! There are some little babies who do go to God just as they are if they have been baptised, and we call them 'Innocents', and God loves to have them with Him in Heaven. There is a Special Day all about the little babies whom cruel Herod killed when he was trying to kill the Baby Jesus—it comes three days after His Birthday (Christmas Day) and we call it Holy Innocents' Day.

But most of us have grown up; and most of us grow up more and more until we become men and women and go out to work. We all grow up to do something. Some children grow up to drive trains, to be soldiers, sailors or airmen, or clerks in offices and people say, 'Oh! he's something in the City', and, instead of going on sitting in desks at school and being taught any

more, some children grow up to be teachers themselves. Of course, some children grow up to be monks or nuns, and, most wonderful of all, some little boys grow up to be priests. But most boys and girls grow up and get married and have homes of their own.

What are you going to be when you grow up? Perhaps you don't know yet; but God knows. I expect He will tell you one day; and He may even have told you already. But you can be sure that He has His plan for you.

★   ★   ★

God never does anything without knowing why He does it. After all, even WE know why we do things. If we go into a sweetshop, we know WHY we go—it is to buy SWEETS and NOT boots! God knows exactly why He made you. He made you for Himself!

FOR HIS GLORY THEY ARE AND WERE CREATED ('created' means 'made out of nothing'). These words come from the Bible.

God has put us into this world so that we can know Him, love Him and serve Him (that means 'do things for Him')—and God loves us so very much that He says to us, 'My Child, when you have tried hard to know, love and serve Me on Earth, then I will take you to be with Me in Heaven, where you will be with My Angels and Saints, and specially with the Blessed Mother of My Son Jesus, in wonderful happiness for ever. And if you will try, then I will always help you'.

You will remember, then, that if someone says to you, 'Why did God make you?' you will be able to answer quite easily:

GOD MADE ME TO KNOW, LOVE AND SERVE HIM HERE ON EARTH AND TO BE HAPPY WITH HIM FOR EVER IN HEAVEN.

All that is the reason why God made us. Don't you think that we ought to try our very best to do what God wants us to do? Suppose you were to make a book-case or to knit a scarf for a friend. You would do it so that your friend could keep his books in it, or wear it. But you would be very sad if you found your friend using your gift to put coal in, or to keep the cat warm at night.

You know, God is sometimes very sad when He sees His children doing things they were not made to do; or not doing the things they were made to do. God made us to know, love and serve Him. Let us try to do this just because God loves us, and wants us to love Him too. You will learn how God wants us to know Him, love Him and serve Him if you will read right through to the end of this book. So don't stop half-way, will you? Or don't only look at the pictures.

SAINT RICHARD'S PRAYER

St RICHARD WROTE THIS PRAYER

O HOLY JESUS, Most Merciful Re-
deemer,
Friend and Brother,
May I KNOW Thee more clearly,
LOVE Thee more dearly and
FOLLOW Thee more nearly.

ANOTHER PRAYER

Teach me, dear Jesus,
To KNOW Thee better,
To LOVE Thee more,
And to SERVE Thee more faithfully,
That with Blessed Mary and all the Saints
I may be happy with Thee for ever in Heaven.
Amen.

WE CAN PRAY IT TOO

BLESSED BE GOD

BECOMING FRIENDS WITH GOD

How do we get to know people? Suppose you were always to meet a boy as you go to school. Every day you see him going in the opposite direction to you. There he is going along on the other side of the road. You get to know him ever so well BY SIGHT. He is short and fat, he has thick glasses and a squint! He has long black hair coming almost to his shoulders, and a crooked nose! These are all things you know ABOUT him. But you cannot say that you KNOW him, any more than you can say that you know the King and Queen or the Royal Princesses, although you do know quite a lot about them.

How would you get to know him properly? I expect he is much nicer than he looks; people often are! There is only one way, and that is by talking with him—not just talking TO him, but also by listening to what he has to say to you—and, of course, the more you are with him the better you will get to know him, until you are really friends with him.

* * *

We get to know God, to love Him and serve Him in the same sort of way. We learn about God first of all—by HEARING ABOUT Him, and, perhaps, by READING ABOUT Him too. We shall never know God really well if we only hear and read ABOUT Him. But when we have got to know something about God then we talk with Him. We call talking with God PRAYING.

PRAYING

To pray—that is to talk with God—sounds quite an easy thing to do, doesn't it? I expect that you have been taught to say your prayers every morning and every night, and you probably do that quite well. But you know how easy it is to forget, or to say them without thinking what you are saying—so it isn't quite as easy as one would think, is it? It does mean that you have to try really hard. When you were a tiny child—much smaller than you are now—I expect your mother taught you to say some very little babyish prayers—something like 'Gentle Jesus, meek and mild, look on me, Thy little child'—and very nice too for a baby of four or five. But you are growing up, and, of course, your prayers have to grow up with you. Some people get into the habit of always saying the same prayers they said as small children—and they never go on learning how to pray better. It is as if a grown-up person never tried to count higher than five and, when she has to count her stitches in knitting, has to count up to five and then start at one again!

There was once a priest who went to visit a large, fat, red-faced old man—and the old chap thought that he ought to say something to the priest that he would like to hear. So he said, 'Well, Father, I always say my prayers.'

'Oh!' said the priest. 'What prayers do you say?'

'Ah!' said the red-faced fat man. 'I always say that little prayer my mother taught me, which starts, "We are but little children small"'! Of course he had never learned to pray as he grew older, and he certainly wasn't a 'little child' any more. We have to learn how to pray just as we have to learn how to do anything else.

* * *

Now the first thing to remember is that we don't have to see God with our eyes in order to speak with Him. In fact, we cannot see God at all in this life on earth because—

GOD IS A SPIRIT

But we can speak with Him anywhere and at any time; we can talk to Him by our bedside, in church, out in the street, in school or on the top of a 'bus or in the back-yard because—

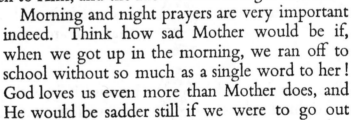

GOD IS EVERYWHERE:
HE FILLS HEAVEN AND EARTH

Wherever we are God is always there, ready to listen to us and to help us.

MORNING AND NIGHT PRAYERS

But there are times when God our Father specially loves to listen to us. Our Heavenly Father wants the FIRST WORDS of the day to be spoken to Him, and the LAST WORDS at night as well.

Morning and night prayers are very important indeed. Think how sad Mother would be if, when we got up in the morning, we ran off to school without so much as a single word to her! God loves us even more than Mother does, and He would be sadder still if we were to go out without first kneeling down by our bedside and saying a few words to Him from our hearts.

At night when we go to sleep we remember that it is God Who has looked after us all the day, and will look after us during the night—it is God Who gives us our Guardian Angel to be with us always.

We should love to kneel at night and speak with God too.

*   *   *

People have sometimes said to me, 'But I don't know what prayers to say'. I know that sounds rather funny, because we always seem to know what to say to our school friends, and God is the very best Friend we could possibly have. So it ought to be easy to know what to talk to Him about. But to make it easier I will tell you what sort of prayers to say.

THE SIGN OF THE CROSS

When you kneel down to pray either in the morning or in the evening be very careful not to hurry. Think carefully that it is God Who loves you ever so much to Whom you are to speak.

Make the Sign of the Cross; and this is how you do it in case you do not know:

With the fingers of your right hand touch:—

first your forehead because it is with your MIND that you KNOW about God;

then your breast because it is with all your HEART that you are trying to LOVE God;

then your left and right shoulders because it is with your ARMS that you will SERVE God.

When you have done that, you will find that you have made the Sign of the Cross on yourself. At the same time you should say:

'In the Name of the Father, and of the Son, and of the Holy Ghost. Amen.'

We bless ourselves with the Sign of the Cross to remind us that it is only because Jesus died on the Cross that we can ever go to be with God in Heaven.

When the Apostles asked Jesus, 'Lord, teach us to pray', Our Lord said, 'When you pray, say, "Our Father. . ."' That is why we say the Lord's Prayer very often indeed.

★   ★   ★

Our Father, Which art in Heaven,
Hallowed be Thy Name,
Thy Kingdom come,
Thy Will be done,
In Earth as it is in Heaven.
Give us this day our daily bread.
And forgive us our trespasses,
As we forgive them that trespass against us,
And lead us not into temptation;
But deliver us from evil.   Amen.

Then we generally say the 'Hail, Mary'. We shall learn later who first spoke the words:

Hail, Mary! Full of Grace;
The Lord is with thee;
Blessed art thou among women,
And blessed is the Fruit of thy womb, Jesus.
Holy Mary, Mother of God,
Pray for us sinners,
Now and at the hour of our death. Amen.

★   ★   ★

IN THE MORNING there are three special things we should try to do:

TO PRAISE GOD. Perhaps this: Glory be to the Father, and to the Son, and to the Holy Ghost. As it was in the beginning, is now and ever shall be, World without end. Amen.

or Holy, Holy, Holy, Lord God of Hosts. Heaven and Earth are full of Thy Glory. Glory be to Thee, O Lord Most High.

or perhaps some other prayer of Praise which we know by heart.

BB   17

TO THANK GOD specially for keeping us safe during the night. O God, I thank Thee with all my heart for keeping me safe during the night, and for bringing me to the beginning of this day.

TO ASK GOD'S HELP.

O my God, I offer to Thee
All that I shall do to-day.
Please give me Thy Grace
And keep me from sin
For Jesus Christ's sake.

Dear Guardian Angel,
Go with me this day.

You may end your prayers in the morning by making the Sign of the Cross.

IN THE EVENING when we have made the Sign of the Cross and said the 'Our Father' and the 'Hail, Mary' there are four special things we try to do:

TO PRAISE GOD. We may like to use the same Act of Praise we said in the morning, or we can find others for ourselves.

TO THANK GOD for all His Blessings, specially those which have made us happy during the day: O God, I thank Thee with all my heart for all the things that have made me happy to-day (specially for——). Don't forget to think of things like your food and clothing, and all those things we take for granted.

TO BE SORRY for our sins—those wrong thoughts, words and deeds—and to tell God we will try not to do them again.

Try to think if there has been anything specially wrong.

O my God,
I am very, very sorry
For these and all my other sins
Which helped to nail Jesus to the Cross.
Please forgive me;
And help me not to sin again,
For Jesus Christ's sake. Amen.

SIN NAILS OUR LORD TO THE CROSS

TO ASK GOD to bless our Church, our priests, our homes and all our friends. And pray for those who are ill and dying, and for the dead.

It is best to pray in your own words, but here is a prayer you may like to say:

PRAY FOR

THE ARCHBISHOP

ALL BISHOPS

DEACONS & PRIESTS

MONKS

NUNS

ALL FAITHFUL

CHRISTIANS, MEN, WOMEN AND

CHILDREN

Bless, O Lord, the Catholic Church all over the World; bless all Bishops, Priests and Deacons, and all faithful people living and dead. Bless my father and mother, my brothers and sisters, and all my relations and friends (specially——).

Have mercy on all sick and dying people, and on all who are in need, for Jesus Christ's sake. Amen.

It is good to ask your Guardian Angel to look after you during the night, and Blessed Mary and all the Saints to pray for you. And you may finish your prayers with the Sign of the Cross, saying:

May the Souls of the Faithful, Through the mercy of God, Rest in Peace. Amen.

19

Then we fall asleep feeling that we have done everything properly. Of course, God wants us to talk to Him from our hearts, so that we need not always say the prayers which I have put down here. But the 'Our Father' and the 'Hail, Mary' are two special prayers which we say whenever we kneel to pray.

ABOUT GOING TO CHURCH

OUR LORD MISSES US WHEN WE MISS MASS

As well as speaking with God the first thing in the morning and the last thing at night there is another special time when we should pray to our Heavenly Father; and that is in church on Sunday mornings at Holy Mass. Never miss Mass on Sundays—we shall learn why later on—for if we do, then God misses us.

And as well as going to Mass on Sundays there are some other days when we must go as well. Here is the list of them; and we call them HOLIDAYS OF OBLIGATION.

All Sundays in the year.

Christmas Day—our Lord's Birthday—December 25th.

The Circumcision—New Year's Day—January 1st.

The Epiphany—when the Wise Men came to see the Baby Jesus—January 6th.

Ascension Day—when Jesus went up into Heaven again—and it comes 40 days after Easter, which is the day our Lord rose from the dead.

Corpus Christi—the great Festival of the Blessed Sacrament—and it comes on the Thursday after Trinity Sunday.

Saints Peter and Paul—the Prince of the Apostles and the greatest of all Missionaries—their day is June 29th.

The Assumption of our Lady—when Blessed Mary was taken up to Heaven by God—this comes on August 15th.

All Saints Day—when we thank God for all the Saints, and ask their prayers. This day is November 1st.

21

All good Catholic children try hard to go to Mass on these days, and I expect that your Parish Priest or your teacher will remind you when they come. It is a good thing to go to Mass on your birthday, and on your baptism day, and perhaps on the birthdays of your mother and father, brothers and sisters and special friends.

'I SHOT AN ARROW'

Of course, God does not want us only to speak to Him or think about Him at these times. God is everywhere, so that we can speak to Him anywhere and at any time. We need not always kneel down to speak with Him, and we need not say anything out loud. Just a thought in our heart is known to Him. God loves small acts of prayer to be sent to Him—and they are almost like ARROWS which we send straight to His Heart, not to wound Him, but to tell Him we love Him. Saint Francis spent a whole night just saying again and again the Holy Name of JESUS. Just that one word and nothing else. And he loved our Lord very much indeed. If something very nice happens to us we can say in our heart, 'Jesus, I thank You for that', or if we see someone who is in pain, 'Jesus, help him', or someone who is being naughty, 'Jesus, save him'. And if we are going along the road, why should we not say inside us again and again, 'Jesus, I love You with all my heart, make me love You more and more', or any other words or thoughts which come into our minds? No one else need know anything about those little arrows, but we can know that they do go straight to the Sacred Heart of Jesus.

THE TWO ANGELS

Two Angels were sent by the Father in Heaven to a certain place at the time of prayer, to collect the prayers of the faithful in baskets. As they flew back to Heaven, one Angel said to the other, 'Why is my basket so heavy that I can scarcely fly, while yours seems to be so very light and easy to carry?' 'Why,' said the other Angel, 'you were sent to collect all the "Please Give Me's" and "I Want's", but I was sent to collect the "Thank You's" of all the people to whom our Heavenly Father has given blessings; but see how few have remembered to give their Thanks!'

VISITS

How lovely it is if we are able to 'pop' into church ever so often, and ever so quietly, just for a few moments, to say a little  prayer in front of the Tabernacle. Perhaps it might be to give our Lord a 'Thank You' for something which we have enjoyed very much, or to ask Jesus to bless someone who is ill. Or it may be to tell Him again that we love Him; or it may even be to tell Him that we have been naughty about something.

And then, perhaps, we might pay a little visit to our Lady's Shrine to tell her that we love her, too, because she is His Mother.

Always remember that the Church is your Father's House.

BE AT HOME IN IT

The last few pages have been about getting to know God by learn- ing to pray—every day in the morning and at night, and at Mass, and at odd times as well. But I want you to try hard to do something else, and that is to go to Sunday School or Catechism because there you learn a lot more things about God and your Religion which there isn't room for in this book.

23

GOD AND THE WORLD

I EXPECT you remember why God made you? It was to know, love and serve Him here on Earth and to be happy with Him for ever in Heaven.

Do you think that it is easy or hard to know, love and serve God here on Earth? It is hard, yes. But don't you think it is rather funny that it is NOT easy to be Perfectly Good, just as God wants us to be? God is Perfectly Good, and God made the World and us. It ought to be easy! Suppose you were a really good carpenter, and all your work was first class; you would find it hard to make a crooked and lop-sided box! Well, surely God Who is Perfect Goodness could not make a world that was not good, nor would He have anything to do with anything that was not good. It is hard to be good because of Sin, because the devil *tempts* us—that means tries to make us do things that God does not want us to do. This is hard to understand, so let us try to know a little more about God and how He made the World.

Long, long ago before there was anything anywhere, before the World was made and even before Heaven itself was made there was still God. God never began: He just WAS and IS and ALWAYS WILL BE. We call that being 'Eternal'. You might think that God must have been very lonely all by Himself. But God can never be lonely, because, although there is only ONE GOD, yet in God, the Father always Loves God the Son, and the Love Which the

Father has for the Son is the Holy Ghost. I know that is hard to understand, but perhaps this picture will help you to understand it better.

THERE IS ONE GOD. IN GOD THERE ARE THREE PERSONS, THE FATHER, THE SON AND THE HOLY GHOST. GOD IS LOVE.

we call this

THE BLESSED TRINITY

I know that is very hard to understand, and there are a lot more things to do with our religion that are hard as well.

SAINT AUGUSTINE AND THE LITTLE BOY

Once upon a time there was a very good and holy man called Augustine who lived at a place called Hippo (a funny name, isn't it?). He was very clever and wrote learned books. And he was trying ever so hard to write a book about God so that people when they read it would understand more about Him. One day he was walking by the seaside trying to think how he could explain to people that God is One, yet there are Three Persons in God. As he walked he suddenly saw a little boy. This little boy was carrying water in a shell from the sea and was pouring it into a little hole he had made in the sand. 'What are you doing?' Saint Augustine asked him. 'Oh!' said the boy, 'I'm just emptying the sea into this hole.' 'You can't do that,' said the Saint, 'because the sea is so very, very big, and that hole is so very, very small.' Then Saint Augustine knew that he was trying to do something rather like that. He was trying to put into

26

his tiny little mind all the wonderful things about God. God is too Great, too Perfect, too Holy to go into our minds so that we can understand *all* about Him.

★   ★   ★

I hope you will remember that story as you go on reading about your holy Religion. God tells us lots of things, but He does not always show us why things happen as they do.

I wonder if you have ever tried to look at the Sun when it has been shining brightly. If you haven't, I don't think I should, because it hurts your eyes. Sometimes when people want to look at the Sun, perhaps to learn  something more about it, they look through a smoked glass because it takes away the brightness. At the sea-side people often wear what they call sun-glasses—they are coloured so that the sun doesn't dazzle them, and they look rather funny wearing them!

When we think about God and try to understand all He does in the world it's as if we were looking through a dark glass. We are not meant to see everything quite clearly in this world. But when we are in Heaven, then we shall be able to see God face to face, and we shall know everything, and we shall not need a glass at all.

BLESSED BE GOD

Billions of years before there was any Earth, God created the Heavens. Heaven is the Home of God, and God means it to be our home, too, one day. And in Heaven God put the Holy Angels. The Angels are perfect Spirits who always stand in His Presence and worship Him, and they go messages for God, and some of them He has sent to us to be our Guardian Angels. The word Angel means Messenger. And they love serving God. We cannot see them, because they are Spirits and have no bodies as we have, but we try to imagine what they look like. Here is a picture of the Heavenly Hosts of Angels.

But—there's always a 'but', isn't there?—one of the Great Archangels (Arch means 'chief', like Archbishop)—called Lucifer, got jealous of God and wanted to be equal with Him. Of course, no one can ever be equal with God, so it was rather silly of Lucifer, wasn't it? But unhappily some of the other Angels felt the same as Lucifer about it, so they rebelled against God. It was very wicked and ungrateful of them, because God their Father loved them ever so much, and had given them perfect happiness. Then Saint Michael, the Great-Warrior-Archangel who leads the Heavenly Hosts of Angels, fought for God against Lucifer and his wicked angels, and drove them out of Heaven down to Hell. This is what is called 'The Fall of the Angels'. So there was peace once more in Heaven. Saint Michael is, of course, the Special Saint of soldiers and of all who fight for what is right.

★   ★   ★

Then God created the Universe—the Sun, Moon, Planets and all the Stars you can see on a beautifully clear night; and also lots more suns, moons, planets and stars which are so far away that you cannot see them. And on the Earth God made a beautiful garden called the Garden of Eden, and in it He placed Adam and Eve. They were perfectly happy, and knew nothing that was not perfectly good and holy. I expect you know the story of what happened, how the devil (late-Archangel Lucifer), looking like a serpent,

told Eve that it did not really matter if she took the fruit God had told them not to take; how Eve took the fruit and gave some to Adam, and they both ate it. They disobeyed God; they sinned against God, their Heavenly Father, Who loved them so much.

We call this 'THE FALL OF MAN'

Then God sent His Angel with the Fiery Sword to drive them out of the Garden and to guard the gate.

29

Because they did what was wrong and sinned against God, all the people who came after them have the stain of Adam and Eve's sin on their souls. Then evil and wicked things came into God's beautiful world, poverty and unhappiness, illness and pain. And ever since there has been a fight going on between good and bad, between God and the devil.

★　　★　　★

But when Adam and Eve sinned they lost something—they lost the Life and Light of God from their souls and from the souls of all who should come after them. They could not go to Heaven to be happy with God for ever. So every little baby coming into the world has not got the Life and Light of God in his soul—at least, not until he has been baptised. But, worse than that, nearly all people have grown up to do wrong things themselves. So they copy Adam and Eve and disobey God. It is very sad, isn't it, that God's children should have been so ungrateful to Him?

When sin came into the World, it was as though a WALL had been built up between God and man. All the people in the world could not by themselves get MAN SIN GOD back to God. But God promised that in His Own Good Time He would send a Saviour Who would make up for the sin of Adam and Eve and for all the sins which people have done who came after—including your sins and mine.

PUTTING IT ALL RIGHT

God started at once to make the world ready for the coming of the Saviour. He watched the people trying to get back to Him, but I am afraid they did not try hard enough, and they even got worse and worse. At last God chose a man who believed in Him and wanted to do His Will, whose name was Abraham. Through

Abraham's great family which came after him God wanted to teach all the people that came into the world more about Himself. And He was going to save the world through this family. He wanted to tell all the people that He was a God of Love, and that He really wanted them to be with Him in Heaven; and He wanted the Hebrews (the Children of Abraham) to do the telling. But they were not always good themselves. They often disobeyed God. And they went through all sorts of exciting itmes, even being kept for a long time in Egypt by Pharaoh King of Egypt. But God chose Moses to lead them out of Egypt into the Promised Land of Canaan—that is, Palestine. It was as they were wandering through the Wilderness on the way to the Promised Land that God gave to Moses the Ten Commandments. But the Hebrews were often disobedient to God even after they had arrived in the Promised Land. So to try to bring them to know, love and serve Him properly, God

sent the Prophets — like Elijah, Isaiah, Jeremiah, and Ezekiel, and a lot more. Some of them the people put to death, others they would have little to do with. Till at last God sent His Son, the Saviour. I will tell you what happened, but you can read it in the Gospels, specially in Saint Luke's Gospel.

GOD WAS MADE MAN

Once upon a time there was living in a village called Nazareth in Palestine a Maiden named Mary, and she loved God more than anything else in the world. She was engaged to a carpenter called Joseph, who also loved God above all things. And one day God sent one of His Great Archangels—Saint Gabriel—to see Mary. And this is what he said to her: 'Hail, Mary! Full of Grace, the Lord is with thee.' And he went on to tell her that God was going to give her a Son, Who should be called the Son of God; and His name was to be JESUS, because He should save His people from their sins. And Mary said, 'How shall this be?' Saint Gabriel said, 'The Holy Ghost shall come upon thee.' And Mary said, 'Behold the Handmaid of the Lord. Be it unto me according to thy word.' That means: 'I am God's servant, so He can do with me what He thinks best'.

Saint Gabriel knelt before our Lady because she was now the Mother of Jesus Who is God, and then he went from her.

Mary went at once to see her cousin Elizabeth, because she too was to have a son, who was to tell the people about Jesus when they were both grown up; his name was to be John. You  remember Saint John the Baptist, don't you? When Mary arrived, Saint Elizabeth said, 'Blessed art thou among women, and blessed is the Fruit of thy womb' (that means 'blessed is your Child'). So now you know where the first part of the 'Hail, Mary' comes from. The second half was made up by Christians some time later.

Some months afterwards Mary and Joseph, her Protector, had another messenger, and it was not an Angel this time. It was someone who came from King Herod to say that everyone must go to his own town to be counted. When that sort of thing happens nowadays we call it a 'Census'. Now, Joseph belonged to the Royal House of David, although he was only a poor carpenter, and his special city was Bethlehem. There he went, taking Mary with him.

After a very long and tiring journey—they probably had to walk—they found the city very full. There was no room for them in the Inn. At last, seeing how tired and poor they looked, someone took pity on Mary and Joseph and said, 'I've got no room in my house, but there is a stable cave out at the back where the animals are; if you like you can rest there on the straw.'

There, among the dumb animals Joseph made Mary as comfortable as he could. And then in the silence of the night the most wonderful thing since the beginning of the world happened:

O COME LET US ADORE HIM

Jesus Christ, the Saviour of the World, was born. Saint Joseph, the Foster-Father, knelt by Mary's side and worshipped the Holy Babe.

He was hungry and cold; He cried like other babies. The only place where He could lie was in the manger where the cattle usually had their food—although He was God the Son.

He was the King of all kings, and might have been born in a palace with lots of people all knowing about His coming, and with every-thing to make Him comfortable. But no, God wanted Him to be poor, to be born in a stable, to have no com-forts and very few people to know about it. I wonder why? Surely because He had come to make up for our sins. He had to suffer for them, and He started to suffer right at the begin-ning of His life.

There were shepherds in the fields keeping watch over their flocks that night. And the Angel of the Lord came to them and told them, 'Go quickly to Bethlehem, for there is born to you a Saviour, Christ the Lord.' And  suddenly there was with the Angel a multitude of the Heavenly Host of Angels praising God and saying, 'Glory to God in the Highest and on Earth Peace to men of good will.'

The shepherds had been looking forward and hoping that God would send the promised Saviour quite soon. So when the Angels had gone from them they wasted no time, but came with haste and found the place; and they found Mary and Joseph, and the Babe lying in a manger. Of course, they did what we should have done: fell on their knees and worshipped their Lord and their God.

O come, all ye faithful, joyful and triumphant,
O come ye, O come ye to Bethlehem;
Come and behold Him, born the King of Angels.
O come, let us adore Him,
O come, let us adore Him,
O come, let us adore Him, Christ the Lord.

I expect they offered Him some small presents on His birthday
—they were very poor, so they could not afford much—like the

kings who came with their Gold, Incense and Myrrh later on. But I am sure they gave what they could. Perhaps they gave some lamb's wool to keep the Baby warm, and some milk, and some bread as well. But the greatest Christmas Present and the most valuable was their love. And we can always give Him that as well. And it is our love which makes the Babe of Bethlehem smile.

That is why we give Christmas presents and birthday presents to those we love.

*   *   *

> For Thy first coming as a little Child,
> For Thy last coming to judge the world,
> For Thy coming into our hearts now by Grace,
>   Praise and Glory be to Thee, O Christ.

That is a little prayer you can say at any time, but specially during Advent—the four weeks before Christmas.

THE ANGELUS

Jesus being born was such a wonderful thing to happen that now, every day, we try to remember it. Perhaps you have heard a church bell ring early in the morning, at 12 o'clock midday, and again at 6 o'clock in the evening. It does not ring in the ordinary way, but it rings like this—ding, dong, bell—then a pause, and again ding, dong, bell—and another pause, and again ding, dong, bell—and another pause—and then nine strokes—ding, dong, bell, ding, dong, bell, ding, dong, bell. You can remember it quite easily—because three times three makes nine!

While the bell is ringing like that, we say some prayers. Sometimes they are said aloud, and sometimes we say them quietly to ourselves. If we know them by heart, we can say them silently whenever we hear the Angelus Bell ring, wherever we are.

These are the words:

The Angel of the Lord declared unto Mary.
And she conceived by the Holy Ghost.

Then say the 'Hail, Mary'.

Behold the Handmaid of the Lord.
Be it unto me according to thy word.

The 'Hail, Mary' is said again.

And the Word was made Flesh,
And dwelt among us.

'Hail, Mary' again.

Pray for us, O holy Mother of God,
That we may be made worthy of the promises of Christ.

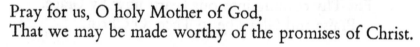

Let us pray

WE beseech Thee, O Lord, pour Thy Grace into our hearts that, as we have known the Incarnation of Thy Son Jesus Christ by the message of an Angel, so by His Cross ✠ and Passion we may be brought unto the glory of His Resurrection; through the same Jesus Christ our Lord. Amen.

But in Easter-tide—that is, from the first Easter Mass on Holy Saturday until Trinity Sunday—the following is said instead:

Joy to thee, O Queen of Heaven, Alleluia.
He, Whom thou wast meet to bear, Alleluia.
As He promised, hath arisen, Alleluia.
Pour for us to God thy prayer, Alleluia.
Rejoice and be glad, O Virgin Mary, Alleluia.
For the Lord hath risen indeed, Alleluia.

Let us pray

O God, Who by the Resurrection of Thy Son our Lord Jesus Christ, hath vouchsafed to give joy to the whole world; grant, we beseech Thee, that with the help of His Mother, the Virgin Mary, we may obtain the joys of everlasting life; through the same Christ our Lord. Amen.

MAKING UP FOR SIN

'God so loved the world, that He gave His only-begotten Son, that whosoever believeth in Him should not perish, but have everlasting life.'

God sent His Son to be a little Baby at Bethlehem because God loved His children and wanted to save them and open the gates of Heaven to them.

I hope you will read the whole story of Jesus for yourself in the Bible—specially in Saint Luke's Gospel. Some people have called his gospel 'the Children's Gospel', because it has more about children in it than either Saint Matthew's or Saint Mark's or Saint John's Gospels. If you read the story you will see how Jesus began to grow up. After the Wise Men had been to see Him, and after the Holy Family had had to flee to Egypt to escape from cruel Herod, He went to live with His Mother and Saint Joseph at Nazareth. There He went on growing up, and learned to be a carpenter like Saint Joseph. When He was twelve years old  you can read how He went with His Mother and Saint Joseph for the first time to Jerusalem for the Passover Feast, and how He got lost and was found in the Temple. He lived at home at Nazareth till He was thirty years old. All that time He was known only to a very few people, and only two or three of them knew that He was anything more than an ordinary young man. But all the time He was God the Son. So He did live a hidden sort of life, didn't He?

But at last the time came for Him to leave His home

to found His Kingdom; we shall learn how He did this quite soon. What I want you to understand now is that from the time He left home He had no house of His own to live or sleep in, and for three years He went about teaching people about the Love of His Father, how they must be sorry for their sins, join His Kingdom, and learn to love God truly, so that they could go to Heaven. He never forgot, though, that He had come to MAKE UP FOR the sins of the world. So He went on suffering nearly all the time.

Now we come to the last week of His life on Earth. We call this week 'Holy Week', and we remember it specially every year.

It begins with Palm Sunday, when Jesus rode into the city of Jerusalem on an Ass—which was the animal kings of old used. Again, I want you to read all about this wonderful week in the Gospel. We shall learn about Maundy Thursday later on, and, of course, you know that on Good Friday, having been betrayed by Judas and condemned by the Chief Priests of the Jews and by Pontius Pilate, the Governor, He was nailed to a Cross on Mount Calvary, just outside the Walls of Jerusalem. There He offered His life to make up for all the sins of the world. Jesus died to save you and me, because He loves us.

He died that we might be FORGIVEN,
 He died to make us GOOD,
That we might go at last to Heaven,
 Saved by His Precious Blood.

There was no other good enough
 To pay the price of sin;
He only could unlock the gate
 Of Heaven and let us in.

O dearly, dearly has He loved,
 And we must love Him too,
And trust in His redeeming Blood,
 And try His works to do.

But it did not all end there, with Jesus dead on the Cross. We know that when we die we shall rise again and go to Heaven if we are worthy, because Jesus rose again from the grave on the Third Day (we call that day Easter Sunday); and forty days later He went up into Heaven (Ascension Day). He went to get a place ready for us. Isn't it wonderful that God has done so much for us?

The Third Day He rose again

The devil still tempts us—tries to make us do what is wrong, and tries to stop us being like Jesus Christ and going to Heaven.

But by dying on the Cross Jesus won the battle against the devil, which had been going on since Adam and Eve first disobeyed God. So if we try hard, and really hope and trust in our hearts that God does help us to fight against the devil, then WE SHALL CERTAINLY WIN. Remember we are to be God's Knights, and wherever we are we are to be His Champions, and stand up for the Faith that is in us. It is not always easy, but if we have as our Standard the Cross, we shall win every time.

Jesus also won something else for us by dying on the Cross, and that is God's Special Grace. We are going to learn later on how we get that Grace, and it is very important because it is nothing less than the Life and Light of God which God puts in our souls. You remember how Adam and Eve lost it for us when they sinned. But Jesus won it back for us.

It is Grace—the Life and Light of God—which makes our souls like the pure, sinless Soul of Jesus Christ, and which makes us fit to go to Heaven.

OUR SAVIOUR SUFFERED TO MAKE UP FOR OUR SINS, AND TO WIN FOR US ETERNAL LIFE

We adore Thee, O Christ, and we bless Thee,
Because by Thy Holy Cross Thou has redeemed the world.

TWO PRAYERS

THE DIVINE PRAISES

Blessed be God
Blessed be His holy Name
Blessed be Jesus Christ true God and true man
Blessed be the Name of Jesus
Blessed be His most Sacred Heart
Blessed be Jesus in the most holy Sacrament of the Altar
Blessed be the great Mother of God, Mary most holy
Blessed be her holy and immaculate conception
Blessed be the name of Mary, Virgin and Mother
Blessed be Saint Joseph, her most chaste Spouse
Blessed be God in His Angels and in His Saints.

THE ANIMA CHRISTI

Soul of Christ, sanctify me
Body of Christ, save me
Blood of Christ, inebriate me
Water from the side of Christ, wash me
Passion of Christ, strengthen me
O good Jesu, hear me
Within Thy wounds hide me
Suffer me not to be separated from Thee
From the malicious enemy defend me
In the hour of my death call me
And bid me come to Thee
That with Thy Saints I may praise Thee
For ever and ever.   Amen.

Try and learn these by heart and use them often.

OUR HOLY MOTHER THE CATHOLIC AND APOSTOLIC CHURCH

THE CATHOLIC CHURCH

JESUS came to teach us how to live, to make up for sin, and to win for us the Grace which can make us like Him and ready to go to Heaven. But Jesus did all this nearly *two thousand* years ago! A long time, isn't it? We might say, 'However can it have anything to do with us who live *now*?' We are going to see how our Lord made it all have a lot to do with us now.

★   ★   ★

Pretend you are with our Lord nearly two thousand years ago. You are listening to Him as He teaches a crowd of people. He is thinking of the way He is going to save people from their sins—and not only those people around Him, but all the people who would live on the other side of the world hundreds and thousands of years later as well!

What is His way? It is what we call the Catholic Church—its full name is

THE ONE HOLY CATHOLIC AND APOSTOLIC CHURCH.

Sometimes, when I have asked children, 'What is the Catholic Church?' they have said to me, 'God's House', and I have had to say, 'No'. Certainly it is true that we call the place where we go to Mass 'a church', and we shall see why later on. But the Catholic Church is not a building made of bricks. Let us see what we *do* mean by it.

★   ★   ★

When Jesus was grown up and had left His home at Nazareth He was baptised by Saint John the Baptist, and after He had been in the Wilderness for forty days and forty nights being tempted by the devil, He came out and started to teach the people.

He taught them a lot of very wonderful things about the Love of their Heavenly Father, and the Kingdom of Heaven, and also

43

that people must be sorry for their sins and try to know, love and serve God properly, so that they could go to be with Him in Heaven.

Crowds of people used to come and hear Him, and they used to follow Him from place to place. Sometimes He taught them in

Parables—those wonderful earthly stories with Heavenly meanings—and He made better many people who were ill, and also forgave many people their sins.

THE APOSTLES

Now, from among all those thousands of people who came to hear Him, Jesus chose twelve men whom He knew to be the best for the work He had to do. And He called them APOSTLES— which means 'those who are sent'. These are their names:—

Simon Peter, the Prince of the Apostles. Matthew.
Andrew, his brother. Thomas.
James and James (*another one*).
John, his brother. Jude.
Philip. Simon (*another one*) and
Bartholomew. Judas the traitor.

Jesus chose the Twelve so that they could be with Him always, and He could teach them all the wonderful things they were to teach others about God. It is wonderful how well the Apostles listened to Him and handed on His teaching, because we know exactly what we must believe if we are to be saved. It is all in the Apostles' Creed. Here it is:

THE APOSTLES' CREED
(the word 'Creed' means 'I believe')

I believe
In God the Father Almighty,
Maker of Heaven and Earth;
And in Jesus Christ His only Son our Lord,
Who was conceived by the Holy Ghost,
Born of the Virgin Mary,
Suffered under Pontius Pilate,
Was crucified, dead and buried.
He descended into Hell;
The Third Day He rose again from the dead,
He ascended into Heaven,
And sitteth on the right hand of God the Father Almighty;
From thence He shall come to judge the quick and the dead.
I believe in the Holy Ghost;
The Holy Catholic Church;
The Communion of Saints;
The Forgiveness of sins;
The Resurrection of the body,
And the life everlasting.   Amen.

Yes, all that is what the Apostles learned from our Lord. Some of the words are rather hard for you, but you will learn what they mean later on.

Jesus also taught the Apostles how they were to give other people the Special Grace which was to fit them for Heaven. And He gave them special POWERS: power to Baptise, to Confirm, to give God's Forgiveness and, most wonderful of all, power to consecrate His Body and Blood. We shall see what all these things mean quite soon now. Of course, Jesus did not give the Apostles all these powers at once. The power to say Mass was given to them on Maundy Thursday, the day before He was crucified; the power to Forgive Sins was given on the first Easter Sunday when He had risen from the dead. And they were not able to use any of those powers till the Holy Ghost came on them on the first Whitsunday. When Jesus went back into Heaven He told the Apostles to wait in Jerusalem till they had got the 'power from on high'. I expect you know the story, how they were sitting all together, and the room was suddenly filled with a 'mighty rushing wind', and tongues of fire sat on the head of each of them, and 'they were all filled with the Holy Ghost'. After that wonderful happening, they started to do their work. They were really strong to do it then, which they had not been before. You remember how they all ran away from Jesus when He was taken prisoner in the Garden of Gethsemane on the Thursday night; Judas had betrayed Him and had lost his place in the band of the Apostles; and even Saint Peter had said he did not know our Lord. But now all was different, they were filled with the Holy Ghost; they were strong; and they understood a lot of things which Jesus had told them but which they could not understand at the time.

So the Apostles started to tell people about Jesus having risen from the dead, and anyone who really believed in Jesus, who wanted to know, love and serve Him and to be happy in Heaven, came and was baptised. They joined the new Way of Life—the Catholic Church—which Jesus had started. It was not a secret society—but a holy society which was to spread all over the world and to bring all men to loving obedience in God's Kingdom.

The Apostles were the first bishops and priests of the Church. And all who loved our Lord came to be baptised, confirmed, and to receive Holy Communion—just as we do now.

In a very short time the number of people joining the Church became so large that the Apostles had too much to do. So they chose out others to help them, just as our Lord had chosen them. And they handed on to them the powers they had from our Lord. Of course, they had to be careful whom they chose. The people they chose to help had to know what to believe and teach, they had to love our Lord more than anything in the world. Then the Apostles laid hands on their heads, and in their turn they received the Holy Ghost. So they had the powers too. That is how bishops and priests have been ordained right from the beginning of the Church. After the death of the Apostles, these bishops and priests took their places, and when they died or were killed they had been careful to see that there were always others who had the powers of bishops and priests to go on with the work of bringing into the Church 'all who would be saved'.

ABOUT BISHOPS AND PRIESTS

I expect you have seen a bishop. Perhaps you have been to a Confirmation in your church, and you may have noticed the special hat he wore. It looks like this→ and it is called a MITRE. It is made in that shape because it is meant to remind us of the 'cloven' tongues of flame which sat on the head of each of the Apostles when the Holy Ghost came to give them the power to be bishops and priests on the first Whitsunday. The bishops are the successors of the Apostles because they have been given all those powers which Jesus gave to them.

The bishops are the rulers of the Catholic Church, and they have to see that people are taught the proper things to believe, and that they have the true Sacraments, which we shall learn about very soon now.

I expect you have seen several priests, and I expect you know one or two very well indeed. When a man is made a priest he has to answer some very important questions and make some

47

very important promises. Then he kneels in front of the bishop who, by laying his hands on his head and praying, makes him a priest. He is given those same powers that our Lord gave to the Apostles, which have been handed down to all other bishops. But a priest is not quite as high as a bishop, because there are a few things which he is not given power to do. A priest cannot ordain (or make) other bishops or priests, and he does not confirm either. But he is made a priest so that he will be able to do the most important things of all: to say Mass, to forgive sins, and to bless people and things. Of course, there are lots of other things a priest has to do, like preaching and teaching people about God and His Church, baptising people, and teaching children—which is very important indeed.

When you see a priest doing any of those things it is just as if Jesus Himself was doing them. In fact Jesus really does them through His priests because of the powers He has given them.

We call our priests 'Father' because they bring us into the Catholic Church—the Special Family of Jesus Christ, and they give us all the things we need for our souls just like our own fathers do for our bodies.

Now we have learned quite a lot about the Catholic Church and I want you to learn this short sentence by heart, because it puts in a few words what the Catholic Church is:

THE CATHOLIC CHURCH IS MADE UP OF ALL THE PEOPLE WHO ARE BAPTISED AND BELIEVE THE TEACHING WHICH OUR LORD GAVE TO THE APOSTLES, WHOSE SUCCESSORS ARE THE BISHOPS.

All of us belong to the Catholic Church because we are baptised, and we ought always to try to get other people to know more about it; because, you see, it is the special way God works in the world and makes people ready for Heaven.

THE COMMUNION OF SAINTS

The baptised people who are on Earth now are not the ONLY people who belong to the Catholic Church. There are all the people who have gone from this Earth. First of all there are all the people who have loved God ever so much and have even been ready to die rather than give up believing in Jesus Christ; we call these the Saints—and they are in Heaven at the Throne of God. Of course, chief of them is Blessed Mary, the Queen of Heaven and Queen of all the Saints, and there are the Holy Apostles, the

Martyrs (those who have actually died for God), the Confessors (who would have offered their lives), and there are the holy Virgins, the Innocents and lots of other holy people who have loved God above all things. They are all in the same Special Family of Jesus Christ. Mary is the Mother of them all, and of us too, just as she was of the Holy Family at Nazareth. We call the Saints in Heaven 'The Church Triumphant', because by God's grace the Saints have triumphed over the devil.

*   *   *

Then there are others who have gone from this world, but who are not yet in Heaven. They are not in Heaven because they are not ready to see God face to face. Most of us when we go from this world will not be quite ready because we shall still have on our souls all the marks left by our sins. Those stains have to be cleaned, and our souls have to be shining white. You will understand this better if you think of God as being a very bright light, thousands of times brighter than the sun. If we were to go straight into His Presence we should be blinded, because the eyes of our souls would not be strong enough to bear His Brightness. So we go to a place where we can be got ready to see God. We call this place PURGATORY—because there we are 'purged' or 'made clean' from our sins, and there we make up for our sins, if we have not tried hard enough in this world. It is also called the CHURCH EXPECTANT or Waiting—and we should pray for the Holy Souls who are there, because they still belong to the same family of the Catholic Church, only they have gone on before us.

So you see the Catholic Church has three parts:

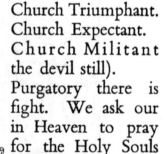

In Heaven — The Church Triumphant.
In Purgatory—The Church Expectant.
On Earth — The Church Militant
(fighting against the devil still).
In Heaven and in Purgatory there is no more devil to fight. We ask our Lady and the Saints in Heaven to pray for *us*, and *we* pray for the Holy Souls in Purgatory. We can often pray, 'May the souls of the faithful through the mercy of God rest in peace'.

We call the place where we go to Mass a 'church' because people who belong to the Catholic Church go there to worship

God. But the Catholic Church is not really a building of bricks.  When you were baptised you did not become a brick in a wall! But you became a member of a Society. When you say that your school is playing football, you do not mean that all the bricks are playing, do you? That would be odd! Of course, you mean that the members—boys—of the school are playing!

THE KINGDOM OF HEAVEN

It will help you to understand better what we mean by the Catholic Church if you remember that Jesus came to found a Kingdom. Not an earthly Kingdom, but a Heavenly. And Jesus Christ is our King, to whom we owe loving obedience, as faithful subjects. There is a special festival about Christ the King, and it comes on the last Sunday in October. We are all Princes and Princesses in His Kingdom.

THE VINE

Jesus once said to His disciples, 'I am the Vine, you are the branches'. Have you ever seen a Vine? There is a wonderful, big one at Hampton Court. It looks something like this:

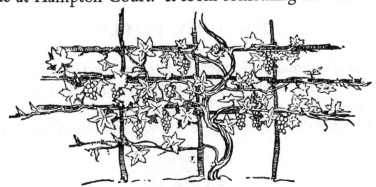

It has a great thick stem, and a number of long branches, which are so long that they have to be fastened to a wall. These branches have lots of smaller ones, and they in turn have smaller branches still, and from them hang the fruit—great bunches of grapes.

The grapes grow in huge bunches, so heavy that

51

they sometimes have to tie them up in muslin bags to stop them falling off and being spoiled.

How do you think a Vine keeps alive so that it can bring out its fruit? It is because of the 'Sap' which comes through the main trunk and goes to every small branch and twig. If the Sap was stopped in any branch, that branch would die. The Sap is rather like the blood in our bodies—it keeps us alive.

GRAFTING Sometimes people make a hole in the side of a tree, and they stick in it a twig from another kind of tree and bind it up. Quite soon the twig takes life from the big tree, and goes on growing because of the sap. This is called being 'grafted'.

Jesus said, 'I am the Vine, you are the branches'. What did He mean? He meant that when we are baptised it is rather like being 'grafted'. The Grace of God flows through Jesus Christ to every member or part of the Church, which is sometimes called the Body of Christ. *You* are a part of the Church. It is the Grace of God which gives your soul the Spiritual Life and Light of God; which makes you a Christian and makes you ready for Heaven.

What is the Fruit? It is to love God above all things, and to be loving and kind to other people as well.

★　　★　　★

THE HOLY FAMILY

I think it is wonderful to remember that the Catholic Church is really the Holy Family. God is the Father; our Lady is the Mother—Saint Joseph is the Protector of the Family—and Jesus is our Elder Brother. And we are all the Children of the Family.

THE SACRAMENTS

I EXPECT you remember that God made us to know, love and serve Him here on Earth and to be happy with Him for ever in Heaven. And do you remember that we said it was hard to do this really well, because the devil is always trying to make us do wrong things and to forget about God?

But God gives us His Special Grace—His Life and Light, and that helps us to fight against the devil, and helps us to become like Jesus Christ and fit for Heaven.

How does God give us His Grace? He gives it to us in two chief ways: through PRAYER; and through the SACRAMENTS. Now we have talked about Prayer, and I hope you are trying really hard to say your prayers. But we have got to learn about the Sacraments.

IHS

What is a Sacrament? A Sacrament is a sign—something you can see, touch or hear, through which God gives us His Special Grace, which you cannot see, touch or hear.

Try and learn these words by heart:

A SACRAMENT IS AN OUTWARD AND VISIBLE SIGN OF AN INWARD
AND SPIRITUAL GRACE

There are seven Sacraments which Jesus gave to His Church:

1. HOLY BAPTISM. We have said quite a lot about this already. Let us see what it really is. I expect that you have, at some time, seen a baby being baptised. You saw the Priest take the baby in his arms at the Font, and he took water and poured it on the baby's head while he said some words. What were

those words? They were: 'Mary (or John or whatever the baby's name was to be), I baptise thee in the Name of the Father and of the Son and of the Holy Ghost'.

HOLY BAPTISM

You see there are two parts. First there is THE OUTWARD AND VISIBLE SIGN—the *Words* which you can hear, and the *Water* which you see the Priest pour on the baby's head. The Priest has to be very careful that he really *does* pour the water on the baby's head and say the right words.

Then there is the INWARD AND SPIRITUAL GRACE, which is the part God does. And there are three things which God does for our souls as the Priest pours the water and speaks the words:

(1) The baby's soul is washed clean of Adam and Eve's sin— and sometimes a grown-up person has to be baptised, and then the wrong things he has actually done himself are washed away too. This is easy to remember, because water is used to wash with.

(2) God puts in the baby's soul the gift of Grace—that Life and Light of God which was lost by Adam and Eve. It is the *seed* of Spiritual Life which has to grow up with the baby.

(3) And the baby is joined on to the Catholic Church and becomes a member of the Holy Family, and becomes a Prince or a Princess in the Kingdom of Heaven. Then of course the baby is able to have the other Sacraments when he is ready for them.

★   ★   ★

When we are baptised we become:

A member of Christ .. a living part of the Body of Christ, the Church.

The Child of God .. a special member of the Holy Family.

An Inheritor of the .. a Prince or Princess of the Kingdom of Kingdom of Heaven Heaven, and ready to go to Heaven.

*   *   *

Being baptised is like being put on to a Racecourse. The course leads to Heaven, and the way on to the course is called Holy Baptism. Being baptised is rather like being brought into a Great Ship, which is sailing to Heaven. Some people have likened the Church to a Ship. Our Lord is the Captain, the bishops and priests are the officers and crew, and all the faithful are the passengers. The gangway which leads on to the ship has written over it 'Holy Baptism'. If you are in the ship, you are quite safe, for the ship is Heavenward Bound; only if you are silly enough to jump out do you stop being safe. I am afraid there are rather a lot of people who have never come into the Church, who have not been baptised. But a lot of them have never had the chance.

When we are baptised it is as if we were sheep being brought into a sheep-fold. Our Lord is the Good Shepherd, and we are the sheep. The Sheep-fold is the Catholic Church. Our Lord knows His sheep all right, because our souls are marked with the Cross. Perhaps you have seen sheep with the shepherd's mark on them when you have been in the country. I once saw a whole flock of real sheep which had a red Cross on every one. It happened to be the shepherd's mark. But it made me think of the Catholic Church, and Jesus the Good Shepherd, and His sheep all brought into the Church with a Cross on their souls.

*   *   *

When you were brought to the Church to be baptised you were brought by your God-parents as well as your father and mother. Every baby boy should have two Godfathers and one Godmother, and every baby girl should have two Godmothers and one Godfather. I wonder if you know who your God-parents were. If you do not know, ask your mother; she is sure to know. Your God-parents had to make three promises for you—or, rather, it was really you making promises through them, as you were not old enough to say anything sensible! And the three promises were these:

You promised to HAVE NOTHING TO DO WITH evil.

You promised to BELIEVE all that God has taught us by His Church.

You promised to DO GOD'S WILL—to do all that is right.

★   ★   ★

Remember God always helps us to keep those promises if we really want to keep them. He gives us His Grace in the other Sacraments to help us to live up to them.

★   ★   ★

On what date were you baptised? It is important to know this, because you should remember every year that it is your Spiritual Birthday, and it ought to be just as important as your ordinary birthday.

It is good to go to Mass on that day.

★   ★   ★

A lot of wonderful things happened to you when the Priest poured the Waters of Baptism on your head and said those words, 'I baptise thee in the Name of the Father and of the Son and of the Holy Ghost'.

Always be thankful for this wonderful gift.

2. CONFIRMATION. Perhaps you have been confirmed as well as baptised; and if you have, then you will know all about it.

56

But you can pretend you know nothing about it at all. Or perhaps you can see if you can find anything you did not know before!

Like all the Sacraments Confirmation has two parts; the part you can see, and the part you cannot see. You can see the Bishop placing his hands on the head of a person who has already been baptised, and you can hear him praying. This is the OUTWARD part of the Sacrament. Perhaps you have seen a Bishop confirming; if you have, then you will remember how in a short service the children, and perhaps some grown-ups as well, went and knelt before him. You may even remember the prayer he said:

Defend, O Lord, this Thy child with Thy Heavenly Grace, that he may continue Thine for ever; And daily increase in Thy Holy Spirit more and more, until he come unto Thy everlasting Kingdom. Amen.

HOLY CONFIRMATION

In different parts of the Church the words are different; but the important thing is the Laying-on of hands. The part which nobody can see is what God does in the souls of those who come to be confirmed. When the Bishop lays on his hands God sends the Holy Ghost to make their souls strong. Sometimes we call the Holy Ghost 'the Comforter'—and that means the One Who

57

makes STRONG. The Holy Ghost comes to our souls to make us strong to keep those three promises which we made when we were baptised.

You cannot see the Holy Ghost coming—but you cannot see the wind, can you? Although you can see the trees moving in the wind. So we should be able to see the result of the Holy Ghost in our souls; the result should be a good and holy life.

When we have been confirmed we belong to God even more than before. The Holy Ghost 'seals' us as His own—as you seal a letter you want very specially to get to your friend. The Holy Ghost seals our souls as His own, to make specially sure we get to Heaven.

The Holy Ghost stays in our souls always, and we should always remember that we have this special strength.

★   ★   ★

When we were baptised we became God's Children.

When we are confirmed we become God's very perfect Soldiers.

When we were baptised we were given the gift of Spiritual Life.

When we are confirmed we are given the gift of Strength.

★   ★   ★

You will understand what a wonderful Sacrament Confirmation really is when you remember Who the Holy Ghost is. He is the Third Person of the Blessed Trinity. He came on the Apostles on the first Whitsunday—or Pentecost; and filled them with His strength so that they could go and do wonderful things for God. Confirmation is your 'Pentecost'. The Holy Ghost fills you with strength so that you too can go and do wonderful things for God.

We can only be baptised *once*, and we can only be confirmed *once*, just as we can only be born once and grow up once. In fact, it is rather like being born and growing up. The new-born baby (the baptised person) needs strength to grow up (confirmation).

If you have not yet been confirmed, look forward to the day when you will be. If you have been confirmed, just think how you are using that wonderful gift of God the Holy Ghost which you have within you.

3. PENANCE is when we go to confess our sins and ask God's Forgiveness. We shall talk a lot about this Sacrament later on, so we need not say any more now.

★　　★　　★

4. HOLY COMMUNION is the most wonderful of all the Sacraments. It is when we go to receive the Body and Blood of Jesus as the Food of our souls. We shall have a lot to say about this Sacrament later on too.

HOLY ORDERS

5. HOLY ORDER is when a man is made a Bishop, a Priest or a Deacon. You remember how the Apostles laid their hands on others whom they wanted to share the work with them? Every Bishop, Priest or Deacon has to be Ordained. The way it is done is just the same to-day as when the Apostles made other Bishops, Priests or Deacons. The outward sign is the Bishop laying on his hands —the Inward Grace is the Power of the Holy Ghost. Holy Order is a very wonderful Sacrament, because in it the Holy Ghost is given so that a man can have the Powers of Bishop, Priest or Deacon. It takes usually at least three Bishops to consecrate another Bishop, because the Church has to be absolutely sure that the Powers are handed on properly; but one Bishop can ordain a Priest or Deacon. The most important Power which is given to a Priest is the Power to say Mass and consecrate the Body and Blood of Jesus. Of course, the other powers which we talked about before are given as well.

HOLY MARRIAGE

6. HOLY MARRIAGE is when people who want to be married come to Church to get the Church's blessing on their new life. The two people make solemn promises before God and His Church, and they are given the Grace to

live their lives together to the end of their days, to the Glory of God.

7. EXTREME UNCTION. When people are very ill indeed, the Priest comes to anoint them with Holy Oil which has been blessed by a Bishop. He anoints them on their foreheads, eyes, nose, ears, breast, hands and feet —that is the Out-

EXTREME UNCTION

ward part. If they are very, very ill, he may just anoint them on their foreheads only. The Inward part is the strength which God gives their souls for their journey to Him, and He forgives their sins. Sometimes this Sacrament also strengthens their bodies so much that they get better again; that is, of course, if God wants them to get better.

Perhaps you now understand a little better what the Sacraments are. We are not meant to receive *all* of them. If you are a little girl, you cannot receive the Sacrament of Holy Order, and whether you are a boy or a girl it may be that God does not want you to be Married. But we all need some of the Sacraments. We must all be baptised, because Jesus said, 'Unless you are baptised with Water and the Holy Ghost, you cannot enter the Kingdom of Heaven'; and we must all receive Holy Communion, because Jesus said, 'Unless you eat the Flesh of the Son of Man and drink His Blood you have no life in you'. Then, if we have sinned, we must have Penance to get forgiven.

What I want you to remember very specially about the Sacraments is this: when you come to be baptised, confirmed, to make your confession or to receive Holy Communion, you KNOW that you will always get God's Grace, because He said He would give it in these ways—and God always keeps His promises.

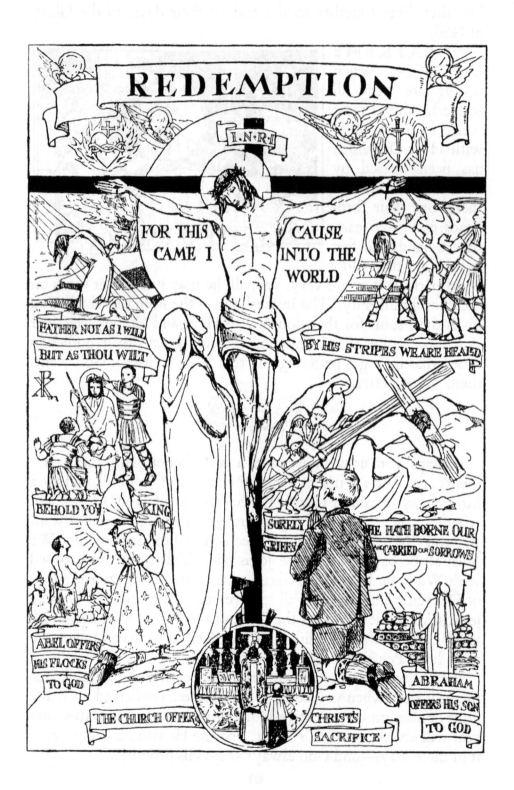

SIN

WHEN we come into this world as tiny babes, we have a *soul* and a *body*; we are rather like a Sacrament—something you can see and something you cannot see. But our soul is the more important part of us, because it never dies. Our bodies will die one day, although it is true they will rise again.

God gives us His Grace specially for our souls. You can see food for your body, because you can see your body; but you cannot see food for your soul, because you cannot see your soul, although it is just as real as your body.

CLEAN AND DIRTY SOULS

When your soul comes into the world, what is it like? Do you think that it is like the Soul of Jesus, lovely and bright, full of the Life and Light of God?

No, I am sorry to say, it is not like that, though it would have been if Adam and Eve had not sinned against God and so lost the true life of their souls. Because of their sin, all souls come into the world empty of the Life and Light of God, and that is such a dreadful thing that it is called THE STAIN OF ORIGINAL SIN. Only Jesus and Mary have been without it; Jesus, because He is God's own Son, and Mary because God kept her free from it so that she could be a worthy Mother for His Son. This stain of sin is done away in Baptism, when God fills the dark and empty soul with His Life and Light.

Do you see why we say that a little baby, who can't have done anything

63

wrong himself—there hasn't been time, and he doesn't know how!—is in A STATE OF SIN before his Baptism and in A STATE OF GRACE after it?

★   ★   ★

It sometimes happens that children are not baptised when they are babies, and they may even grow up to be men and women before they receive this Sacrament. Then we find, I am afraid, that there are other stains on their souls which they have made themselves; the stains of sins which they have actually done. So they have to confess their sins and say they are sorry for them, and then the waters of Baptism wash away every sort of stain or sin. Their souls are filled with God's Grace and all their sins are forgiven. When once God has made a soul so bright and beautiful and clean by Baptism we must remember that He wants us to stay like that and even grow more lovely still.

★   ★   ★

It's a horrid thing to think that when we do sins after we have been baptised we are really doing our best to spoil God's beautiful work in our souls. That is why we who are baptised should be willing to do anything to stop spoiling the souls which God has made so fair and clean.

THE SOUL IS LIKE A LOOKING-GLASS

When you look into a looking-glass what do you expect to see? Your own face, don't you? I expect you look in one every morning when you do your hair, or put your tie on! I want you to pretend that your soul is a looking-glass. If you could possibly look into your 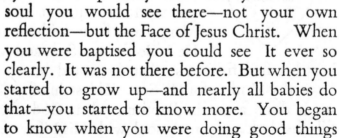 soul you would see there—not your own reflection—but the Face of Jesus Christ. When you were baptised you could see It ever so clearly. It was not there before. But when you started to grow up—and nearly all babies do that—you started to know more. You began to know when you were doing good things and when you were doing bad things. And you started to know more about God as well. Then it was that you started to make that looking-glass dirty. You know if you leave

64

your glass without dusting it for a few days it gets a thin coating of dust on it, and it makes it hard to see yourself clearly.

All those naughty things are like specks of dust which gather on the Mirror of your soul, and make the Face of Jesus Christ less clear. You are quite old enough now to understand when you sin against God. You know that it is wrong when you do not bother about your prayers, or stay away from Mass when you  could quite easily go, or when you are 'cheeky' to your mother, or tell lies, or use bad words, or take things that do not belong to you. All these things are sins against God, and they spoil that clean glass, and make it dusty.  When we sin against God it is just as if we were helping the cruel people who nailed Jesus to the Cross. You can no longer see the Face of Jesus Christ clearly.

Sometimes people do things that are very, very wrong indeed; when they know all the time that it is wrong, but still go on sinning. Then it is just as if someone put a big black mark right across the mirror, so that you could not see the Face of Jesus at all. Pray God that He will keep you from ever spoiling your soul like that.

* * *

O Saviour of the World, Who by Thy Cross and Precious Blood hast redeemed us:

Save us and Help us we humbly beseech Thee, O Lord.

You can say these words if you ever feel the devil is tempting you to do what is wrong.

SIN IS SEPARATION FROM GOD, YOUR BEST FRIEND

I expect you have a special friend with whom you go about and with whom you play. Suppose you were to say something rather unkind to your best friend—he or she would be rather sad and hurt. It is much the same with God. Jesus died on the Cross because God loves us so much; because God wants us to be friends with Him. He is our Best Friend. He made us, He gives us all the things that make us happy, all the things we need such as our food and clothing. And, most wonderful of all, He asks His friends to be with Him in Heaven for ever. And then, perhaps, we sin. Oh! how sad it is! Because it spoils, and sometimes even stops, our friendship with God Who loves us more than anything else in the world. It separates us from Him, just as if a wall had been built up between us and God.

★　　★　　★

When we have sinned against Him, we have to do our best to become friends again. We don't really like quarrelling with our ordinary friends, do we? We feel much happier when we have made it up, and are playing together again. Of course, we want to be friends with God again when we have sinned, so we must do our best to make it up. I say *we* must do our best, because of course God will always do His part—that is, He is always ready to forgive us. That is why He is such a wonderfully good Friend. But it takes two to be friends, and if God is ready to forgive us, then we must be ready to be sorry for anything that has spoilt our being friends with Him. We must try to make up for it, and be careful never to do it again.

★　　★　　★

What is Sin?

SIN IS ANY THOUGHT, WORD, DEED (THING WE DO) OR THING LEFT UNDONE WHICH IS AGAINST GOD'S WILL

★　　★　　★

We can sin against God in *four* ways:

1. We can THINK horrid thoughts inside our minds, like hating people, being jealous of them, wishing something hurtful might happen to them. Or we can be sulky and grumble inside ourselves.

2. We can SAY wrong things, like telling lies, or calling people nasty names, or by using swear words. And we can speak wrongly about God and holy things.

3. We can DO wrong things, like hitting other people in a

66

temper, or taking things that do not belong to us, behaving badly in church, in school or at home or in the street, or by disobeying.

4. And we can LEAVE THINGS UNDONE or do them without taking trouble, like staying away from Mass, NOT saying our prayers, or not being careful when we are at Mass or saying our prayers; perhaps by not owning up to something we have done at school or at home, and letting someone else be punished for it; not trying to help people who need our help.

★   ★   ★

It is sad to think that there are so many ways in which people do sin against God, but I have only put down some of them here, so that you will know how you can please God—by NOT doing them, and by keeping right away from them.

I hope you will never do any of them, and I am sure you are trying to love God very much indeed, and that you would hate even to think of joining those who nailed Him to the Cross.

Blessed Mary loved Jesus perfectly and never sinned at all.

Saint John, the Beloved Apostle, loved Jesus nearly as much, and I do not think he sinned very badly.

Saint Mary Magdalene loved Jesus very much as well; she had been a sinner, but had made up for it.

★   ★   ★

O my God, because Thou art so good, I am very sorry that I have sinned against Thee, and I will not sin again.

67

REPENTANCE

THAT is a strange word, isn't it? We are going to find out what it means. And the first thing to do to understand what it means is to read this story, which I expect you have heard before. It is one of the Parables which our Lord told to the disciples, and it is about someone who sinned and was separated from his father, his best friend. We shall see what he did to become friends again.

THE PARABLE OF THE PRODIGAL SON

Once upon a time there was a nice kind man. He was very rich, and had a lovely big house to live in, and lots of servants and people to do things for him, who loved to do the things for him because of his being so nice and kind. He did not live in a big town; he lived in the country. Perhaps you are lucky enough to live in the country, or at least you have visited the country, with its lovely green fields and woods and hills, with beautiful rivers and lakes. Well, he lived in a lovely part of the country. There was no nasty smoke or dirt. All was beautiful and fresh. Of course, he had lots of sheep and cows and other animals; and he specially had many very nice friends who used to come and see him. He loved all his servants very much, and the friends who used to come and see him, and he even loved the animals in the farmyard. But, above all, he had two sons, whom he loved ever so much—much, much more than anything else in the world; and they were all ever so happy together at home. But one day the father thought his younger son was not quite so happy, and he did not like him to be unhappy. At last he found out what was the matter, for his son came to him and said, 'Dad, I'm getting tired of staying at home. I know you are all most kind to me, and I have been happy, but I want to go and see what things are like in other parts of the world. I want to go and see towns and all the other things that are so exciting. I know you will be sad about me, but I want now the money that you are going to leave me when you die, and I want to go and have a good time doing as I like.'

Yes, the father *was* very sad. But he would not force the boy to stay at home and so he let him go. One morning he watched his son set off with the things he needed, his pockets full of money, and carrying plenty of food. It was a lovely bright morning, and the sun was shining, and nothing could have been nicer. He set out happily, walking quickly, enjoying every moment of it.

His father watched him go very sadly; and every morning after that he used to go up to the top of his house and look. What do you think he used to look for? For his son coming back again. Day after day he went up to look; day after day he came down; there was no sign of his son.

What happened to the son? Well, after travelling for a very long time, he got to a town in the far-away country. There he settled down and started to make friends with people. That was very easy because he had lots of money. They all used to spend a lot of time together eating and drinking and living wickedly. They were not very nice friends really, and only liked him as long as he had any money. At last, after he had gone on living in this bad way for some time, he found he had no money—he had spent it all. He found also that he had no friends either—they had all left him. He was poor, he was alone and he was hungry. Now what was he to do? He was in want, and there was no one to help him. He wondered how his father was, but he did not like to go back home now. So he had to get a 'job'. Things were rather bad in that country, and there was a famine (i.e. when crops fail and there is not enough to eat), so 'jobs', particularly good ones, were not easy to get. He got so 'down and out' that he had to take a 'job' of feeding pigs. He did not like that at all, and the worst of it was that he was still very hungry, so very hungry that he would have eaten the crusts and things he was given to

throw to the pigs, if he had dared. His clothes were now in rags. No longer were they the bright, smart clothes he was used to, and of course he could not buy new ones without money. After this had been going on for a long time, and he had sunk as low as he possibly could, he started to think. This is what he thought: 'I wonder how Dad is. I was terribly wrong to leave him like that, and I am very, very sorry for it now. I am much worse off than even the least of his servants. They all have enough to eat, and clothes to wear. And above all I know that I have hurt my father very much indeed. What shall I do? I know! I will get up, and I will go to my father, and I will say to him, "Father, I have sinned against Heaven and against you, and I am not fit to be called your son; make me like one of your servants, so long as I can come back."' So the son started on the painful journey home, a journey very different from that on which he had set out so very cheerfully one lovely bright morning long ago. He found it ever so hard for now he was thin and weak, dirty, ashamed of himself and terribly unhappy.

Now the father still used to go every day to look for his son coming back. At last he went up one day as usual to the top of his house and looked right away in the distance. 'What is that tiny speck in the distance? Is it moving? Yes. It looks like a bundle of rags and bones moving slowly along.' So the son crept home very, very slowly. He was almost crawling on his hands and knees he was so down and out.

His father did not wait long when he knew that it was his son.

 He ran as fast as his old legs would carry him to meet his son, and he flung his arms around him and cried because he was so happy. But the son meant to say what he had made up his mind to say. So he said: 'Father, I have sinned against Heaven and against you, and I am not fit to be called your son. I am so sorry that I ever went away from you, and I know that it was terribly wrong.' What do you think the father did? He called his head servant and told him to take his son indoors, and said, 'See that he has a good bath, brush his hair, and put on him the best clothes he used to wear before

70

he went away. Put a ring on his finger, and shoes on his feet, to show that he is not to be a servant, but one of the family again'. The cook was told to get ready a wonderful dinner, so that they could all sit down and have a lovely feast to celebrate the boy's return. 'For,' said the father, 'it's as if my son had died and has now come to life again.' You see, he had sinned very much, but was so very, very sorry that he wanted to make up for it by being like one of the servants. But the father loved him so much that he forgave him and took him back into the family. The son lived happily with his father at home after that and never wanted to go away again.

★　★　★

I want you to think about six things in this story:

1. The son sinned, and was separated from his father.
2. He felt sorry he had hurt his father.
3. He came back and owned up that he had sinned.
4. He wanted to make up for it.
5. The loving father forgave him, and
6. Told his servant to put him back near him where he was before.

God is like the father, and we are all like the son in the story.

Now think about six things to do with us:

1. When we sin and do wrong things, they separate us from God our Heavenly Father.
2. Then we must try to be sorry that we have wronged God by our sins.
3. We must own up—go and tell our Heavenly Father that we have sinned.
4. We must try to make up for our sins by being better.
5. Then God gives us His forgiveness through
6. His priest who puts us back in our proper place in the Special Family of Jesus Christ.

★　★　★

Always remember that God did not HAVE to forgive the sins of men, because it was their own fault that they sinned; but He

71

DOES forgive our sins, He puts us back into the Family, and makes our soul shining bright again; all because Jesus died on the Cross to make up for them. And He loves us even when we are a long way from Him in sin.

O dear child of God, if you have gone from Him at all in doing wrong, run to Him and own up. Never think your sins don't matter. They may not seem very big sins, but remember how they hurt your Saviour on the Cross. You will always find that He will forgive you if you want Him to.

SIN NAILS OUR LORD TO THE CROSS

I shall tell you very soon now how to get your sins forgiven, but for the moment remember there are three things we should do when we have sinned:

BE SORRY—OWN UP—MAKE UP FOR

These three added together mean

REPENTANCE

* * *

Jesus said, 'There is joy in the presence of the Angels of God over one sinner that repenteth'.

THE SACRAMENT OF PENANCE

I wonder if you have ever thought how babies are brought to church and are baptised each one by itself, and God brings them into the Catholic Church through His priest who baptises them. When we come to be confirmed, although others may be confirmed at the same time God uses His bishop to give us, each one by himself, the gift of the Holy Ghost. God gives us the Food of our souls in Holy Communion through His priest who comes to each one of us separately. Naturally when we have sinned God forgives us, each one by ourselves, through His priest.

* * *

When Jesus appeared to the Apostles when He had risen from the dead on the first Easter Sunday, He gave them the Power to forgive sins. He said, 'Peace be unto you. As My Father has sent Me, so send I you', and He breathed on them and said, 'Receive the Holy Ghost; whose sins you forgive they are forgiven, and whose sins you refuse to forgive they are not forgiven'. By doing this Jesus made the Apostles able to go on with His work.

* * *

He often forgave people their sins. You remember how He forgave Saint Mary Magdalene who had been very wicked before she knew Jesus. And of course you remember the paralysed man who was brought to our Lord by four friends who carried him on his bed. Jesus said to him, 'Son, be of good cheer, your sins are forgiven'. And the other people who heard Him grumbled saying, 'Who can forgive sins but God alone?' Of course they did not know that Jesus is God as we know.

* * *

Our Lord has handed on that Power to all the priests of His Church. I don't expect that you have ever seen a priest being given the Sacrament of Holy Order. The bishop says, as he lays his hands on the new priest's head, 'Receive the Holy Ghost, ——; whose sins you forgive they are forgiven, and whose sins you refuse to forgive they are not forgiven'.

* * *

When we have sinned and been naughty, then we go to Confess or own up to those sins to God in front of His priest. And the priest is able to give us God's Forgiveness because He has the Power. This is called the Sacrament of Penance.

73

WE RECEIVE THIS SACRAMENT WHEN WE GO TO CONFESSION TO
TELL OUR SINS BECAUSE WE ARE SORRY FOR THEM, AND RECEIVE
GOD'S FORGIVENESS.

I am going to tell you exactly how to do that.

GETTING READY FOR CONFESSION

If you have never been to Confession
before, I expect that someone will help
you to get ready. But in case no one
does help you, here are a few things to
remember.

Always go somewhere by yourself so
that you can think what your sins really
are. The church is the best place if you
can go there.

Ask God the Holy Ghost to tell you
what your sins are. You can do that by
saying something like this:

O my God,
I know that I have sinned against Thee
And have hurt Thy dear Son Jesus Christ on the Cross;
Show me my sins!
Those wicked thoughts;
Those wrong words spoken;
Those things I have done wrong;
And the things I have left undone;
Since my last Confession.

You may like to say that lovely hymn, 'Come, Holy Ghost, our
souls inspire', which you can find in any hymn-book.

Then think of Jesus dying on the Cross for you. Think
carefully over the time since your last Confession. Or, if it is your
first confession, think back as far as you can.

Some people find it easier to write down their sins on paper;
it helps them to remember. Of course, you can please yourself.

Try hard to remember everything, and never leave anything
out on purpose, because it would be no good going to confession
at all if we did that.

When you think you have remembered everything, think of your sins one by one, and tell our Lord in your heart how sorry you are. You can say a little prayer something like this:

O Jesus, my Lord and my God;
I come to confess
These my sins at Thy Cross,
Hoping for Thy Forgiveness.
Help me to be truly sorry;
Help me not to do them again;
Help me to make up for them
For Thy dear sake. Amen.

AT CONFESSION

Then, when you see no one else is with the priest at the confessional, go and kneel there and ask for his blessing: 'Bless me, Father, for I have sinned.' Make the Sign of the Cross when he blesses you. Then say, 'Since my last Confession which was — — weeks ago, I have——' and then say quite simply what you remember having done wrong. Try to say how often you have done things; it may be 'a few times' or it may be 'a lot of times'.

If you have written your sins down, you can read them; then you won't leave out anything.

Be very careful to burn the paper afterwards, in case anyone else should read it. Remember your sins are only to do with God, yourself and the priest who hears your confession. When you have finished you can say, 'That's all'. Later on you may like to say the 'I confess' and the little prayer which begins, 'For these and all my other sins', and you can find both in most little prayer books

*　*　*

Listen ever so carefully while the priest talks to you. He will try to help you to love God better, and to overcome the sins you have confessed.

Then he will tell you to do a 'Penance'. A penance is something we do which helps to make up for our sins. It may be a prayer or a psalm or a hymn which we are to say. Or it may be something we are to *do*. But, whatever it is, remember you must do it very carefully indeed afterwards. Don't forget it! Of course, the penance cannot really make up for all that Jesus suffered on the Cross; but by doing it we can do our bit to make up for our sins.

★ ★ ★

Then listen for the words of Forgiveness—we call 'Forgiveness' 'Absolution'. It really means *being loosed from* our sins.

The words are: 'I ABSOLVE THEE FROM ALL THY SINS IN THE NAME OF THE FATHER AND OF THE SON AND OF THE HOLY GHOST'.

You will see the priest make the Sign of the Cross over you at those words, so you can make the sign on yourself to remind you that it is only because Jesus died on a Cross that you can be Absolved or forgiven.

AFTER CONFESSION

When the priest says, 'Go in peace. The Lord hath put away thy sins', go back to your place in church and thank God from the bottom of your heart for being so good to you. He has made your soul just as it was when you were baptised, beautifully clean and white, filled with the Life and Light of God; all sins have been taken away from you. You could say a prayer something like this:

My God,
I thank Thee with all my heart and soul
for taking away my sins,
Through the Blood of Thy dear Son Jesus.
I promise
that I will try my very best,
with the help of Thy Grace,
Not to sin again.
Help me for Jesus Christ's sake. Amen.

★ ★ ★

76

Don't you think that it is worth going to confession when you know God forgives you in such a wonderful way?

Do your penance carefully, and then go quietly out of church, remembering that the devil may try at once to make you do again the same things you have just confessed and for which you have been forgiven. So, as the Scouts' motto says, 'Be prepared'.

★   ★   ★

When ought you to go to confession? When you have sinned and been *very* naughty—that is, when you think you have a really black mark on your soul.

But it is also a good thing to go to confession about every month or six weeks, so that your soul can be 'dusted'. You can fit your confessions in so that they come just before such times as Advent, Christmas, Lent, Easter, and Whitsun, and at regular times during the rest of the year. Most people make their Holy Communion as soon after their confession as possible, so that their souls are still clean to receive our Lord.

MASS AND HOLY COMMUNION

THERE are three things which Jesus said all Christians must do if they are to be good Christians. He said that everyone must be baptised when He told the Apostles, 'Go and teach all nations, baptising them in the name of the Father and of the Son and of the Holy Ghost'. He also said, 'When you pray, say "Our Father"'. That is why the Our Father is the prayer which every Christian says very often. The third thing is very important too. He said, as He took the bread and wine, 'This is My Body', 'This is My Blood', 'Do this in remembrance of Me'. We are going to learn what that means.

THE FEEDING OF THE FIVE THOUSAND

Jesus was on a mountain near the sea of Galilee with His Apostles, and there was also a great crowd of people. They had been following Him from place to place, listening to His wonderful teaching. Probably most of the people had come a long

way from their homes, and the little food they had with them had long ago been eaten. They had not worried about food for their bodies while they were listening to Jesus, Whose words were food for their souls. But they were a long way from the shops, and it was Jesus Who thought of food to eat. Isn't it wonderful how He looks after our bodies as well as our souls? Of course, Jesus knew what He would do. Philip said to Him, 'Two hundred penny-worth of bread would not be enough for everyone to have a little'. A penny in those days was worth much more than it is to-day; it was a day's wages; so it would have been very expensive. Andrew said to Him, 'There's a lad here who has five little loaves of bread and two small fishes, but what are they among so many?' There was a lot of grass in the place, so Jesus said, 'Make the men sit down', and there were about five thousand of them. Jesus took the loaves and two fishes, and broke them, and gave thanks and gave them to the Apostles to set before the people. They kept coming back to fetch more, and there was always more when they came back, so that everyone in that crowd had enough. The Apostles then gathered up all the crumbs, and they filled twelve baskets. The people, when they saw the wonderful miracle that Jesus had done, naturally wanted to make Him their king. Jesus was already their King really, but they hadn't learned as much about Him as we have, so they did not know that. They wanted to make the King of Heaven and Earth an ordinary earthly king. But Jesus went away from them further into the mountain to pray to His Heavenly Father.

Jesus, by a miracle, fed five thousand people so that everyone had enough. He only started with five little loaves and two small fishes. But that was food for their bodies. Jesus was getting them ready to understand that He would give them Food for their souls, which is much more important.

BREAD FROM HEAVEN

It was the day after the feeding of the five thousand, and Jesus was in Capernaum, on the other side of the sea of Galilee. Again He was teaching a crowd of people. Many of them had been with Him the day before and had seen the miracle; and the Twelve Apostles were standing round Him. Some of the people had only come to hear Him because of the miracle. So Jesus told them, 'Don't worry so much about the food that perishes', and He went on to tell them that He would give them Bread from Heaven. This Bread would be His Flesh, so that if they ate It their souls would live for ever. They thought it very strange, and some of them asked, 'How can this man give us His Flesh to eat?' You see, they did not know that He was God as well as Man, and could do what He said. They thought He was only the son of a carpenter. But Jesus was not angry with them, for He knew they did not understand as you and I do. He just said to them, 'If you do not eat My Flesh and drink My Blood you will have no life in you'. Some of them were rather annoyed at this and would not follow Him any more, because they did not understand. Then Jesus turned to His own Apostles and said, 'Are you going away too?' They said, 'No. Of course not. To whom shall we go? We know that what You say is true'. They trusted Jesus although they did not quite understand. They trusted Him so much that they knew that in some wonderful way He would really give them His Body and His Blood as the Food of their souls.

MAUNDY THURSDAY

Palm Sunday was some time later, probably a month or two, when Jesus rode into the City of Jerusalem like a King sitting on an Ass. The time for Jesus to offer the Sacrifice of His Life was coming very near. It was Thursday in Holy Week—the first Holy Week there ever was—and also the great festival of the Jews called the Passover was on Saturday. Jesus wanted to eat a Passover Supper with His Apostles. I expect you know the story very well indeed. Two of the Apostles went to an upper room in Jerusalem and laid the table. Then in the evening Jesus came with them all and sat down to the sacred meal.

The Apostles were wondering what was going to happen to Jesus and them all, because the Jews, the Scribes and the Pharisees and the Jewish Priests were hating Him a lot and were stirring up the people to hate Him too. The Apostles loved Him dearly, at least all except one. That one was Judas, and he had made up his mind to betray Jesus to the chief priests for money. Then a very solemn thing happened. Jesus washed their feet, like the servants used to do in those days. He did it to show that the most important people should be the servants of the others. After that He sat down at the table again, and the Apostles were all wondering what was going to happen, when He took bread, and gave thanks and blessed it and said, 'THIS IS MY BODY WHICH IS GIVEN FOR YOU, Do this in remembrance of Me'. Then He

took the cup—or chalice, as we call it—with wine in it mixed with a little water, and He gave thanks again and said, 'THIS IS MY BLOOD WHICH IS SHED FOR YOU'. And He gave to each of them what *looked* like ordinary bread and wine, but what was really no longer bread and wine, but His Sacred Body and Precious Blood. So the Apostles received their First Holy Communion, and the First Holy Communion that anyone had ever received. Jesus gave Himself to them in this wonderful way. It was the Bread which came down from Heaven about which He had told them.

But what is so wonderful is that He gave them the Power to do the same thing, when He told them, 'Do this in remembrance of Me'.

When our Lord had been crucified, and had risen again the Apostles did what He told them to do. Whenever they met together to worship God, one of them took the place of our Lord, and did exactly what He had done. He took bread and wine, and gave thanks and said exactly the same words over them, 'This is My Body—this is My Blood'. Then they were no longer bread and wine, although they looked like them, but the true Body and Blood of Jesus. Then all who had been baptised received the Body and Blood of Jesus as the Food of their souls, just as the Apostles had done on Maundy Thursday, from the hands of our Lord Himself.

As more and more people came into the Catholic Church, the Apostles handed on this power to others, by giving them the Sacrament of Holy Order, so that wherever in the wide world there were Christians, there would always be a priest to do what Jesus had commanded; and Christians could have Holy Communion.

To-day when you go to Mass you see exactly the same thing happening: Christians going up to the Altar to receive Jesus Himself as their Spiritual Food, exactly as the first Christians did. When you come to Mass on Sundays or any other day, you see the priest standing at the Altar. What is he doing? Just what our Lord did on Maundy Thursday, and what priests have done ever since. You know that in the middle of the service when the bell rings and everyone is very quiet the priest is taking the bread  and saying those same words, 'This is My Body', and he lifts It up for us to see; and he is taking the Chalice and saying, 'This is My Blood'.

Then you know that there is no longer ordinary bread and wine, but the true Body and Blood of Jesus, and that Jesus is really there at His Altar.

GOING TO MASS IS LIKE GOING TO BETHLEHEM

The Shepherds came to Bethlehem to see the Baby Jesus lying in the manger. They saw with their eyes just a tiny baby. But with their inside eyes—the eyes of their souls—they saw God the Son, Jesus, the Saviour of the World.

When we go to Mass we are like the Shepherds—we come to worship God. We see with our eyes what looks like a little white wafer of bread; but with our inside eyes—the eyes of our souls—we see Jesus Himself, our God and our Saviour.

GOING TO MASS IS LIKE BEING AT THE CROSS ON CALVARY

Blessed Mary, Saint John and Saint Mary Magdalene stood by the Cross of Jesus as He offered the Sacrifice of His Life to make up for the sins of the world. At Mass we stand by their sides, and join in offering to God the same sacrifice. That is why we sometimes call the Mass 'THE HOLY SACRIFICE'. Jesus is just as really on the Altar as He was on the Cross, but in a different way. Of course He does not die again—that could never happen—but His Death is offered in every Mass, just as He is always offering it in Heaven.

I know this is hard for you to understand, but remember it was hard for the Apostles too, to begin with. I think this might help you to understand better. If you are going to give a present to your best friend you want to give him something really good, the very best you can afford, don't you?

By ourselves we have nothing fit for God—but there is one thing—Jesus Himself. When we come to Mass we come to give something to God, and the only really good thing we have is Jesus, really there on the Altar. So we give Him through the hands of the priest.

That is why it is so very important that we should never miss coming to Mass on Sundays. It is our duty to give to God the best we can. The best we can give is the Mass—Jesus Himself.

We go to Mass to do four things:

To praise and worship God
To thank Him for all His blessings
To ask forgiveness for all our sins
To ask blessings on our friends living and dead and on ourselves.

Remember we should love to go to Mass because there we are joined with all the Angels and Saints of God in worship. We are all one family with them, specially at Mass.

RECEIVING HOLY COMMUNION

I expect you have often seen people going to the Altar to receive Holy Communion. You have seen the priest come down and give them the Precious Body and Blood of Jesus. Perhaps you go to Communion yourself; if so you will know a lot about it. When we go to Holy Communion it is just as if we were with the Apostles in the Upper Room at Jerusalem, and Jesus is giving us His Body and Blood Himself.

Think what a wonderful thing it is to go to Holy Communion! Don't you think it is ever so important to be properly ready to receive Jesus into ourselves? Let us see how we can best be ready.

GETTING READY

I want you to imagine that your mother and father are going to have a very important visitor to see them. He is coming to have tea at your house. Your mother is all 'put about' in the morning seeing that everything is spick and span for the important visitor. The floor is scrubbed, every tiny speck of dust is cleaned from the pictures on the wall and the table and the legs of the chairs. The crockery is carefully washed and all the spoons made to shine nicely. And your mother sends you off to get some nice flowers to make the room look cheerful, and a warm fire is burning in

Drawing on this page by Jennie Oliver Dick

the grate. Then the great moment arrives. You have all been watching the clock for the time, and you hear a step outside—no, it's only the afternoon post!—then at last, just at the right time he comes. How you look after him! You see he has all he wants, and you never leave him by himself. You talk to him and listen to what he has to say to you. And when it is time for him to go, you ask him to come again; and you will always love his visits; and your parents will often ask him to come.

But in Holy Communion we receive as our Special Visitor Someone Who is more important than all the Kings and Queens and Princes and Princesses in the whole world all put together. It is Jesus Christ Himself, your Lord and your God Who is to be your Special Guest. You must be ever so much more careful about getting the House of your Soul ready for Him.

First of all the HOUSE MUST BE CLEANED. It must be scrubbed clean—by being really sorry for your sins, and if you have been very naughty by going to Confession.

Then, as you know, a house which is *only* scrubbed clean is not very attractive or nice really, the House of your Soul must be ADORNED AND MADE BEAU- TIFUL. How shall we do that? By having a really nice bunch of flowers in our souls! These are some of the flowers Jesus loves to find in that bunch: We must really BE LOV- ING HIM more than anything else. We must WANT Him to come really and truly. We must BELIEVE that it is Jesus Himself Who does come. If we are trying to Love Him, to Want Him and to Believe in Him then we shall have a really lovely bunch of flowers which will make the House of our Soul beautiful.

★   ★   ★

Then there is one other thing: our bodies must be ready too, as well as our souls. We must never have anything to eat or drink, however tiny it is, before coming to Holy Communion. We call this keeping the FAST, and we must keep it from Midnight. It is very easy to forget and to have a cup of tea before coming out in the morning.

I am not going to write out all the prayers you might say before Holy Communion, because I expect that you have a little book with prayers in it, which you are used to. All you should remember is never go to Holy Communion without getting the House of your Soul ready.

EXACTLY HOW TO RECEIVE HOLY COMMUNION

When you get up in the morning on which you are to make your Communion, be specially careful to have a clean outside, as well as inside. Say your morning prayers as usual, adding a little prayer asking God to help you to make a good Holy Communion. Then set off for church. It is best not to talk to other people as you go, because you want to be thinking of Him Who is to be your Guest. When you get into church and are nicely in your place, spend as long as you can before the Mass starts on your knees making quite sure you are ready. Follow the Mass in your book, listen carefully to the Collects, Epistle and Gospel, and join in all the prayers of the Mass either by following them in your book or by saying the parts you are meant to say. Remember as the Mass goes on that you are really 'With Angels and Archangels and all the company of Heaven' and are offering your very best with them.

You will know when the Consecration takes place—when the priest says those words of our Lord, 'This is My Body', 'This is My Blood', because a little bell will ring to warn you that It is going to happen. Then later on the bell will ring again to tell you when to go up to the Altar. Be very specially reverent after the Consecration, trying to tell our Lord how much you want Him to come to you. Then when the time comes, leave your seat, genuflect—that is, bow your knee to the ground in worship of our Lord —and go up to the Altar with all the others, and kneel at the Altar rail. You can tell our Lord in your heart, 'Lord I am not worthy that Thou shouldest come under my roof, but speak the word only and my soul shall be healed'. You may remember that it was the Centurion who said that to our Lord, when Jesus said He would come to his house to heal his servant who was ill. He is coming to you now, and you are not really worthy. Tell Him you want to be worthy, and that you really do love Him more than anything else in the whole wide world. Then the priest comes down to give Holy Communion. He comes to you first with the Host—that is, the Sacred Body of Jesus. Keep your hands to-gether, lift up your head, and put your tongue just over your lower lip. When the priest has put the Sacred Host on your tongue you can swallow It quite easily. Then remember Who you have within you as your Guest. Then the priest comes with the Chalice. Don't touch it, but just lower your head a little as the priest brings it to touch your lips. Don't try to drink, but just let your lips touch the Precious Blood. Be careful not to wipe your mouth afterwards. Don't move from your place till the priest has given the Precious Blood to the person on your left, in case in moving you should jolt his arm and perhaps cause an accident. But when the priest has passed the person on your left, then get up, genuflect and go quietly back to your seat.

In some churches people may receive the Sacred Host on their hands. If they do this in your church this is how you do it. Place your right hand on your left with the fingers stretched out. Lift them up as high as you can while keeping them quite flat and steady. Then the priest will put the Host on your hand. Take It into your mouth by using your tongue; and be specially careful that you do not leave even the tiniest crumb on your hand. Look very carefully.

When you get back to your place after receiving Holy Communion, kneel quite still for a few moments, and REMEMBER you have Jesus Him- 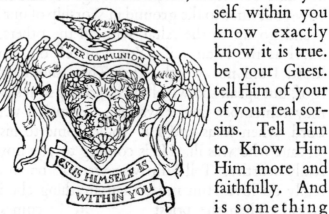 self within you —you don't know exactly how, but you know it is true. He has come to be your Guest. Talk with Him: tell Him of your Love for Him, of your real sorrow for your sins. Tell Him you really want to Know Him better, Love Him more and Serve Him more faithfully. And perhaps there is something special you want to talk to Him about—perhaps something to Thank Him for or to Ask Him for. It may be that a friend of yours is very ill; or it may be someone's birthday. Now is the time for you to talk to Him about these things.

When you think you have finished, turn to your book, and use some of the prayers marked 'Thanksgiving after Holy Communion'. It is ever so important to say 'THANK YOU' to our Lord for coming to you. So be just as careful about it as you are to get ready for His coming.

Don't hurry away as soon as you see the priest going away from the Altar. I have been in some churches where this happens. Suddenly everyone in church jumps up and rushes to the door of the church, and at once start talking as hard as they can! I don't think that is very nice, do you? I think we should want to go home as quietly as possible, remembering for as long as we can what a wonderful thing God has done for us.

In the early days of the Catholic Church, people who had not been able to receive Holy Communion in the morning, when they saw people coming from church, used to go to them and kiss them. This sounds rather funny to us, but they knew that Jesus had come only a very short time before to dwell in their souls, and it seemed the only thing for them to do. It was a sign of love for our Lord. Any way we can remember that as a story, and as we go home from Mass we can remember we have Him within us.

Why does He come to us in this wonderful way? He comes to make us more like Him; to give us His Life and Light; and to help us to live for Him. So we shall want to come to Holy Communion as often as possible. Never think you can come to Holy Communion too often. Our Lord wants His children to come to give themselves to Him very often indeed. So don't think you can only go once a month, because you can go whenever you like, if you prepare yourself properly.

THE WOULD-BE THIEF

There was once a Parish Priest who was in charge of a very small parish in the country. One night about midnight, a man came to his house and said, 'There is a woman dying at the little house in the woods, will you come at once and give her the Last Sacrament?' So the Priest got up and went to the church, and got the Blessed Sacrament from the Tabernacle and set off to walk through the woods. The man  had gone on before to say he was coming. The woods were very lonely, but the Priest was not frightened at all because of Whom he was carrying. He thought, though that he could hear footsteps behind him. It was very dark and there was no moon. He kept stopping to listen; and whenever he stopped the footsteps stopped too. At last he arrived at the house. There was no light in the house at all. He knocked and there was no answer. He knocked several times till at last someone put his head out of the window. The Priest said, 'Isn't there someone ill here?' 'No', was the answer. 'We are all quite all right.' So he went back home, carrying with him the Most Holy Sacrament. As he walked he again thought he could hear footsteps—whenever he stopped they stopped too, and whenever he started again they started. He put the Blessed Sacrament back into the Tabernacle and went to bed again. Very strange, he thought!

Many years later this same Priest was a Bishop, and he was called to a big prison to see a man who was to be hanged for murder. The poor man had asked to see him. As soon as he came into the man's cell, the man said, 'Do you remember a night many years ago?' And he went on to tell the story of that night. How he had come to tell the Priest someone was ill, how there never was anyone ill really, but that he had followed him all the way in order to steal the silver vessels in which he carried the Blessed Sacrament. 'But why did you not steal them?' asked the Bishop. 'Why?' said the man. 'Because you had someone with you all the time!'

*   *   *

When you come away from Holy Communion remember you 'have Someone with you all the time'.

*   *   *

The devil is never so strong in his attacks upon us as when we have just been to Confession or to Holy Communion.

So always be on your guard.

SAINT TARCISIUS

When the Catholic Church was being persecuted in the City of Rome many hundreds of years ago, there were a lot of Christians in Prison, waiting to be put to death. One thing they wanted above all else was to receive Holy Communion. The Christians who were still free used to have Mass in the great underground passages which are called the 'Catacombs'. When the Bishop heard what they wanted, he told the people about it and said, 'How are we to get the Blessed Sacrament to them? It is dangerous for anyone to go to the prison.' But there was a little Altar Server named Tarcisius who used to get into the prison to see some of his friends; he was only ten, so the gaolers didn't mind. When the Bishop asked, 'Whom shall we send?' he piped up, 'Please send me!' So the Bishop said, 'Yes.' And the Holy Body of Jesus was wrapped in a fair linen cloth, and the boy carried It in a little bag round his neck. Very reverently he hugged the precious little bag to him as he went quickly towards the prison. But suddenly he met some soldiers.

He hoped it would be all right. But it wasn't. The soldiers started to mock him, and when he said nothing to them, they said, 'Oh! he's a Christian. Here, what are you carrying?' Tarcisius ran as hard as he could. But the soldiers threw stones at him, and one hit him on the head, and he fell  to the ground and died. The soldiers, who were very cruel, went to see what he was carrying, but they found only a beautifully clean piece of fair linen.

*　　*　　*

How reverently we should behave whenever we go into church! Because there in the Tabernacle is Jesus Christ in His Sacramental Presence.

THE TABERNACLE

I expect you have noticed a white light in a lamp hanging in front of one of the Altars in your church. It may be the high Altar, or it may be in a side chapel. And you have noticed, perhaps, a box in the middle of the Altar, or it may even be in the wall near an Altar. And it has a curtain hanging in front of it. There is kept a number of Hosts consecrated at Mass so that people who are ill may have the Blessed Sacrament taken to them at home; or people who are not able to be at Mass may come at some other time and still have Holy Communion. Of course, there in the Tabernacle is Jesus Himself in His Sacramental Presence. So we shall often go there to pray before the Tabernacle.

If you are ill you know that you have only to ask your Priest, and he will bring you your Communion. You simply have to get a table ready, with a clean white cloth on it, and if you have them a Crucifix and a pair of candlesticks with candles in them and a little bowl with some water in it. If you are ill for several weeks you should certainly have your Communion brought to you; and if you have read the last few pages you will understand why. Of course it really is the same as though you were receiving Holy Communion at Mass in church; because the Blessed Sacrament is always the same Jesus.

★　　★　　★

Will you try to remember all your life that Holy Communion is the great Heavenly Meal in which all Christians all over the world are joined together? Whether you are in your own church at home, or in a tiny little Mission church in some out-of-the-way part of the country, if you are a Missionary in the Arctic, or in the middle of Africa, it is always the same Mass, and the Holy Communion is always the same. Wherever there is a Priest and an Altar, there is the Mass. It may be very rich, with lots of servers, and lights and incense and processions; or it may be on a battle-field with a soap box acting as an altar, but Jesus is there under the veils of bread and wine just the same.

A very sad thing happened some little time ago. A girl who had been very regular in coming to Confession and Holy Communion for several years moved away from her church to a new part of a big city. About a year later she came back to see her friends at her old home, and her Priest met her and said, 'Hello,

Mary. How are you getting on?' 'All right, thank you, Father.' 'What church do you go to now? Do you go to the one I told you about?' asked the Priest. 'No. I did not like that one at all, so I haven't been to Mass or Communion since I left here, except once!' Oh dear, how our Lord must long for that child! I know outward things may be different, and we may not like them quite as much as the outward things we are used to. But we must remember all our life that it is really the same Church inside, it is the same Mass—inside; and it is the same Holy Communion always.

GOING ON A JOURNEY

We are Heavenward Bound—we are going on a journey to Heaven. It is not always an easy journey, because the devil does seem to try his best to stop us going on with the journey. There are lots of side turnings which seem ever so much nicer than the narrow straight road; and even on the narrow straight road there are lots of big stones, and holes to be avoided. We've simply got to get to the end of the road, because there God is waiting to give us our reward, a Crown in Heaven. But we've got to win it. He won't give it to us if we never arrive. How could He? Our Lord once said, 'He that endureth to the end the same shall be saved'. See that you go on, and on, and on, and on . . . Heavenward Bound. Jesus is always there to help, and the Blessed Mother Mary and the Angels and Saints are there to help us on our journey.

* * *

I hope you have enjoyed this book. I know there is a lot in it, and perhaps you have found bits of it rather dull. But when we are learning REALLY IMPORTANT THINGS it cannot all be made exciting, although the things themselves are exciting. To be Heavenward Bound is thrilling; because all the wonderful Saints of God have been Heavenward Bound, too, and it was

Jesus Himself Who first showed us the way. But the Saints didn't always find it easy or exciting. Learning *how* to be Heaven-ward Bound is HARD WORK. But we shall want to go on—because we know that God made us, that God loves us and that He wants US to love HIM for ever in Heaven.

STEAM BOILERS

(CARE AND OPERATION)

A PRACTICAL GUIDE TO THE CARE AND OPERATION OF
SUPERHEATERS, FEED-WATER HEATERS, STOKERS,
AND OTHER BOILER ACCESSORIES, AND THE
EFFICIENT HANDLING OF STEAM
BOILERS

REVISED BY

ROBERT H. KUSS, M.E.

CONSULTING MECHANICAL ENGINEER
FORMERLY SALES MANAGER, EDGE MOOR IRON COMPANY, CHICAGO
AMERICAN SOCIETY OF MECHANICAL ENGINEERS

ILLUSTRATED

Merchant Books
1920

INTRODUCTION

A S a rule, there are more chances to effect desirable economies in the boiler room than in all other places around the plant.

¶ Yet how can one do it? What is the procedure? How is it that Bill Thompson over in his plant can always make the same coal last longer, get more results—and frequently bring the factory superintendent down to the boiler room with a smile on his face at what is being accomplished? How does Bill do it?

¶ It's this way: Getting the good out of a good boiler consists not merely in shoveling coal in the front door, or turning on the stoker. Nor will starting the feed pumps once in a while, or moving the drafts and dampers occasionally, do all the work.

¶ A good boiler-room man knows not only the apparatus which happens to be set up in his particular plant, but he knows also the good and bad apparatus in the plants of his brother engineers. He keeps thinking all the time about what his particular equipment is doing, what it might do, what he can *make* it do—if he just changes this or that a little, or coaxes along such and such a pump, or stoker, or blower, or grate, or—anything else of the kind in his domain. He first knows apparatus and principles—and then sets out to apply what he knows to his own particular establishment. He does not necessarily change everything around, but he goes at his work sanely, intelligently—and proceeds to work out better and more result-getting solutions than anybody on his job ever did before. That is the way the Bill Thompsons of the business have gotten where they set out to go.

¶ It is the purpose of this little book to give the practical man on the job help toward what we have called the Bill Thompson class—in other words, the best boiler men in the field. The book takes up the infinite detail of boiler rooms and explains clearly, adequately all features. There are two sections. The first discusses boiler accessories—the feed-water heaters, pumps, superheaters, safety valves, fusible plugs, and such that are found in current boiler room equipment. The second section deals with boiler *practice*—the firing, stoking, cleaning, setting, testing and general care of boilers in all their relations.

¶ In the book the practical boiler man will find his own equipment and that of others explained. By borrowing an idea here, and another there, and *studying* how the whole plant works, the boiler-man should be able to get very much more good from his equipment in the future.

CONTENTS

PART I

BOILER ACCESSORIES

CONTENTS

CONTENTS

PART II

BOILER PRACTICE

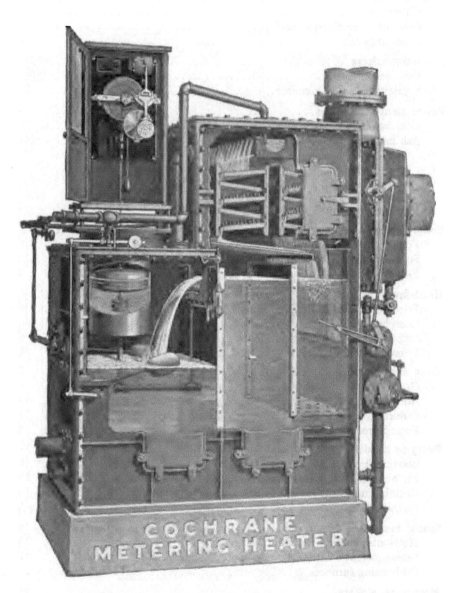

PART SECTION OF COCHRANE METERING HEATER
Courtesy of Harrison Safety Boiler Works, Philadelphia

BOILER ACCESSORIES

INTRODUCTION

A proper consideration of the subject of "Boiler Accessories" presupposes the reader to possess a fairly complete understanding of the purposes for which boilers are used, and of their main characteristics as to design and arrangement. In order to operate a boiler successfully many devices have been developed. Some of these devices are primarily concerned with the routine operation of the boiler and are those which make it possible to operate it at all. Many others are used in conjunction with boilers with the purpose of promoting a more economical performance, although these same devices may also contribute to greater safety. In the present treatment it is thought best to deal with the several items of the subject by taking up first the parts which have to do with the *pressure*, that is, with all of the devices which are included in the steam and water side of the steam-generating system, thus leaving the devices used in the generation and delivery of heated gases to be treated in the last part of this paper.

BOILER ATTACHMENTS

MANHOLES AND HANDHOLES

Characteristics of Manholes. A manhole allows access to the boiler for cleaning and repairs. It is elliptical in form and large enough to admit a man. About 16 inches for the major axis, and 12 for the minor axis, is a good size. The manhole is closed by a plate or cover made of cast iron or forged steel. This plate is held to the seat by a yoke, or yokes, and bolts, the pressure inside of the boiler pressing the plate against its seat. Fig. 1 shows one form, Y being the yoke, L the cover, and N the bolt. The joint between the cover and the shell is made steam tight by packing.

Reinforcing Plates. The strength of the boiler should always remain unimpaired; so, whenever a large hole is cut in the plate, the edge should be strengthened, for the tension is concentrated there, and the plates, moreover, are likely to become weak by corrosion. The strain put upon the plate by screwing up the cover, if no packing is used, is considerable, especially if a piece of scale gets between the faces before the joint is made tight.

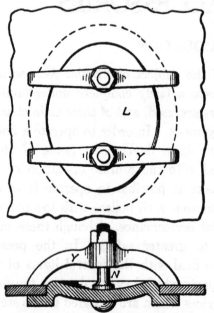

Fig. 1.   Plan and Section of Manhole Cover

Fig. 2 shows the section of a strong and simple manhole. The edge of the plate is strengthened by a broad ring of steel, which is flanged and riveted to the shell, its edge forming the seat. The cover as shown in the figure is shaped for strength. The edge of the ring which forms the seat, and the cover, are machined to make a tight joint without packing. The strengthening ring should be at least ⅝ inch thick and 4 inches wide, so that the rivet holes may not be too near the edge.

Location.   In some types of boilers, such as horizontal water-tube boilers, when it is possible to place the manholes in the ends of the drums, the elliptical opening is flanged in and a reinforcing ring is shrunk around the flanged metal for strength, and then both the edge of the flange and the face of the reinforcement are faced off to provide a true seat for a gasket between the seat and the manhead.

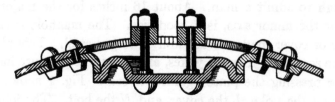

Fig. 2.   Section of a Strong but Simple Type of Manhole

It is important to note that the major axis of the manhole should be so placed that the removal of the metal weakens the structure as little as possible. In shell boilers, if the manhole is placed on the cylindrical part, the major axis is placed in the same direction as the girth seam because the danger of rupture due to internal pressure is only half in girth what it is longitudinally.

Use of Handholes. Handholes are commonly placed in boilers to give access to parts where a man cannot enter; for instance, in many horizontal return-tube boilers there may be a handhole in each end near the bottom. They are convenient to admit hose for washing out the boiler and for the removal of scale and sediment. Handholes are similar to manholes in construction, but usually require only one yoke and one bolt to keep them in place. Handholes greatly facilitate cleaning the fire-box water leg of locomotive and small vertical boilers.

Individual and Group Handholes. The development of water-tube boilers has brought about a great variety of schemes for giving access to tubes for their renewal and cleaning in such cases where the tubes are expanded into headers or manifolds not large enough to admit a man (Fig. 50, "Types of Boilers"). Provision is usually made for access by providing a hole opposite each end of the tube. These holes are not always elliptical but may be circular, provided the plates can be removed from the boiler head at some other location. In one type, the plate which makes the closure is placed on the outside of the opening, with the yoke on the inside, thus compelling the plate to resist the pressure in lifting it from its seat. In this case no gasket is used in the joint, but dependence is placed upon ground joints both where the plate meets the seat and where a blind nut presses against the plate to hold it in place.

Some water-tube boiler designers try to overcome the difficulties of having separate holes for each tube by having handholes large enough to serve groups of tubes; others provide separate holes for each tube, but shape the handhole slightly different than elliptical in order to obtain the advantage of interchangeability having the plate on the inside of the header or box. In fact, the problems arising from the necessity of providing access to tubes have given rise in their solution to a great variety of boiler designs, in many cases determining the main features which enter into boiler construction.

SUPPORTS

Importance of Adequate Supports. Since a boiler is constructed of heavy materials and contains a great deal of water, and at the same time is subjected to high and varying temperature stresses, it should be carefully supported. It is not good practice to depend upon

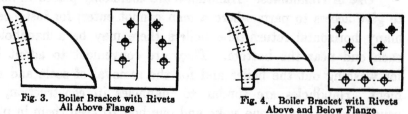

Fig. 3. Boiler Bracket with Rivets
All Above Flange

Fig. 4. Boiler Bracket with Rivets
Above and Below Flange

masonry above the fire line for holding the boiler in position, though of course this is permissible, if the operating conditions are not severe, and if due diligence is practiced in the inspection of the brickwork after a good design has been selected. Not a few severe boiler explosions have been attributed to improper supporting designs. This is espe-

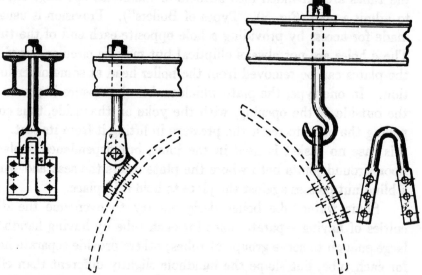

Figs. 5 and 6. Two Methods of Supporting Boilers by Suspending from Overhead Beams

cially true in cases of boiler and pipe failures where boilers have settled, thus drawing heavy steam piping of a rigid form down with them.

  Types of Construction. There are two common methods of supporting boilers: (1) by means of brackets; (2) by suspending from beams.

Bracket Supports. In horizontal tubular boilers it is customary to use two brackets on each side. The front brackets rest on the brickwork, but the others rest on small iron rollers to allow for expansion. Brackets are so arranged that the plane of support will be a little above the middle of the shell. There are several forms of brackets. The form shown in Fig. 3 is usually made of cast iron and is provided with rivets above the flange of the bracket. It is better to have the rivets both above and below the flange, as shown in Fig. 4.

Suspension Supports. Fig. 5 shows one method of suspending from beams. A lug made of wrought iron is riveted to the plates of the boiler. A bolt having one end bent like a hook holds

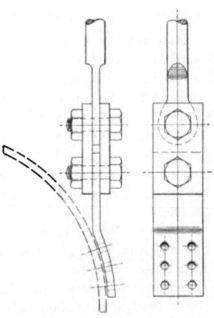

Fig. 7. Flexible Support for Suspended Boiler. Flexibility Secured by Means of Two Pieces of Boiler Plate Bolted Together

the lug from the beam. In Fig. 6 the lug is replaced by a loop of wrought iron. Fig. 7 shows another method of suspension, the connection between the rod and the boiler plates being short pieces of boiler plate arranged for flexibility.

When the boiler is of small diameter, it may be suspended as shown in Fig. 8.

Water-tube boiler supports are as numerous as the types of boilers manufactured. The tendency is to provide a form of support which permits the erection of the entire boiler before constructing any of the enclosing masonry. Suitable facilities must be provided for the

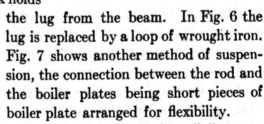

Fig. 8. Illustrating Methods of Suspending a Boiler of Small Diameter

expansion of the boiler proper by leaving space between the boiler and the masonry, which is filled in with some more or less pliable material, such as mineral wool, which at the same time will exclude air from entering the setting.

FUSIBLE PLUGS

Necessity for Use. Fusible plugs are used as a safeguard against the effects of carrying water at too low a level in the boiler. They are especially serviceable in such cases as they provide a warning when the water over the crown sheet of a fire-box boiler becomes too shallow. The best municipal and government regulations include requirements stating exactly the form and position of plugs on all kinds of boilers; these regulations, if carried out as intended, are of considerable service although it must be understood that too much reliance should not be placed upon a device of this character.

Types of Plugs. There are two main forms of fusible plugs: those which on blowing out require the immediate shutting down of the boiler, and those which act as a warning only, being capable of replacement without shutting the boiler down. The tendency of practice is to allow only the first kind, and also to avoid the use of valves which may shut off the escaping steam after a plug has blown out. The latter remark applies to the form of fusible plug which is in communication with a pipe projecting below the water line, a type frequently used in the drums of water-tube boilers. These plugs consist of a core composed of an alloy of tin, lead, and bismuth, with a covering of brass or cast iron. The United States inspection law requires at least one fusible plug to be put in every marine boiler, with the exception of water-tube boilers, the plug to be made of a bronze casing filled with good quality Banca tin from end to end. While this plug is kept at a comparatively low temperature by water on one side, the fire on the other side will not melt it; when the water level becomes low enough to leave one end of the plug uncovered, the alloy core of the plug, having a comparatively low melting point, will fuse and run out of its casing, thus relieving the pressure in the boiler and allowing the excess of steam to extinguish the fire, which otherwise would be likely to destroy the crown sheet.

Unreliability. Fusible plugs are frequently unreliable. Sometimes they will blow out when there is no apparent cause, and sometimes remain intact when the plates have become overheated. If a coating of hard scale is allowed to accumulate over the plug, it may stand considerable pressure even after the core has become melted. To provide against this, the plug should be replaced frequently. If allowed to remain in the boiler for any length of time, the composition of the alloy is likely to change, the plug thus becoming more or less unreliable.

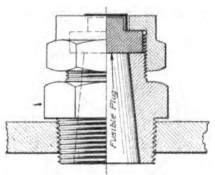

Fig. 9. Part Section of Fusible Plug Attached to Crown Sheet of Boiler

Construction. Figs. 9 and 10 illustrate the ordinary plug. It should be so made that, when screwed into the crown sheet, it will project 1½ or 2 inches above the plates, so that when the alloy melts there will be a sufficient depth of water over the crown sheet to prevent injury from heat.

Sometimes the core is covered with a thin copper cap, as shown in Fig. 9, which protects the alloy from contact with the water, thus preventing a chemical change and the formation of scale. It does not necessarily follow that a hole ½ inch or ¾ inch in diameter will liberate steam fast enough to prevent excess of pressure. If, however, the quantity of escaping steam and water is considerable, combustion will be retarded and the fire will be partly extinguished. This will operate to warn the fireman of what has happened; and, if the escape of steam is not too rapid, he may throw wet ashes or fresh coal over the entire fuel bed and thus

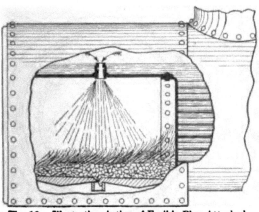

Fig. 10. Illustrating Action of Fusible Plug Attached to Crown Sheet

deaden the fire. By almost closing the damper, combustion will be reduced to such a point where the boiler can be taken out of service without endangering the boiler crown sheet.

STEAM GAGES

Working Steam Pressure. The steam pressure in the boiler is measured in *pounds per square inch*. When we say the boiler is working or steaming at 80 pounds pressure, we mean that the gage pressure is 80 pounds; that is, the pressure in the boiler is 80 pounds above *atmospheric pressure*. It could be measured by a water or mercury column; but, as these would need to be very high to measure the pressures used at the present day, they are not practicable, and for this reason a spring pressure gage is used instead.

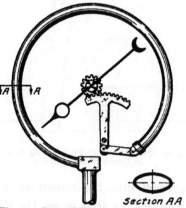

Fig. 11. Steam-Filled Curved Tube Indicating Pressure in Bourdon Steam Gage

Bourdon Dial Gage. The dial gage, now used almost universally, was invented by M. Bourdon. It is designed in accordance with the principle that a flattened, curved tube closed at one end tends to become straight when subjected to internal pressure.

The tube, which is usually oval in section, is bent into the arc of a circle as shown in Fig. 11. One end is fixed, and is in com-

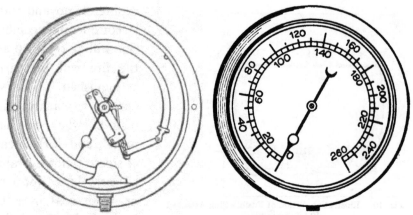

Fig. 12. Interior Mechanism and Dial of Standard Type of Steam Gage

munication with the boiler. The other is closed and free to move. By means of levers, a curved rack, and a pinion, the motion of the

free end is multiplied and indicated by a needle, which is attached
to the pinion. The needle moves over a dial which is graduated
to agree with a mercury column, or with a standard gage. The

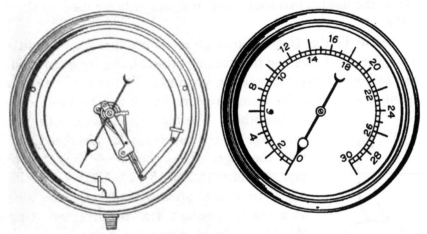

Fig. 13. Interior Mechanism and Dial of Low-Pressure Gage

backlash of the levers is taken up by a hairspring. Fig. 12 shows
the interior and face of a Bourdon steam gage manufactured by
the American Steam Gage Company.

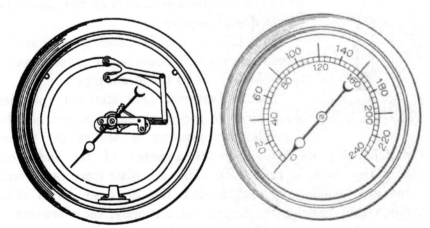

Fig. 14. Steam Gage for Use on Locomotives. Excessive Vibration of Needle Prevented
by Use of Two Short, Stiff Springs

Fig. 13 shows the exterior and interior of a steam gage. The
face of the dial is graduated. The only difference between this
gage and a vacuum gage is that in the latter the curved tube is

turned in the opposite direction, so that the needle will move clockwise with a decrease of pressure.

Locomotive Steam Gages. On account of the jarring, the gage for locomotives must be very strong. To prevent excessive vibration of the needle, two short, stiff coil segments are used, as shown in Fig. 14.

Use of Testing Gage. Sometimes two pressure gages are fitted to a boiler; one indicating the working pressure, and the other graduated to about twice the working pressure. The latter is useful in testing the boiler under water pressure, and also serves as a check on the other. The pipe which connects the pressure gage to the boiler should have bends in it near the gage. These bends—or, better, a coil pipe, as shown in Fig. 15—are filled with water, which transmits pressure and keeps the spring at a nearly constant low temperature. Gages should be placed where the water in the coiled pipe will not freeze; also, the gage should not be exposed to a high temperature. In order that the gage may be removed from the boiler for examination, repairs, or calibration, while the boiler is under pressure, the connection should be provided with stopcocks.

Fig. 15. Water-Filled Coil Pipe for Connection to Steam Gage

In a battery of boilers, each should have its pressure gage, which should be connected directly to the boiler, not to the steam pipe.

Special Features. For stationary practice many kinds of gages are manufactured, but the principle of operation is always the same; the differences are mainly in the accuracy of the indicators and in the enclosing cases. To make the dials more easily read lights are sometimes placed behind the dials so as to shine through, thus bringing the figures out distinctly; these are termed illuminated dial gages. To preserve the accuracy of the instrument the mechanism is usually enclosed in a dust-proof case. Where the distance between the observer and the dial is considerable, the dials should be large in diameter and the figures made very distinct.

WATER COLUMNS

Description. A water column is a boiler attachment used for the purpose of determining the level of the water. A complete column consists of a cylindrical chamber, Fig. 16, in direct communication with the boiler in two different places, viz, the steam space and the water space, carrying on one side, with connections in the upper and lower parts of the cylinder, a glass tube called a *gage glass*, three quick-opening cocks in direct communication with the interior of the column cylinder at three levels, and a spherical enlargement beneath the column which is intended to provide a place for sediment collection. Exterior connections to both the column proper and the gage glass, containing valves to permit blowing down, are also essential.

In certain types of boilers it is more convenient to attach the gage cocks and the gage glasses direct to the boiler sheets without the use of an independent column. The principle of operation and use of the separated attachments is, of course, the same as though the column were used. The advantage of the column is that it reduces the number of openings in the boiler proper, and by its use a number

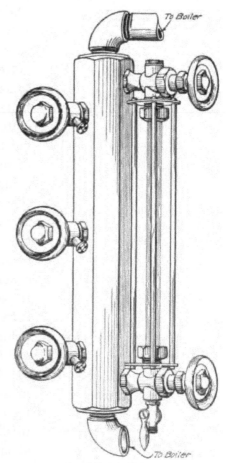

Fig. 16.   Water Column Carrying Gage Glass and Try Cocks

of other attachments are made possible. The latter remark refers to high and low water alarms, feed-water regulator attachments, etc.

Alarm Systems. When a water column carries an alarm system, the usual method is to provide floats in the cylindrical portion of the column which, upon being displaced from their normal positions, open needle valves leading to whistles. The normal positions of the floats cover a range of water height within which the boiler can be safely operated; when the water is either above or below this height, one or the other float opens its valve and a shrill whistle calls the attention of the water tender. There is a difference of opinion as to whether or not shut-off valves should be located in the pipe lines joining the water column with the boilers

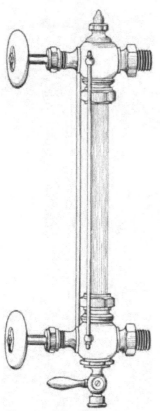

above and below the column. Such valves are of service when it is desired to replace a broken gage glass—should better means be lacking—or to perform some other kind of a repair while the boiler is under pressure. Municipal and state regulations are gradually recognizing that it is better to object to the use of such valves, as there is danger of their being closed when not so intended and thereby greatly increase the hazard. In any case, if these valves are used, facilities should be provided for locking them *open*. The pipe work in making water-column connections should be such as to permit access throughout without difficulty; this is accomplished by the use of straight pipe connected up with *crosses* and *tees*.

Gage Glasses. In order that the fireman may know the water level without trying the cocks, a water-gage glass is used. It consists of a strong glass tube about one foot in length, having the ends

Fig. 17. A Good Type of Water Gage Glass

connected to the boiler or column by suitable fittings.

As both ends of the tube are in communication with the boiler, the water level in the glass will be the same as in the boiler, and is always in sight when properly connected. Fig. 17 shows a good form of gage glass. The glass is protected by rods which are parallel to it. As the glass often needs cleaning, repacking, or renewing, cocks are provided for shutting off communication with the boiler. A drain cock is also placed at the lower end to empty the glass when the attendant wishes to ascertain whether or not the glass is working properly.

The drain cock is often provided with a drain pipe. The steam and water passages should be at least one-half inch internal diameter.

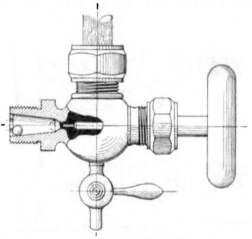

Fig. 18. Automatically Acting Ball Valve to Prevent Injury to Workmen and Loss of Water on Breaking of Gage Glass

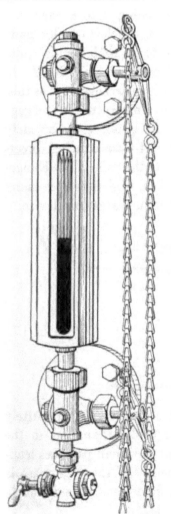

Fig. 19. Klinger Patent Gage Glass

Precautions in Case Gage Glass Breaks. The glass is likely to break because of accident or of changes in temperature. To prevent serious injury to the fireman and loss of water as a result of the breaking of the gage glass, automatic valves may be placed in the passages. In Fig. 18 a ball valve is shown in detail. If the glass breaks, the pressure of the steam drives the ball outward, filling the conical passage. When a new glass is put in, the balls are forced back by slowly screwing in the stems. This, like other safety devices, is very likely not to work when it should.

In boilers where the steam space is small, as in locomotives, the allowable variation of water level is slight; but the greater care with which the glass is watched makes up for the small margin of safety. If dirty water is used, or if the water foams, the level in the glass will be unsteady and unreliable, since dirt clogs the passages unless they are large, and the foaming causes a fluctuation of the water level. A small pipe connecting with the steam space where no ebullition occurs will insure a steadier water level.

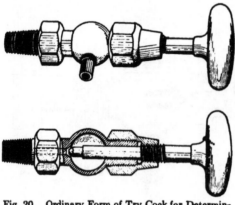

Fig. 20.   Ordinary Form of Try Cock for Determining Water Level in Boiler

The chief objection to the gage glass—namely, its breaking — may be overcome to some extent by attaching it to a gage column, which is usually made of brass and stands quite clear of the boiler itself. In such an arrangement as this, the temperature in the gage glass cannot vary as widely as if it were attached directly to the boiler. The Klinger Patent water gage glass is not easily broken, and possesses many advantages over the common glass. Fig. 19 illustrates this device.

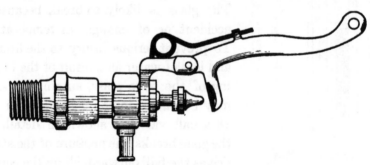

Fig. 21.   Try Cock Operated by Means of Lever

Blowing Out Gage Glass. The water gage is not absolutely reliable, for the water in the gage, being cooler than that in the boiler, may not indicate the true level, and the small passages leading to it may become choked with sediment. If the gage glass is frequently blown out by the engineer and kept clean, this difficulty will be reduced.

Try Cocks. Try cocks are of widely different forms, and may be either like the general type shown in Fig. 20, which is the ordinary locomotive form, constructed in two parts so that they can be separated for the purpose of repacking without detachment from the boiler; or they may be of the lever type shown in Fig. 21. There are usually three cocks—one at the highest desired water level, one at the lowest, and one midway. More cocks may, of course, be used if desired. The water level can be determined by opening the cocks in succession and observing whether dry steam or hot water blows out. In some types of boilers the try cocks must be placed on the boiler sheets direct; in other types their use is prevented unless they are attached to a water column. Water-tube boilers enclosed in brickwork, and fire-tube boilers similarly set, would impose making the direct connections quite long, in which cases the try cocks are always attached to water columns.

VALVES

Characteristics and Uses of Cocks and Valves. Of all boiler accessories, perhaps the most important are the cocks and valves, by means of which the flow of steam or water may be shut off completely or only partly so. The valve operates by moving a disk across the pipe in a transverse direction, or by bringing a cap tight upon the seat in a fore-and-aft direction. A cock consists of a block inserted in the passageway, with an opening cut through in one direction. When the handle of the cock is in line with the pipe, the opening allows the steam to pass through; but if turned crosswise, the opening is closed.

Classification. Valves are of two kinds—those which are manually operated and those which are automatic. All control valves are manually operated, while those which are used for safety are automatic. Automatic valves may release when the pressure becomes excessive, like safety valves, or they may prevent the pressure becoming excessive by closing against steam coming from an external source, like automatic stop and check valves. Reducing valves are really one type of automatic stop and check valves, though their construction to meet the requirements of their particular service is usually somewhat different.

Application. The application of valves depends upon the severity of the service and, to a large extent, upon the opinion of the designing engineer as to the equipment as a whole. In general, the practice is growing into favor of using valves to permit the temporary removal from service of a part of the general equipment for the purpose of repairs and of employing by-passes around portions of the equipment and double service lines or loops of the same line.

MANUALLY OPERATED TYPES

Fig. 22.   Standard Globe Valve
Courtesy of Crane Company

Globe Valve. *Construction.* The valve shown in Fig. 22 gets its name from the globular shape of the casing which encloses the valve. Extending across this whole casing is a substantial diaphragm, the central portion of which is in a plane parallel with the length of the pipe. The opening is cut in this portion (horizontal in the figure) through which steam or other fluid may pass when the valve is opened. When the valve is closed, a cap is forced down to close its opening. The rim around the opening is known as the valve seat. The valve cap is operated by a spindle, which passes through the bonnet of the valve, and is mounted at the upper end by a small wheel or handle. To prevent the escape of steam around this spindle, a stuffing box is provided. The valve cap may or may not rotate as the spindle turns; usually it does not.

Replacements. The valve shown in Fig. 22 is a standard globe valve known to the trade as the Crane Navy valve. It is a good valve of the type and is tested up to 250 pounds hydraulic pressure per square inch. If the disk or seat becomes scored, the valve may easily be reground.

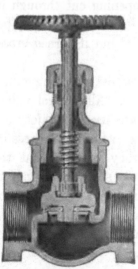

Fig. 23.   Extra Heavy Copper Disk Globe Valve
Courtesy of Crane Company

A valve shown in Fig. 23 has a detachable valve cap. Instead of relying for tightness upon the valve and seat coming together, metal to metal, a removable disk is provided, which, being softer than the metal valve seat, easily takes up the wear, and the valve not only can be closed tighter but, if anything happens to impair the tightness of the valve, the copper disk can be replaced by another at a trifling expense. In cheaper valves, when the cap is scored, the valve is worthless. The valve seat sometimes has a slight bevel, as in Fig. 22, the valve cap being shaped like the frustrum of a cone.

It is impossible to close a valve tightly if the slightest particle of scale or grit gets between the disk and the seat. If this happens, the valve seat is likely to become scored, and so does not hold tight; but it may be reground and, if the valve disk itself is damaged, can readily be replaced.

Angle Valve. An angle valve, shown in Fig. 24, is similar in construction to the ordinary globe valve, and is sometimes used in place of the straightway valve and an elbow. Both these styles of valve should be so placed in the steam pipe that the entering steam comes beneath the valve seat. If this is done, the

Fig. 24. Angle Valve
Courtesy of Crane Company

valve stem may be easily repacked simply by closing the valve. If the steam enters in the opposite direction, a leaky valve stem cannot be packed, as loosening the stuffing box would permit the escape of the steam. There are, however, exceptions to this rule.

Gate Valve. The gate or straightway valve gives a straight passage through the pipe, and, when open, offers very little resistance to flow. The globe valve, of course, offers much resistance, because the fluid has to change its direction of flow completely.

There are two forms of gate valve— one with wedge-shaped sides, and the other having the valve sides parallel. Fig. 25 shows a Crane valve with wedge-shaped sides. A collar holds the valve spindle at a fixed point, and to open or close, the valve is drawn up or lowered by turning the

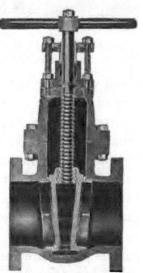

Fig. 25. Crane Wedge Gate Valve, with Non-Rising Stem
Courtesy of Crane Company

spindle. When the gate reaches the bottom of the pipe, a wedge on the lower end of the spindle causes the sides to move laterally with sufficient force to bring a strong pressure against the valve seat. For heavy work these valves are made with a rising spindle instead of a stationary one. This possesses the distinct advantage of indicating at a glance whether they are opened or closed, while one cannot tell by looking at the ordinary gate valve whether it is open or not.

Check Valve. When it is necessary that the flow should always take place in the same direction, as in the feed pipe of a boiler, check valves are used. There are several forms shown in Fig. 26, one of which is of a pattern similar to a globe valve. This check valve is of a ball or flat type, the seat being parallel to the direction of flow. The valve is held in place by its own weight, and by the pressure of the fluid in case of a reverse flow. In the swinging

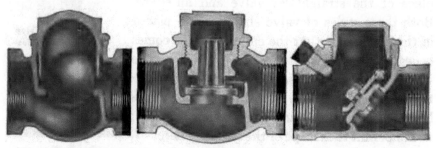

Fig. 26. Horizontal Check Valves. Left, Ball Type; Middle, Cup Type with Flat Seat; Right, Swinging Type

check valve, the seat is at an angle of about 45 degrees to the direction of flow. It is fitted somewhat loosely where it is fastened to the swinging arm, so that it may properly seat itself. This form is usually preferred, as it offers less resistance to flow, and there is less chance for impurities to lodge on the valve seat. When a check valve is used in the boiler feed pipe, there should be a stop valve between it and the boiler which can be shut in case the check valve should get out of order.

Materials Used in Construction. For pressures under 200 pounds per square inch, cast iron may be used for the body of the valve; but, for economy, it should be used only when the pressure is over 130 pounds. For heavy work it is frequently necessary to have a massive valve that cannot be broken easily. In such a case a cast-iron body is the most suitable thing. The valve seat, valves, spindles, stuffing box, glands, and nuts are usually made of gun metal or brass.   For very high pressures, especially on steam mains, cast steel is generally used, with gun metal fittings similar to those enumerated for the cast-iron valves.

AUTOMATICALLY OPERATED VALVES

Safety Valves.   Safety valves are used for relieving the boiler when the pressure exceeds a certain limit, and to give warning of high pressure.   There are several different types, but the essential feature is a valve opening upward, held on its seat by a weight or spring.   When the pressure in the boiler exerts a force greater than that holding down the valve, the valve will open automatically.

Lever Safety Valve.   The lever safety valve shown in Fig. 27 is a common type for stationary work, especially for small boilers.

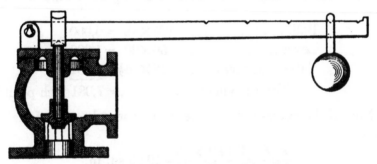

Fig. 27.   Common Type of Lever Safety Valve

The valve is held in place by a weight at the end of a lever.   The force required to lift the valve is governed by the location of the weight on the lever arm.   The body of the valve is usually made of cast iron, the seat being of brass.   An opening on the side of the valve may be connected with the feed-water heater or drain, if the escape of steam into the air is undesirable.   If the valve becomes leaky, it should be reground; but no attempt should be made to make it tight by increasing or moving the weight on the lever.

The amount of necessary weight on the lever, and its distance from the fulcrum, can be determined in the usual manner of computing leverage forces and moments, remembering that weight times weight arm is equal to power times power arm.   In such a valve as this, power is the steam pressure, and the power arm is the distance of the center of the valve from the fulcrum.   There are four weights acting downward—the ball, the lever arm, the valve, and the spindle—and in the process of computation the weight and leverage of each must be taken into account.

Suppose, for example, that we have a lever safety valve such as is illustrated in outline in Fig. 28, and that we know the following conditions: the ball weighs 125 lbs., and is suspended at the end of the lever 48 inches from the fulcrum; the valve and valve spindle together weigh 18 lbs., and are 4½ inches from the fulcrum; the lever arm itself weighs 50 lbs. If the valve seat is 5 inches in diameter, at what pressure will the valve blow off, ignoring the friction of the stuffing box and fulcrum pivot?

The center of gravity of the lever arm must be determined from the drawing, Fig. 28, and this is found to be 20 inches from the fulcrum. The leverage of the weights acting downward is then as follows:

$$\text{Ball} \ldots\ldots\ldots\ldots\ldots 125 \times 48 = 6{,}000$$
$$\text{Lever} \ldots\ldots\ldots\ldots\ldots 50 \times 20 = 1{,}000$$
$$\text{Valve and Stem} \ldots\ldots 18 \times 4\tfrac{1}{2} = \underline{81}$$
$$\text{Total moment} \ldots\ldots\ldots = 7{,}081 \text{ inch-pounds}$$

Now, if the valve-seat diameter is 5 inches, the area of the valve will be

$$\frac{\pi D^2}{4} = \frac{3.1416 \times 25}{4} = 19.63 \text{ sq. in.}$$

The total moment to be overcome is 7,081 inch-pounds, and its distance from the fulcrum is 4½ inches. Therefore, the necessary

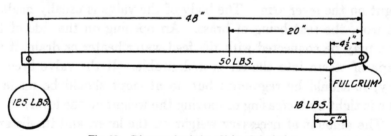

Fig. 28. Diagram for Safety-Valve Calculations

upward pressure on the valve will be $\dfrac{7{,}081}{4\tfrac{1}{2}}$ or 1,573.5 pounds. If the area of the valve is 19.63 square inches, then the necessary pressure in pounds per square inch would be $\dfrac{1{,}573.5}{19.63}$ or 80 pounds, approximately. That is, this safety valve would blow off when the boiler pressure reached 80 pounds per square inch.

If it is desired to design a valve which will blow off at known pressure, the same principles will apply, but the computations will be figured in the reverse order. The area of the valve, times the boiler pressure, would give the total lifting force; and this, multiplied by its leverage, would give the lifting moment, which would be resisted by the downward moment of the combined weights of valve, valve stem, lever, and ball. If the moments of the lever, valve, and valve stem were known, the remainder, of course, would be made up by the ball. If the length of the lever arm were known, then the weight of the ball would be varied to correspond; and, conversely, if the weight of the ball were fixed, the length of the lever must be made to correspond.

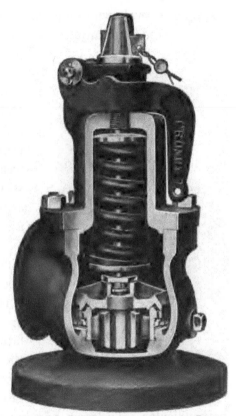

Fig. 29. Crosby Pop Safety Valve for Stationary Boilers

The lever safety valve has several defects. It does not close promptly when the pressure is reduced; and it is likely to leak after it is closed, and may be readily overloaded, or even wedged on its seat. It is essential that a safety valve should be automatic, certain in its action, and prompt in opening and closing at the required pressures. It must be one which can be relied upon under all circumstances and not easily tampered with.

Pop Safety Valve. The pop safety valve fulfills the above requirements better than those of the lever type. Pop valves open when the steam pressure is sufficient to overcome the tension of the spring. Fig. 29 shows a Crosby pop safety valve for stationary service. The valve is connected by a flange to the central spindle and is held down on its seat by the pressure of the central spring. The valve is provided with wing guides and an annular lip. The guides fit smoothly into the seating upon which the valve rests. The seats of the valve have an angle of 45 degrees. The under face of the lip, together with the seating, forms a small chamber through which all the steam must pass in order to reach the open air.

The valve shown in Fig. 30 for stationary boilers is made by the Ashton Valve Company. The general principles are those of all pop safety valves. The valve seat is made of composition or nickel, and with a bevel of 45 degrees, as is the United States Government standard. The pop chamber is surrounded by a knife-edge lip, which wears down in proportion with the seat, thus keeping the outlet of the same relative proportions and giving a constant amount of pop.

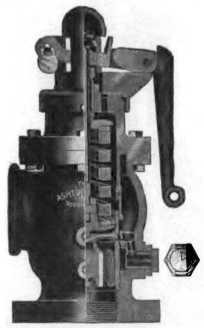

Fig. 30.   Improved Lock-Up Pop Safety Valve

The amount of pop—that is, the difference of pressure between the opening and the closing of the valve —is regulated from the outside by means of the screw-plug pop regulator shown in section and plan at the lower right hand of Fig. 30. If more pop is desired, turn the regulator so that S will be more nearly perpendicular. To lessen pop, make O more nearly perpendicular. The springs are made of Jessop's best steel and are held by pivoted disks at the top and bottom to insure a true bearing on the valve.

The inlet and outlet are both on the same casting, so that the valve may be taken apart to be cleaned or repaired without disturbing the boiler connection. It has a lock-up attachment, so that the regulating parts cannot be tampered with, either by accident or by design. The spring is encased, in order to protect it from the steam.

The Crane Marine pop safety valve is shown in Fig. 31. It has a bevel seat, and is provided with a cam lever, by which it may be raised from its seat one-eighth of the valve opening. The lever can be thrown over far enough to lock the valve open when there is no steam pressure. The outlet of the valve, if desired, may be piped to the supply tank or to any other point.

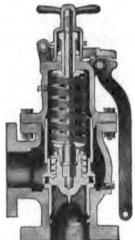

Fig. 31. Crane Marine Pop Safety Valve

Locomotive Safety Valves. Safety valves for locomotive boilers must be made of heavy material to stand the severe usage. They should be so constructed that they will not cock or tilt. The Ashton valve shown in Fig. 32 is constructed so that the amount of pop can be regulated by merely turning the two posts marked *2* and *3* to the right or left. The noise of the steam escaping from the ordinary safety valve is disagreeable, and in some States the law requires the use of the muffler safety valve. The Ashton valve shown in Fig. 32 has a top muffler.

Safety valves should be connected directly to the boiler without any pipe or elbow. They should be tried every day by means of the lever. It is best not to locate safety valves on the steam outlet main leading from the boiler.

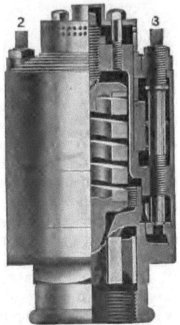

Fig 32. Ashton Locomotive Increased-Lift Muffled Pop Safety Valve

Blow-Off Cocks. It is customary and good practice to locate between the boiler and the blow-off valve a cock known as the blow-off cock, which answers the purpose of carrying the boiler pressure and receiving the worst service of scale and muddy sediment at times when the boiler under pressure is being blown down. Simplicity of construction and tightness are the main requirements sought. Fig. 33 illustrates the Homestead blow-off cock.

This valve is so constructed that when it is closed it is at the same time forced firmly to its seat. This result is secured by means of the traveling cam A, through which the stem passes. The cam is prevented from turning with the stem by means of the lugs B, which move vertically in slots. Supposing the valve to be open, the cam will be in the lower part of the chamber in which it is placed, and the plug will be free to be easily moved. A quarter of a turn in the direction for closing it causes the cam to rise and take a bearing on the upper surface of the chamber, and the only effect of further effort to turn the stem in that direction is to force the plug more firmly to its seat. A slight motion in the other direction immediately releases the cam, and the plug turns easily, being arrested at its proper open position by contact of the fingers of the cam at the other end of its travel. E and D are balancing ports.

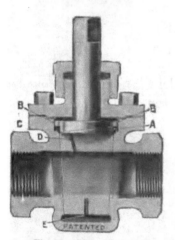

Fig. 33. Blow-Off Cock
Courtesy of Homestead Valve Manufacturing Company

Blow-Off Valves. The severity of the service mentioned in a preceding paragraph which all blow-off valves have to withstand, owing to the cutting action of scale and other gritty sediment, has caused designing engineers to pay particular attention to these valves. Many forms have been devised which, while they are bound to have the essential features of globe, angle, straightway, or Y valves, are so constructed that the danger of scoring the valve disks or seats is materially reduced.

Fig. 34 illustrates a straightway blow-off valve known as the Everlasting. It consists of a top and bottom bonnet, a disk, and a lever and post. To open, the disk is simply drawn away from its seat to one side by moving the lever arm. The Faber blow-off valve is shown in Fig. 35. One feature of this valve is a separate half-inch pipe line connected with the boiler above the mud drum or to the steam main joined to the valve at C. It will be seen that the seat of the valve is still in communication with steam or water at boiler pressure even after the valve disk is about to close on its

Fig. 34. Views of Everlasting Blow-Off Valve
Courtesy of Scully Steel and Iron Company

seat; this steam, as it blows over the valve seat and disk, is intended to cleanse both. This half-inch line, while it contains a valve, should always be open during normal operation.

Automatic Stop and Check Valves. Where several boilers in service are attached to the same steam main, there is the possibility that a failure on the part of one of the boilers will relieve the steam pressure in the steam main very quickly unless provision is made automatically to cut the boiler affected out of service from the remainder of the boilers. To meet this service, a type of valve has been developed known as the automatic stop and check valve. It is located immediately adjacent to the boiler as close to the steam space as possible, with no valves intervening, separate and distinct from the control valve of the boiler, which is located adjacent to it or as close as may be.

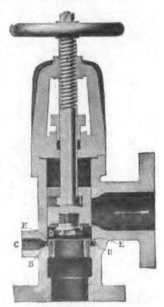

Fig. 35. Faber Blow-Off Valve
Courtesy of Elliott Company

It will be readily understood that, should a boiler fail so as to let its steam and water out quickly, and should this boiler be equipped with a valve of the kind mentioned, the remainder of the boilers could go on with their work without disturbance, while, without such provision, the steam coming from the unaffected boilers would flow to the affected one and pass through its rupture. Many munici-

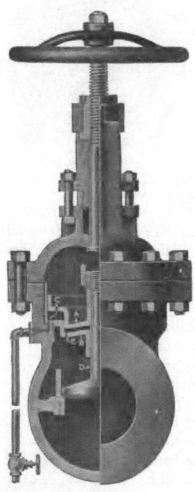

Fig. 36. Golden-Anderson Double-Cushioned Non-Return Valve

palities and States require the use of automatic stop and check valves when more than one boiler is attached to one main, and the practice is gradually becoming universal. The valve shown in Fig. 36 is one of a great many intended for use in such places as mentioned, and is made by the Golden-Anderson Valve Specialty Company. An inspection of the illustration shows that, while the stem can be turned down to close the valve should it be open, it cannot raise the valve disk from its seat should it be closed, there being no fastening between the stem and the disk. The requirement that a valve of this character must be unerring in its service demands the best material and workmanship.

Reducing Valves. Sometimes steam is desired at a lower pressure than that of the boiler. For instance, a small low-pressure engine may be run by steam taken from the same boiler that supplies a higher-pressure engine. This reduction is accomplished by throttling the steam by means of reducing valves. These are arranged to be operated automatically, so that the pressure can be reduced and a constant pressure in the steam pipes maintained. There are several forms in general use.

In the Holt valve, Fig. 37, the low-pressure steam acts on the lower side of the diaphragm; and the weight, which may be set so as to cause the desired pressure, acts on the other. The movement of this diaphragm causes a balanced valve to move to or from its seat. The valve opens until the steam pressure equals the weight above. The pressure in the main steam pipe does not affect the movement of the valve. It depends only upon the pressure on the two sides of the diaphragm.

In the Mason valve, Fig. 38, a spring, which may have its tension altered by a key, takes the place of the lever and weight in the

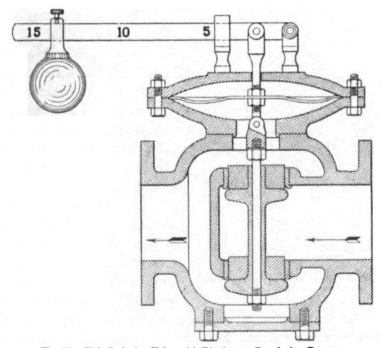

Fig. 37. Holt Reducing Valve with Diaphragm Regulating Pressure

Holt valve. When the pressure in the low-pressure system has risen to the required point, which is determined by the spring, the valve closes, and no more steam is admitted until the pressure falls sufficiently to open the valve again.

In another form of valve, a piston acted on by the low-pressure steam regulates the opening of a balanced valve, and this maintains a constant steam pressure.

In the Foster reducing valve, the valve is held open by the spring and levers, until the steam pressure at exit presses on the diaphragm sufficiently to close the valve. The valve is held open so as to admit just the proper amount of steam to maintain the required pressure.

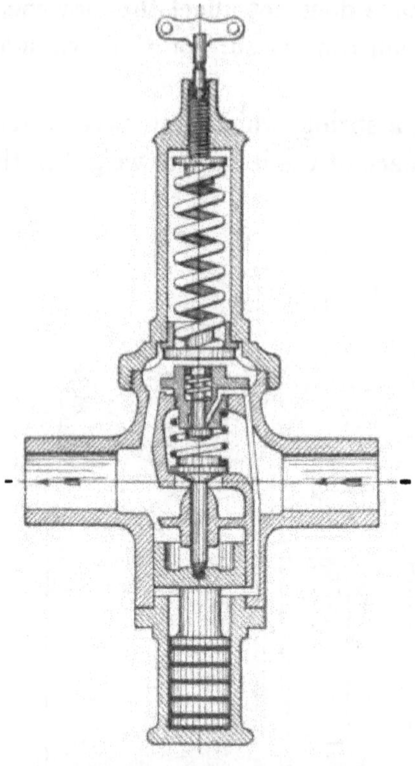

When a reducing valve is used, a stop valve should be put in to prevent flow when steam is not in use.

STEAM PIPING

The subject of steam piping in its entirety is one far beyond the scope of this treatment of boiler accessories, but it is essential that it be brought up to the extent of emphasizing its importance, especially as concerns the steam connections from the boilers to the main steam header.

Precautions. *Provide for Drainage.* The first requirement is that all piping must be so arranged that the condensation can be drained. A failure to provide drains may be responsible for the rupture of engines and any other apparatus located in line with the engine. For the same reason, it is customary to locate control valves in the high parts of steam pipes connecting boilers and steam mains so that the condensation may flow freely in either direction.

Fig. 38. Mason Reducing Valve. Pressure Regulated by Means of a Spring

Flexible Connections. As a second requirement, ample provision should be made for flexible steam pipe connections to the main header. This is accomplished by the use of long sweep bends. It is especially important that attention be paid to the flexibility of the blow-off connections, as the distance between the blow-off openings and the blow-off main is usually short. If the connections are rigid, a stress is thrown upon the flange connecting the blow-off pipe to the boiler, resulting in a leaky joint. It is well to remember that the blow-off main is subjected to wide ranges of temperature which cause a corresponding deformation in length, which is distributed among the various branches and attachments.

Proper Strength of Pipe and Allowance for Expansion. Pipes must not only be of sufficient size and strength, but should be so installed as to make ample provision for expansion due to the high temperature when they are filled with steam. The supports for long pipe lines should be arranged somewhat as shown in Fig. 39, which allows the pipe a considerable amount of lateral motion.

Expansion Joint in Long Pipes. If the pipe line is long, an expansion joint must be provided. Sometimes a curved U-bend may be inserted in the pipe line, which of itself will have flexibility

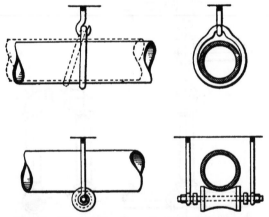

Fig. 39. Side and Transverse Sectional Views Showing Methods of Arranging Supports for Long Pipe Lines

enough to provide for reasonable expansion. Or, if the steam main is not all in one line, a similar bend may be provided, with elbows and nipples, Fig. 40. In this case, any expansion of the steam main will cause the nipples to turn slightly in the elbows. This motion, of course, is slight, but it is sufficient to prevent rupture. For large pipes a slip joint, made tight by a stuffing gland, is usually provided. If this is done, great care must be taken that the steam main is straight and in perfect alignment, as the pipe may otherwise bind in the expansion joint and cause much damage from leakage.

Straight and Sloping Runs to Avoid Condensation. In marine work, especial care must be taken that the pipe lines are not so rigidly connected together that they will be injured by the working of the ship. This can be readily provided for by laying the pipe in such a way as to provide a simple form of swivel joint.

The pipe lines should be as straight as possible, to prevent unnecessary friction of the steam and unnecessary condensation; and they should, if possible, be so installed as to leave no pockets wherein condensation may collect. If such a pocket is unavoidable, a drain must be provided, leading from the pocket to the steam trap, whence the condensation may be discharged into the hot well or filter box, because the collection of water in steam pipes is a source of inconvenience and danger.

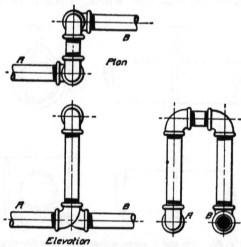

Fig. 40. Method of Forming Swivel Joint in Steam
Piping to Counteract Effects of Expansion
and Contraction

The pipe lines should be installed with sufficient slope, so that the condensation will readily drain to a convenient point, whence it may be drawn off. This slope should be in the direction of the flow of the steam, as the water will not readily flow otherwise. Great care should be taken that the pipe lines nowhere sag, as such a depression will collect condensation. This may cause very little disturbance unless the pressure of the steam is suddenly raised, in which case the water is likely to flow bodily along the pipe; and if it does not enter the cylinder of the engine and cause damage there, it will cause a serious water hammer, which may rupture the elbows of the pipe and endanger life.

Materials for Piping. Formerly, when low pressures were used, cast iron was a common material for a main steam pipe leading from the boiler to the engine, but the higher pressures of today require the best wrought iron or steel. In marine work, copper is commonly used; but with the advent of higher and higher pressures, copper fails to give the requisite strength, and it has to be reinforced with wire or iron bands. According to the British Board of Trade Rules copper pipes 15 inches in diameter may be used at pressures not over 150 pounds; but at 200 pounds, copper pipes over 10 inches in diameter are not allowed as there is always danger that the large copper pipe will burst. For large sizes, riveted iron or steel pipe may be used. For high pressures, cast-steel fittings are required by the U. S. Steamboat Inspection rules. It is now the common practice to use steel for such purposes.

Pipe Connections. *Gasketed Joints.* Large steam pipe is made in sections which can be riveted together. The small sizes are fitted with the ordinary type of flange, and the sections may be bolted together, a suitable gasket being used between the two flanges to make a steam-tight joint. The flanges are machined perfectly smooth, and the packing may consist of rubber and fiber reinforced with wire insertion; of asbestos; or of corrugated copper.

Flanges and Unions. As the pressures used have become higher it has been necessary to construct tighter and stronger connections in both steam and water mains attached to boilers. This is especially true since the use of superheated steam has become general. Only a few of the methods in use can be brought up here. Fig. 41 shows the Edward flange, which is intended to avoid the use of gaskets between the two adjacent flanges. To accom-

Fig. 41. Edward Flanged Union
Courtesy of Edward Steam Specialty Company

plish this, the annular V-shaped projection shown in the upper flange is inserted into the companion groove of the lower, both being drawn together by bolts. The narrow slot in the edge of the upper V serves to insure a tighter joint. An application of the same principle in the making of a box union is shown in Fig. 42.

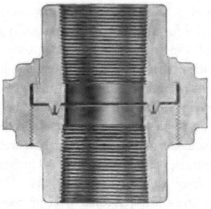

Fig. 42. Edward Box Union

Pipe Sizes. The true inside diameter of steam, gas, or water pipe is not always the same as the size by which the pipe is designated. For instance, what is called "3-inch" pipe has an actual inside diameter of 3.067 inches, and 3.5 inches outside diameter. The actual sizes of pipe, inside and outside, are to be found in any handbook or steamfitter's catalogue.

WATER END AUXILIARIES

FEED WATER REQUIREMENTS

Adequate Provisions Important. Perhaps the most important of all auxiliaries connected with a boiler is its feed apparatus. This is vital; for, if the feed is interrupted and the water runs low in the boiler, not only is there danger of damaging the boiler itself, but a disaster may follow of far greater concern. For marine purposes—and the same is true to a considerable extent in stationary work—at least two independent feed systems should be provided. In marine work, the main feed pump draws water from the filter box or feed-water heater, and pumps it into the boilers under ordinary conditions. There should be a by-pass around this pump, and the feed line should be connected by means of a valve to what is known as the "donkey" pump, which may be used for auxiliary feed purposes in case the main pump is damaged or in need of repairs.

Both of these pumps draw from and discharge into the same feed line; but, to provide against emergencies, there is usually a cross connection to the sea, so that sea water may be had if necessary. While in port, when the main engines are not running, and consequently when the feed water cannot be heated economically, an injector is almost invariably used. On land it is usually considered sufficient to install an injector in addition to the feed pump, although ·n large plants an auxiliary feed pump should be installed as well. In a small plant the fireman usually attends to the water; but on board ship and in large plants, a water tender is usually provided, whose business it is to keep the water in the boiler at the proper level. His task may be materially lessened by some automatic arrangement, so that if the water discharged into the hot well from the condenser rises above the normal level, a float will open the valve leading to the feed pump and increase the rapidity of its stroke. This will reduce the level of the hot well or filter box, as the case may be.

Such an arrangement as this will keep a fairly uniform level of water in the boilers; and if a surface condenser is employed, and all the condensation is pumped back into the boilers, the water level will remain constant except for slight leakages of steam, and for the possibility of improper action of the feed pump. Leakage of steam can be made up from the supply of fresh water. At sea, salt water may have to be used for this purpose, although its use is very objectionable.

Location of Feed-Water Connection. There is considerable difference of opinion as to where the feed water should be introduced into the boiler, although the consensus of opinion seems to be that it should enter not far from the water line. In stationary practice, where the marine type of boiler is used, the feed water is introduced at the rear of the boiler near the bottom; but this is open to grave objections, for the feed water, being comparatively cool, and being introduced into the coldest part of the boiler, naturally tends to become dead water and to retard proper circulation, which is essential to economical steaming and often essential to the safety of the boiler itself.

Location Depends Upon Type of Boiler. The best place for introducing the feed water will naturally depend upon the type of boiler, and the service for which it is intended. If the entering water is of high temperature, it might enter near the bottom of the boiler. But if the feed water is comparatively cold—and it is always colder than the water in the boiler and the surrounding steam if the circulation is good—great care must be taken that it does not strike directly against the hot boiler plates, as it might thereby cause local contraction and possibly a serious leak, and it should be introduced in such a way as to make sure of its aiding the natural circulation of the boiler.

Practice in High-Pressure Work. The higher the steam pressure in the boiler, the more difficult becomes the problem of feed, and the more danger there is of injury to the boiler by the comparatively cold feed water striking hot plates. It is a universal practice in marine work, and a common practice on land, especially for internally-fired boilers, to cause the feed to enter above the water level near the center of the boiler; then branching off into two pipes, one leading to each side through the steam space until the side of the boiler is reached; and then running downward toward the bottom. The feed water, which very likely has been previously heated by a feed-water heater, is still further heated by its passage through this feed pipe, which is in direct contact with the live steam of the boiler. This internal feed pipe, turning down at the sides, causes the water to strike the outer shell of the boiler, which is the most remote from the fire, and this downward motion materially assists the circulation in the boiler. When this arrangement of feed is adopted, Fig. 43, care must be taken that the lower end of the feed pipe is well below the low-water level. If the end of the pipe is alternately immersed in water and then exposed to steam, violent explosions in the pipe are likely to follow, although nothing more serious may result than breaking an elbow or frightening the attendants.

Practice in Stationary Work. In stationary practice, it is quite common to admit the feed water into the steam space through a horizontal pipe which enters this space through the tube plate a few inches below the low-water level and terminates in a perforated pipe of large diameter. This method distributes the feed water admirably, and allows it to become considerably heated before it reaches the bottom of the boiler. If the feed water contains a considerable amount of magnesia or calcium carbonate, holes so arranged in the feed pipe are likely to become clogged and the feed consequently interrupted. Water of this sort should be fed into a trough, or the feed pipe be opened at the top by a long slot, so that the feed water may overflow. The trough, in this case, forms an admirable mud drum or sediment collector.

Practice with Internally-Fired Boilers. In internally-fired boilers of the Cornish or Lancashire types, the feed is usually delivered near the bottom through a horizontal pipe—either through the

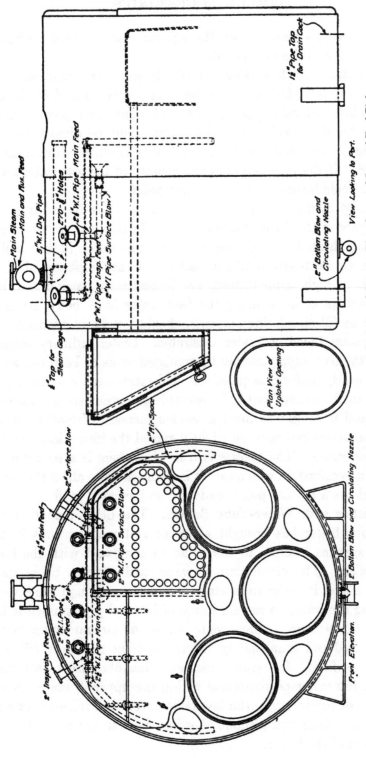

Fig. 43. Scotch Boiler of Marine Type Showing Arrangement of Surface and Bottom Blow-Outs, and Internal-Feed Piping

front end or by a vertical pipe through the crown. This method is not conducive to the best circulation.

In addition to these effects on circulation, there are other grave objections to introducing feed water near the bottom of the boiler; for, should anything happen to the feed pump, or a piece of scale lodge under the check valve, the water might be almost entirely blown out of the boiler before the difficulty could be discovered or remedied. If the pipe enters in the vicinity of the low-water level, no water could be drawn out below this point.

Use of Spray. Sometimes the feed water is forced into the steam space in the form of a fine spray. In this way it not only is thoroughly heated before mingling with the water in the boiler, but the air is taken out, and salts, such as sulphate of lime, insoluble at high temperatures, are immediately precipitated; but the advantage of introducing the feed water in a body, so as to produce useful circulating currents, should not be overlooked.

Constant Level of Water Desirable. Under ordinary circumstances the feed supply should be regulated so as to keep the water level as nearly uniform as possible. This statement requires modification to the extent that it is desirable to permit stored water to be reduced in height to meet a sudden increase of load until the firing conditions can equal or slightly exceed the immediate requirements for steam. The reverse is true when there is a reduction of the steam required, in which case it is permissible to allow the water to rise above a normal point ready for an increased load.

Practice with Water-Tube Boilers. The development of the water-tube boiler has brought about several modifications in the feeding systems internal to the boiler as compared with the large shell boilers. The circulation of water within them being more positive makes it easier to locate proper outlets, though the scheme of forcing the water to remain inside of internal piping until it has risen in temperature is preserved. Under no circumstances is the water introduced immediately before reaching the most effective heating surface. In some instances manufacturers introduce enlarged internal pipe structures within the upper drums with the intention of precipitating the low temperature precipitates, expecting to blow these out without allowing them to enter the general circulation of the boiler.

Separate Feed Control with Boiler Battery. If several boilers are attached together in the form of a battery, each boiler should be supplied with an independent connection to the feed pipe, otherwise a damage to the feed pipe in one boiler might affect the others. Moreover, if several boilers are fed from one pipe, the pressure in each of them being slightly different, an excess of water will naturally be fed into the boiler having the least pressure, whereas it is usually the case that the most water is needed in the boiler having the greatest pressure. The foregoing is equivalent to saying that each boiler should have its own feed-control valve. Where one boiler unit has several drums, one feed-control valve in one line may serve all of the drums, but the best practice requires that each drum shall have its own branch feed. Each branch feed should also have a check valve and a control valve, or a combination of a check and control valve.

Internal Piping. Internal piping should be substantial and so constructed that it is either easily taken apart for cleaning or easily cleaned while in place. This piping is preferably made of brass, and some boiler laws make this a requirement.

PUMPS

Reciprocating Pumps. *Characteristics.* Boilers are usually fed by a small, direct-acting steam pump placed near the boiler. Although these pumps require a large steam supply per horsepower per hour, the total amount of steam used is small because the work done is small. If a feed-water heater which can use the exhaust from the pump is used, the disadvantage of uneconomical steam use in a reciprocating feed pump disappears. A more economical pump is a power pump driven by a large steam engine; but in this case the rate at which water is supplied is not easily regulated to the demand of the boiler. Power pumps are usually arranged to pump a larger quantity of water into the boiler than is required, the excess of water being allowed to flow back into the suction pipe through a relief valve.

Method of Action. The Worthington duplex pump shown in Fig. 44 is well adapted for feeding boilers. In Fig. 45 is shown a section of the same pump. Steam, controlled by valves, drives the

Fig. 44.   Straightway Piston Pattern Duplex Pump
Courtesy of Henry R. Worthington, New York City

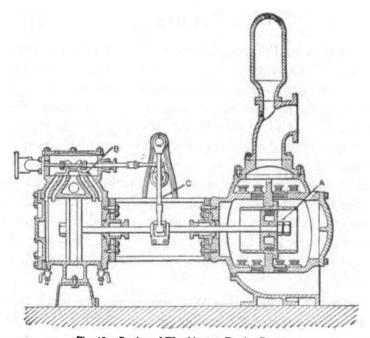

Fig. 45.   Section of Worthington Duplex Pump

piston in the steam cylinder, which moves the plunger in the water cylinder, since both are fastened to the same rod. The movement of the plunger forces a part of the water in front of it up through the valves into the air chamber, and through the pipes into the boiler. On account of the partial vacuum caused by the movement of the plunger, water will be drawn from the suction pipe, through the valves, into the pump cylinder, filling the space left by the movement of the plunger. During the return stroke, this water is forced up into the air chamber, and a like quantity enters the other end of the pump cylinder. The valves are kept on the seats by light springs, until the pressure on the bottom side is sufficient to lift them and allow water to flow through.

When two pumps are placed side by side, and have a common delivery pipe, the machine is called a duplex pump. It is usual to set the steam valves so that when one piston is at the end, the other is at the middle of its stroke. A duplex pump having a large air chamber and valves set to act in this manner delivers water with an approximately constant velocity.

Injectors. *Energy of the Jet.* Water may be forced into a boiler by an injector, or inspirator. By means of this instrument, the energy of a jet of steam is used to force the water into the boiler. That there is sufficient energy to do this work is evident from the fact that each pound of steam, in condensing, gives up about 1,000 B. t. u., and a B. t. u. is equivalent to 778 foot-pounds. Not all the energy of the jet of steam is used in forcing water into the boiler; some is wasted, and much is used to heat the feed water.

Method of Action. The action of the injector is briefly as follows: The steam escapes from the boiler with great velocity and, as it passes through the cone-shaped passage, draws air along with it, thus creating a partial vacuum in the suction pipe. Atmospheric pressure forces water up into the suction pipe, and the jet of steam which it meets is partly condensed. The energy of the jet carries the water along with it into the boiler.

Experiments show that the injector, if considered as a pump, has a very low efficiency. When used for feeding a boiler, it has a thermal efficiency of nearly 100 per cent, since all the heat of the steam passes to the water except the slight amount lost in radiation. The pump, however, has one great advantage over the injector. It can force hot water from a heater into the boiler, while an injector can be used only with cold or moderately warm water.

Fig. 46 shows the exterior and the interior section of a Hancock inspirator. To inject water into the boiler, first open overflow valves *1* and *3;* close valve *2;* and open starting valve in the steam pipe. When the water appears at the overflow, open *2* one quarter-turn, close *1*, and then close *3*. The inspirator will then be in operation. When the inspirator is not working, open both *1* and *3* to allow water to drain from it.

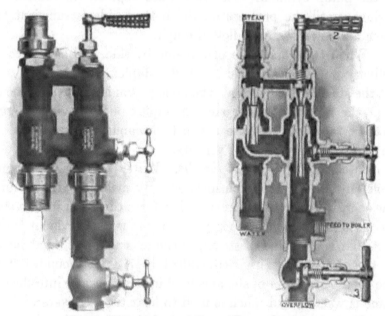

Fig. 46. Full and Sectional Views of Hancock Injector
Courtesy of Hancock Inspirator Company, Chicago, Ill.

Both the temperature and the quantity of delivery water can be varied by increasing or decreasing the water supply. When the water in the suction pipe is hot, either cool off both pipe and injector with cold water, or pump out the hot water by opening and closing the starting valve suddenly.

Centrifugal Pumps. Within recent years a method of feeding boilers by means of centrifugal pumps has come into favor. As the name implies, the action of the pump depends upon the centrifugal force obtained in the rapid revolution of a system of vanes attached to a shaft overcoming the pressure exerted in the discharge line. The accompanying illustration, Fig. 47, shows a section of a centrifugal pump without the driving motor or engine. The water intake is shown at the lower left-hand part of the cut; the revolving shaft is here shown carrying three vane systems or impellors placed alternately in series with stationary parts. Each pair, made up of a revolving disk and a stationary disk, is called a stage. When the shaft revolves, the water carried around the shaft by the first disk is thrown by centrifugal force away from the shaft and is guided into the next stage by the stationary disk. The next revolving disk receives the feed water at a pressure higher than that of the water at the source, and in turn impels it to the third stage at a still higher pressure.

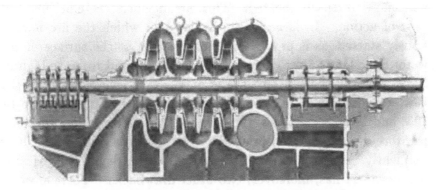

Fig. 47. Typical Section of a De Laval Multi-Stage Centrifugal Pump
Courtesy of De Laval Steam Turbine Company

The third stage performs the same service, and, when leaving the tips of the vanes of the third revolving disk, the water pressure is sufficient to overcome the pressure in the discharge pipe feeding the boiler.

Use for Boiler Feeding. In order to obtain success with the use of a centrifugal pump for boiler feeding, the design of the passages and the facilities for preventing communication between the stages, except by way of the ports provided, must be especially well cared for. In the illustration, note should be taken of the lubricating rings and the annular wearing rings on the faces of the disks. When a pump of this kind is directly connected to an electric motor or steam turbine, the whole constitutes a compact piece of apparatus.

Circulating Apparatus. There is always more or less danger in starting a fire under a boiler. If the circulation is poor, the result will be that not only will the water be of an uneven temperature—hot near the top and cold at the bottom—but the boiler shell is likely to be subjected to severe strain, owing to the difference of temperature arising from the stagnation of the cold water near the bottom. The fire must be started slowly, and considerable time consumed in getting up steam. To overcome the difficulty of poor circulation, several mechanical devices have been applied.

Injector. The first device tried was a hydrokineter—a sort of injector—in which jets of steam driven through a conical nozzle drew in the surrounding water. This was so arranged as to induce the cold water to flow from the bottom toward the top, where it was more intensely heated. This arrangement is efficient, but slow of action. In large marine boilers—in which the fire is cautiously started, as is proper—the temperature at the surface of the water, four hours after lighting up, has been found to be as high as 205°, while at the bottom it was only 73°. Several observations with a hydrokineter in action have shown the temperatures to be 205° and 144°, respectively. It was six hours more before the temperature was equalized throughout. In naval vessels, where it is frequently necessary to raise steam rapidly, this device is altogether too slow. It has, moreover, two other drawbacks. There must be an auxiliary boiler under steam pressure, and it will cease to act when the temperature and pressure of steam in the main boiler have reached those in the auxiliary boiler.

Feed-Water Jet. The steam jet, in the American Navy, has been replaced by a jet of feed water forced through a conical nozzle. This arrangement answers very well so long as steam is being drawn from the boiler; but when the boiler is at rest and steam is being raised, it is inoperative.

Small Centrifugal Pump. The best service is to be had by means of small centrifugal pumps fixed beside the boilers, which take water from the bottom of the boilers and discharge it a little below the water level. The pumps may be turned by hand while raising pressure, and may be worked by steam when sufficient pressure has been attained. A small engine of perhaps 1½ horsepower is sufficient to give a proper circulation to a large boiler. With such a circulating device, steam may be raised with safety in a comparatively short time.

REGULATING AND HEATING FEED WATER

Feed-Water Regulators. Strong claims are made for feed-water regulators as economical adjuncts to boiler equipment. Whether these claims are realized in practice depends largely upon the conditions under which the boiler plant is operated. Many engineers hold, on the contrary, that such devices should be avoided because their use creates a false sense of security in the minds of the operating force, which may give rise to carelessness on the part of the water tender and, at a time when something goes wrong with the regulator, operate to bring about a serious accident. That this is true generally can not be asserted positively, as the evidence seems to prove that feed-water regulators are good in some places and not in others. There are two kinds of regulators for feeding water; at least, the aims of manufacturers have developed along two distinct lines. By far the greater number of regulators are intended to insure a constant water level in the boiler, while there are several, more recently developed, whose object is to permit a varying water level, depending upon the demand for steam.

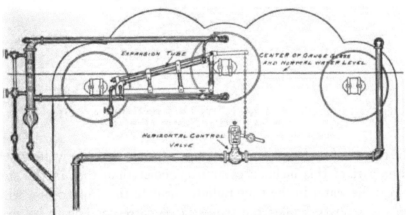

Fig. 48. Copes Regulator Installed for Submerged Tube Regulation on a Stirling Boiler; Feed Valve Horizontal
Courtesy of Northern Equipment Company, Erie, Pennsylvania

Varying Water-Level Regulator. Among the latter may be described the Copes regulator, illustrated in Fig. 48. In this figure the regulator part is shown as an adjunct to the water column.

The moving force is centered in the part "expansion tube", which is really a differential water column.   As the expansion tube changes its length, it actuates a bell-crank lever which, by means of a chain, moves the stem of a balanced regulator valve.   The latter is shown in Fig. 49.   The variation in length of the expansion tube is obtained by the variation of the height of the water in the tube.   When the water is high, the average temperature of the tube is lower than when the water is low; consequently, the length of the tube is less.

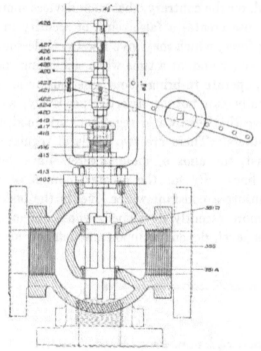

Fig. 49.   Details of Type B H, Copes Feed Valve
Courtesy of Northern Equipment Company

The reason of its lower average temperature is that the water in the lower part of this inclined column is cooler than that in the stem above; the water in the tube radiates heat to the atmosphere, while the steam space retains the temperature corresponding to its pressure.

It is plain that, when the boiler load is light, the regulator tends to keep the water level high.   This water tends to act as storage water against the time when the load becomes heavier.   The reverse is true when the load is heavy, the regulator tending to reduce the

water fed to the boiler to the amount required, until an opportunity
has been given to create more steam by an increase of draft and

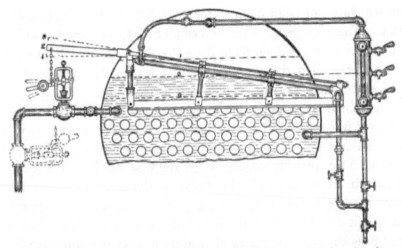

Fig. 50.   Diagram of Copes Submerged Tube Regulator as Installed to Regulate
Feed with Variable Water Level
Courtesy of Northern Equipment Company

greater coal consumption. Fig. 50 shows the Copes Submerged
Tube Regulator, as installed on the usual fire-tube boiler.

Constant Water-Level Regulator. As an example of the type of
regulator intended to maintain a constant water level may be
mentioned the Liberty, Fig. 51. A study
of the illustration will disclose the operation. The column on the left is in communication with the water of the boiler at
such a height that a normal level of water
in the boiler will stand at the middle of
the column. When the water in the boiler
starts to rise, it has the effect of raising
the float, which, in turn, communicates
with the lever system at its upper extremity.
From this point the action is simple enough
to be understood by examining the figure
closely. The regulator control valve is
shown on the right of the float column.

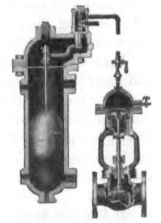

Fig. 51.   Liberty Feed-Water
Regulator
Courtesy of Elliott Company

Evaporators. No boiler can be run without a certain loss of
water, due either to a slight continuous leakage or to blowing off.

In stationary practice, this loss can be readily made up by the introduction of fresh water but at sea it is seldom possible to carry a sufficient amount of fresh water, and the make-up must be had either from sea water, or from fresh water provided by the use of an evaporator.   The evaporator is really a small boiler, the water in which is heated by a steam coil supplied from the main boiler.   The evaporated water—called the evaporation—passes into the condenser and then becomes a part of the regular feed water.

In a single evaporator, if the evaporation passes directly to the condenser, its heat is lost to useful work.   To provide a more economical arrangement, multiple evaporators are installed.   These consist of a series, the evaporation from the first passing into a coil in the bottom of the second; the water in the second condenses the evaporation from the first, while at the same time the evaporation from the first helps to heat the water of the second.   The steam and water pass through the series of heaters in opposite directions.

It is a rule in the French Navy to provide 380 pounds of fresh water per hour for each 1,000 indicated horsepower.   This provides for a loss of about 2 per cent without drawing on the reserve supply, which is 4,500 pounds for the same amount of power.

The evaporator may be arranged to communicate with a low-pressure valve chest, in which case the evaporation may be made to do work in a low-pressure cylinder of a triple-expansion engine before entering the condenser, or it may be connected with the feed-water heater if the exhaust steam is inadequate.

Feed-Water Heaters. *Economy Factor.* The introduction of feed water at a high temperature increases the economy and tends to prolong the life of the boiler.   The injurious effects from unequal expansion are diminished; and when the feed water is warmed by exhaust steam or by the waste gases in the uptake, the saving of fuel is considerable.   It may be safely stated that of all boiler-room accessories, feed-water heaters have the best claim as producers of economy.

If this gain comes from waste gases or exhaust steam, which would otherwise make no return for their heat, the gain is clear; but there is no gain in thermal economy by heating feed water with live steam directly from the boiler.   In the latter case there is a distinct loss.

Methods Used. There are several ways of heating the feed water. In condensing engines, the feed pump discharges from the condenser into the hot well, and the water is drawn from the hot well as boiler feed, at a temperature of 100° to 140° F. This, however, if the pressure is over 100 pounds, is entirely inadequate; and for the best economy, feed water at this temperature should be passed through some form of feed-water heater. With noncondensing engines, it is absolutely necessary that in some way the feed

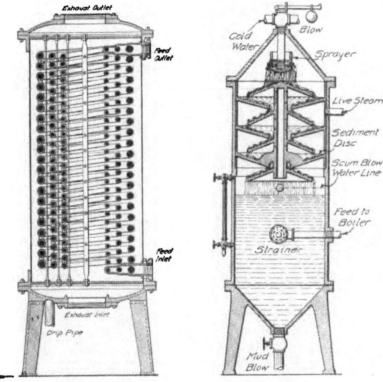

Fig. 52. Feed-Water Heater, Closed Type

Fig. 53. Feed-Water Heater, Open Type

water should be heated by the exhaust steam or by waste gases from the chimney, the apparatus in the first case being called a feed-water heater, and in the second, an economizer.

A feed-water heater may be arranged so that it will not only heat the water, but will at the same time purify it, precipitating the calcium and magnesia salts, which collect on suitably prepared plates, and gathering, at the bottom of the heater, dirt and other sediment which would injure the boiler or cause it to operate uneconomically.

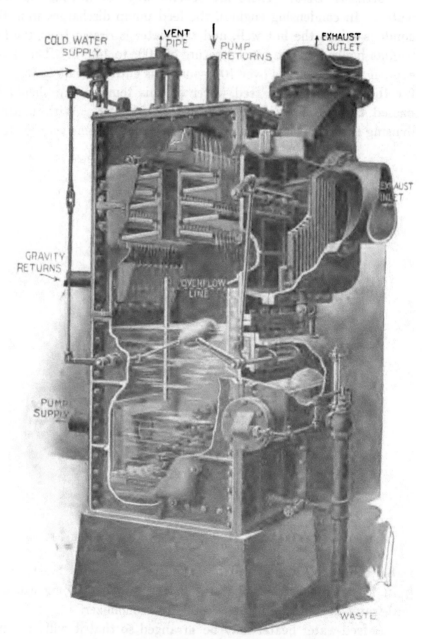

Fig. 54.   Interior View of Cochrane Heater and Receiver
Courtesy of Harrison Safety Boiler Works

Types of Heaters. There are two types of feed-water heater—the open, which is frequently used in land work; and the closed, which may be used either on land or at sea. In the open heater, the steam raises the temperature of the water by mingling with it in direct contact. The closed type of heater resembles in its action a surface condenser; the steam used for heating purposes surrounds tubes which contain the feed water, or the water circulates about tubes through which the heating steam passes.

Fig. 52 shows a feed-water heater of the closed type, the exhaust steam heating the feed water within the tubes. The heater shown in Fig. 53 is of the open type, the feed water becoming heated and depositing sediment while flowing from one tray to another.

The Cochrane heater, Fig. 54, is a combined heater and purifier of the open-heater type, the water entering at the top and flowing in a thin sheet over a series of trays. The exhaust steam enters through the oil separator and, rising among the trays, heats the water to about 210° F, the action being similar to that of a jet condenser.

Skimmers. Boiler feed water, if taken from rivers or ponds, is likely to contain vegetable matter as well as solid materials. The vegetable matter will usually float to the surface, while the solids will collect at the bottom. To keep the boiler free from such impurities, it is customary to provide two blow-outs — a surface blow-out or skim-

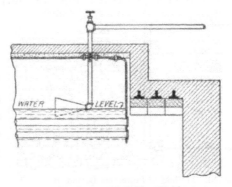

Fig. 55. Section of Boiler Showing Method of Installing Surface Blow-Out

mer, to take care of what rises to the top; and a bottom blow-out, to take out the sediment that collects at the bottom of the boiler. The surface blow-out usually consists of a dish or funnel-shaped receptacle set with its face vertical, as shown in Fig. 55. When the water level is in line with this blow-out opening, the opening of the valve will skim the impurities from the surface of the water. Oil may get into the boiler through the feed water, and a considerable portion of it can be removed in this manner.

Bottom Blow-Out. The bottom blow-out consists merely of a pipe leading from the bottom of the boiler outward. Both these blow-outs may be connected into one outlet.

Water-Tube Arrangement. In water-tube boilers a mud drum is usually installed, which collects the solid matter, and the bottom blow-out is then connected with this mud drum.

Marine Practice. In Fig. 43 is shown an arrangement of surface and bottom blow-outs as usually installed on a Scotch boiler of the marine type. If the feed water contains salt, which may frequently happen in marine practice, it is necessary that the boiler should be blown out frequently in order to remove the excess of salt. The heat losses due to this frequent blowing out are considerable, but they cannot be avoided, except by the use of fresh water, which sometimes may be impossible at sea. The density of the boiler water, if salt feed is used, should be carefully determined by a salimeter.

Protection for Blow-Out Pipe. The blow-out pipe leading from the bottom of an externally-fired boiler through the brick setting, if not properly protected, may be burned off, owing to the heat of the fire. This pipe is fre-

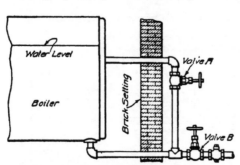

Fig. 56. Method of Protecting Bottom Blow-Out Pipe by Means of Circulation Pipe Connected to Boiler

quently covered with asbestos or other fire-resisting material; but it can be best protected by the means shown in Fig. 56. A pipe connected to the boiler slightly below the water level runs out through the brick setting and connects into the main blow-out pipe. This causes a circulation of water to pass continuously through the system, and prevents destruction of the blow-out pipe. When it is necessary to use the bottom blow-out, the valve *A* is closed, and the blow-off valve *B* is opened; otherwise, *B* is closed, and *A* is open while the water circulates.

Provision for Shutting Off Blow-Out Pipes. The blow-out pipe is usually shut off by a cock, which, although not so easily operated as a valve, is more trustworthy. Usually both a cock and a valve

are provided. Should a small particle of sediment lodge on the
valve seat, it would be impossible to close the valve tightly, and
considerable leakage would result, while an inspection of the valve
would not indicate whether it was completely closed or not. But a
glance reveals the fact whether or not a cock is tightly closed. The
cock is likely to stick because of corrosion or unequal expansion,
but, if it is frequently opened, this difficulty is not of great weight.

Fig. 57.   Typical Twin Strainer
Courtesy of Elliott Company, Pittsburgh, Pennsylvania

The plug and casing of the cock should not be made of the same
material, as, in that case, they will more readily stick if the cock
remains closed any length of time.

Automatic Skimmer Systems. Several skimmers have been
devised which are intended to operate automatically in the sense
that, by their use, the surface impurities are constantly carried away
from the boiler proper through the skimmer funnel and the adjoined
piping. This piping, which is external to the boiler proper, but

carries boiler pressure, leads to a settling chamber, a return lead of piping entering the water space of the boiler below the water surface but above the lower sediment chamber of the boiler. The principle of operation is to set up a slow circulation through the system due to the denser water of the external piping overbalancing a like column of water inside of the boiler, thus slowly carrying the surface impurities down to the settling chamber. Such a system should not be a direct part of the blow-off system to get the best results, and care should be taken that the return pipe will not cause the sediment to return to the boiler, as will occur if its connection with the settling chamber is too low down or too close to the deposit of sediment. In any case, the whole system must be suitably valved and contain facilities for independent blowing down. The blowing down should occur frequently.

Strainers. Where boiler feed water is likely to be taken from a source which permits the entrance of solids, such as ice, sticks, leaves, grass, cinders, wood, fish, eels, or any other kind of refuse, it is highly desirable to install a strainer which is exactly what the name implies. There are many forms of strainers, but all manufacturers aim to provide a device which will give uninterrupted service by so designing the equipment that the parts are easily removed and cleaned of the accumulated débris. The illustration, Fig. 57, shows a *twin* strainer which has the advantage of being two strainers so valved that one side can be operating while the other is opened for cleaning.

STEAM END AUXILIARIES

SUPERHEATERS

Reasons for Use of Superheaters. As the science of steam use has gradually progressed under the constant search for better means for creating and using heat energy, engineers have endeavored to overcome inherent heat losses in the transmission of steam through distances and by reason of cylinder condensation in engines. The early adoption of the *steam jacket* on engines had the same end in view so far as engine performance was concerned, but it was discovered that, while such a scheme would reduce actual cylinder condensation, the net condensation of steam might easily be increased. On the principle that dry metal surfaces convey heat from surrounding media much less rapidly than wet surfaces, it soon became evident that superheated steam would overcome, to a large extent, uneconomical engine operation, because superheated steam is as dry as a so-called permanent gas. The use of superheated steam received its greatest impetus at the time steam turbines were introduced, not only on account of the greater thermodynamic advantage, but also on account of the reduction of the blade wear of both the stationary and moving parts. Its use in reciprocating engines, though recognized as an advantage thermodynamically, has not been so general on account of the difficulties which arise in lubricating the rubbing parts subjected to high temperatures. This introductory statement is made in order to indicate that superheaters are used solely for their economical advantages, and not in any way because they tend to make the work of boiler-room operation less complicated, although it is to be said that a good superheater should not increase the complication of anything except, perhaps, the initial installation.

Types. *Direct Connected and Separately Fired.* There are two types of superheaters: those which form a part of the pressure construction of the boiler and are enclosed within the same structure as the boiler, and those which are separately fired. The latter type differs in no way from the attached type, both consisting of pipe coils placed where high temperature gas impinges upon them. The steam to be superheated passes through the coils on the inside, and the gas among the tubes or coils on the outside. The separately-fired type is necessary where the boiler construction is not adapted

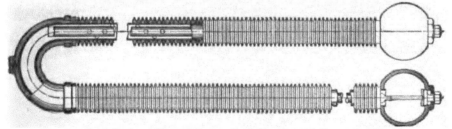

Fig. 58. Cross-Sectional View of Return-Bend Element and Connecting Headers
Used in the Construction of Foster Superheaters
Courtesy of Power Specialty Company

to the attachment of the coils within the path of the gases passing through or around the boiler-heating surface, or in cases where extremely high temperature superheated steam is required in some manufacturing process.

Armored and Bare Coils. Two kinds of coils are in general use—bare tubes or coils and armored coils. Both kinds of super-

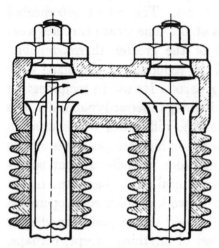

heaters may or may not have internal blind-end insertions of pipe in order to force the steam being superheated to pass along the tube surface in a thin sheet, thus making the coil superheating surface much more effective.

The leading make of armored superheater is known as the Foster, manufactured by the Power Specialty Company, New York City, Figs. 58, 59, and 60. Fig. 58 shows a single element partly cut away to expose the internal tubing. Fig. 59 shows

Fig. 59. Enlarged Section through Return Header Plugs

a larger section through the return header plugs for the holes giving access to the header ends of the superheater element—cast-iron rings

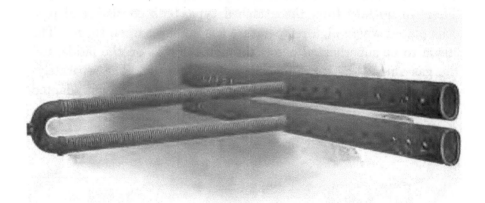

Fig. 60. One Protected Element of Foster Superheater, Showing Inlet and Outlet Headers
Courtesy of Power Specialty Company, New York City

shrunk on a two-inch seamless tube, and the inner tube forcing the steam passing through to hug the coil surface.

Fig. 60 shows one element connected to two headers and a number of openings in both to accommodate a number of elements. The construction shown is that of the Foster superheater. The Babcock and Wilcox superheater is identical in shape, except that the element is not armored. Both superheaters are attached to boilers in practically the same manner and at the same locations. In operation and use, however, they are quite different, in that the Foster superheater, being armored, does not require "flooding"—a term used to indicate that water is introduced into the superheater coils at the starting up of the boiler until steam has actually been

Fig. 61. Foster Superheater Mounted in Edge Moor Boiler

generated. The flooding is resorted to in bare-tube superheaters to preserve the coils from burning out during the time when no steam is given off by the boiler proper. The Foster arrangement, by presenting a protection of cast iron to the heated gases, delays the heating of the superheater tube proper until steam is actually generated and is passing through the superheated coils. The non-flooding type obviates the danger of sediment deposits from dirty water, and the still greater danger that a part of the flood water may remain in the coils even after steam is being delivered by the boiler, which, when a sudden demand for steam arises, may be carried in a mass and cause serious damage to either the piping or the engine.

Fig. 61 illustrates only one of many forms of superheater installations in use. The boiler shown is a water-tube boiler of the horizontal type, and the superheater is shown by the loops or elements placed between the boiler drums and the top row of tubes of the boiler proper. It will be noted that the superheater coils are not subjected to the intense heat of the gases immediately after being generated in the furnace, but receive this gas after passing among the boiler tubes in its first pass. The superheater receives its steam from the steam space in the rear header of the boiler and delivers it from the upper manifold.

STEAM SEPARATORS

Danger of "Wet" Steam. Steam is said to be wet or to be superheated according as it carries entrained moisture, or is of a temperature higher than that of saturated steam at the pressure dealt with. Wet steam is uneconomical to use, not only because it induces cylinder condensation in the engine, but because, if a considerable amount of water gets into the engine, it is really dangerous, for it may so completely fill the clearances that the piston will strike a blow against the cylinder head sufficient to break it. The water in the pipes, moreover, may cause a serious hammering, which not only is annoying, but may be actually hazardous, for a severe water hammer may break the joints of the steam pipes, and a large quantity of escaping steam at high pressure would be exceedingly dangerous to the lives of the engine-room attendants. This is especially true on board ship, where the engine room is small, the supply of air meager, and the means of escape limited.

A considerable amount of water may be deposited in the sag of an improperly built pipe line, and may remain there for an indefinite length of time if the pressure in the boiler does not fluctuate; but a sudden rise of boiler pressure will likely cause this water to pass bodily through the pipe toward the engine.

Priming. When a boiler delivers steam containing entrained moisture, it is said to *prime*. The presence of any substance which tends to increase the surface tension of the water, such as grease, oil, or other foreign matter, increases the priming tendency. If the boiler is such that the steam in entering into the space containing the boiler dry pipe is projected near the dry-pipe openings, the result is much entrained moisture in the steam. When a boiler, working at a fairly uniform rate, is suddenly called upon to deliver a somewhat greater quantity of steam and the fire conditions are correspondingly improved, the water level is raised on account of a greater percentage of steam bubbles in the water mass; and the result may be that the level of the water approaches so close to the steam outlet pipe that the steam, rushing toward its opening, carries large quantities of suspended moisture with it. If the water foams badly and the foregoing event takes place, the amount of moisture carried along with the steam may be quite large.

Priming may be detected from the unusual behavior of the water in the gage glass, or from the hammering in the steam pipes or engine cylinder. To avoid a breakdown under such conditions, the speed of the engine should be reduced, the drain cocks of the cylinders and pipes opened, and the fires eased down. Sometimes, by suddenly shutting the main stop valve, the pressure in the boiler can be increased sufficiently to overcome the difficulty.

Simple Methods of Obtaining Dry Steam. *Steam Dome.* Almost any boiler is likely to prime to some extent; and, to obtain as dry steam as possible, several devices are employed. On the top of stationary boilers and locomotives, a steam dome is frequently built, from which the steam is drawn, the idea being that less moisture will be found here than if the steam be drawn directly from the main portion of the boiler.

Dry Pipe Method. In marine work, and sometimes in stationary plants, a dry pipe is used, Fig. 43. This is merely a large pipe inside the boiler from which the steam is drawn. The pipe is near the top of the boiler, and the upper side of it is perforated with holes through which the steam may pass. In this way a considerable amount of moisture is prevented from leaving the boiler.

The moisture in steam can be reduced by the familiar process of superheating; but if this, for any reason, is impracticable or undesirable, a steam separator may be used for the purpose of extracting the moisture which comes from the priming of the boiler or from condensation in the steam pipe.

Types of Steam Separators. There are several forms of separators; but all are designed on the general principle that if the direction of the steam current is suddenly changed, or if it is diverted upward and then downward, the water will be separated from the steam and will fall to the bottom of a suitable receptacle.   The depth of water collected in the bottom of the separator is readily indicated by a gage glass, and it may be drawn off as desired.   To prevent the possibility of flooding the separator, it is well to connect it with an automatic trap which will empty it without close attention from the engineer.   It is needless, of course, to say that the trap from this

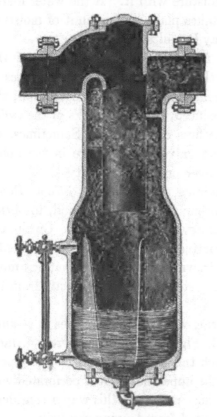 

Fig. 62.   Stratton Separator
Courtesy of Griscom-Russell Company

Fig. 63.   Cochrane Separator
Courtesy of Harrison Safety Boiler Works

separator should be connected to the hot well, and the drip should be returned to the boiler with the loss of as little heat as possible.

In the Stratton separator, Fig. 62, the steam enters at one side of a cylinder, flows downward, and then upward through a pipe in the middle.   Dry steam escapes from a pipe near the top on the opposite side from which it enters.   The separated water is drained at the bottom.

The Cochrane steam separator, Fig. 63, is of the baffle-plate type. The branches for the entrance and exit of the steam project from each side of the spherical head. Another branch from the bottom provides for connection with the well. The baffle plate, which is cast as a part of the head, is ribbed, or corrugated, and has ports at each side for the passage of steam. The area of the ports is large, to prevent loss by friction. A small pipe is inserted in the plate on the outlet side at the bottom of the baffle plate, to drain any condensation in the outlet chamber. Steam, entering at the left-hand opening, strikes the baffle plate and passes to the outlet chamber by means of the two side passages, as shown in Fig. 63.

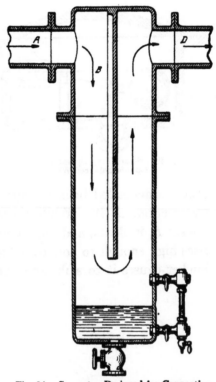

Fig. 64.   Separator Designed for Connection to Main Steam Pipe Near Engine

A form of separator which is fitted to the main steam pipe near the engine is shown in Fig. 64. Steam enters at A and strikes the dash plate B; any water coming with the steam is separated and falls to the bottom. The steam takes the direction indicated by the arrows, and flows out at D. This separator is fitted with a gage glass which is similar to a boiler gage glass.

TRAPS

Steam Traps. Steam traps are used for collecting

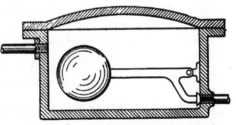

Fig. 65.   Simple Steam Trap Operated by Float

the water of condensation from steam pipes. They consist of a receptacle with an inlet and outlet valve so arranged that the condensation which collects may flow out, but steam cannot pass.

Float Type. In the float trap shown in Fig. 65, the float rises and falls with the change in water level. When the water level rises

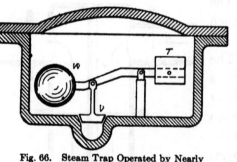

above a certain point, the float opens the discharge valve. The trap shown in Fig. 66 is similar, the float being replaced by a weight W, which is nearly counterbalanced by the weight T. The raising of W by the water opens the valve V.

Fig. 66.   Steam Trap Operated by Nearly Counterbalanced Weight

Bucket Type.   There are other forms called bucket traps. In the one shown in Fig. 67, the water enters at W. While there is only a little water around the bucket F, it floats, and the valve V is closed; but when the water rises high enough to flow over the edge, the weight of water in the bucket causes it to sink, and opens the valve V. Water is forced

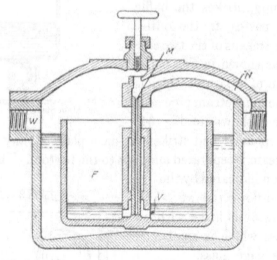

Fig. 67.   Bucket Type of Steam Trap

up the passage M, and out through the pipe N, by the pressure of the steam on the surface of the water surrounding the bucket.

Differential Type. Another form of trap, called the differential steam trap, depends upon a head of water acting on a flexible diaphragm. Water enters at either top or bottom by the pipes E, Fig. 68. When the water level rises it fills the chamber G and the pipe N. This causes a pressure on the under side of the diaphragm greater than that caused by the spring H, which spring acts on the upper side of the diaphragm and tends to keep the valve open. While the pressure below the diaphragm preponderates, the valve P remains closed. When the water rises and fills the chamber J so as to flow down the pipe M, the water pressure on the upper and lower side of the diaphragm will become equal, because the head of water in M is practically the same as that in N. The spring will now open the valve P, and water will be discharged from the pipe I. When the head in M falls, the pressure on the under side of the diaphragm again becomes greater, and the valve accordingly closes.

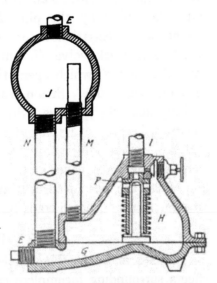

Fig. 68. Differential Steam Trap Operated by Water Pressure on a Flexible Diaphragm

Return Traps. Traps that are used for returning water of condensation to the boiler are called return traps. The object is to

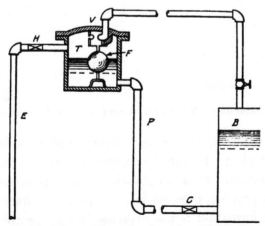

Fig. 69. Diagram Illustrating Operation of Return Trap

reclaim the steam condensed in piping, which would otherwise be lost. There is a variety of forms, but the principle of action is

similar in all and is shown in Fig. 69. *B* represents the boiler
and *T* the trap, which is placed a few feet above the boiler. The
trap is supplied with steam from the boiler. It is also connected
with the boiler by the pipe *P*, in which is a check valve *C*.
Water of condensation enters the trap through the pipe *E*, in
which is a check valve *H*, until it reaches a depth sufficient to
raise the float *F*, which opens the balanced steam valve *V*, called
an equalizing valve. Steam from the boiler then enters the trap
and equalizes the pressure. Since the pressures are equal, water in
the trap, because of its height above the water level of the boiler,
will flow to the boiler until the level in the pipe *P* is nearly the
same as the water level in the boiler. As the water level in the
trap falls, the float *F* drops, and the equalizing valve is closed.
In some forms of return traps buckets are used instead of floats.

SOOT BLOWERS

Causes of Soot. The whole subject of soot arises out of the
effects surrounding incomplete combustion, of whatever form that

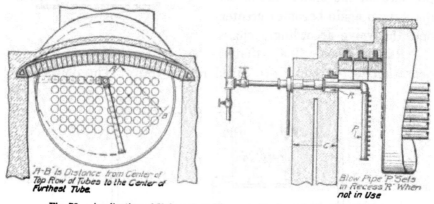

Fig. 70. Application of Vulcan Soot Blower to Horizontal Fire-Tube Boiler

may take. Therefore, the causes, effects, and remedies having to
do with incomplete or partial combustion are inseparably linked
with soot formation. If the combustion process is looked after effectually the soot problem becomes less in extent. Primarily the main
loss from soot formation is the decrease in the absorbing ability of
the heating surfaces rather than the loss due to the amount of fuel
unburned and rejected as soot. Corrosion of boiler parts is sometimes caused by the acid action of a combination of the sulphur

products of combustion uniting with moisture of which the soot acts as a ready absorbent.

Methods of Removal of Soot. The removal of soot presents difficulties which require ingenuity on the part of both the designing and operating engineers of steam plants. It has developed that soot of a given thickness on heating surface is somewhat more serious in the reduction of boiler economy than an equal thickness of scale deposited by evaporated water. The problem in fire-tube boilers is less difficult than with water-tube boilers for the same reason that the reverse is true in the matter of scale removal.

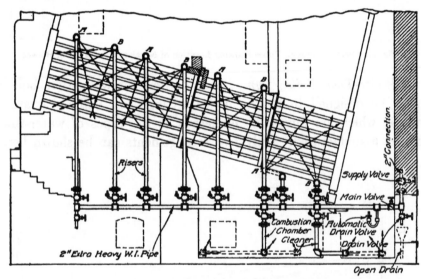

Fig. 71. Side View of Vulcan Soot Blower as Applied to Single-Deck Horizontal Water-Tube Boiler with Vertical Baffles
Courtesy of Vulcan Fuel Economy Company, Chicago

Fire-Tube Boiler Type. In fire-tube boilers the soot cleaning is done by inserting a pipe leading to either air or steam under pressure in the end of each tube, thus creating a high velocity of gas or steam movement in that particular tube which scrubs out the soot. If the process is continued, and soot is not blown from one part of the boiler to another, results are fairly satisfactory.

An improvement in the manual cleaning can be obtained by the device shown in Fig. 70. This blower—shown in the illustration as ready for use—performs the entire blowing service by rotating the blower arm so that jets of steam blow down each tube. The cleaning is done rapidly, and the soot is forced to go in the direction of the gas travel or toward the chimney. When not in use the blower pipe is withdrawn into a recess in the back wall of the boiler setting, thus removing it from the hot gases.

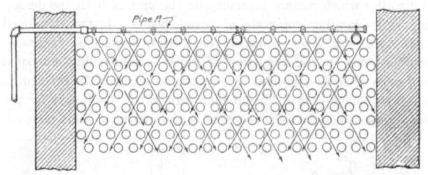

Fig. 72. Section through Tubes Showing Location of Nozzles of Vulcan Soot Blower

Water-Tube Boiler Type. Soot blowers for water-tube boilers must be designed to fit the boiler settings and baffling arrangements, which are almost as numerous as the types of water-tube boilers manufactured. Only two arrangements can be shown here.

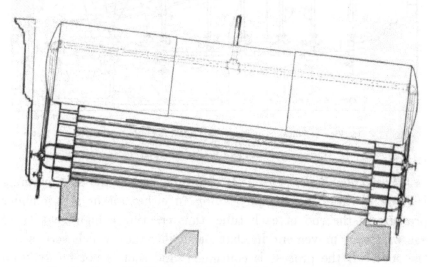

Fig. 73. Type of Double-End Soot Blower Attached to Water-Tube Boiler
Courtesy of Diamond Power Specialty Company, Detroit, Michigan

Fig. 71 illustrates a system adapted for use with a horizontal water-tube boiler. The intention is here to keep the cross blowing pipes out of the heated gases until a part of the heat has been extracted. The number of openings in the setting wall are reduced to a minimum and ample facilities for drainage are provided. Fig. 72 shows the direction taken by the steam jets.

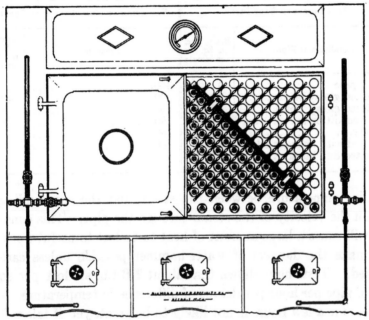

Fig. 74. Single-End Soot Blower for Boilers Having Hollow Stays
Courtesy of Diamond Power Specialty Company, Detroit, Michigan.

Some types of boilers do not permit side access to the boiler tubes, in which case other means must be resorted to than those given in Fig. 71. Figs. 73 and 74 show one method employed where advantage is taken of the hollow stay bolts of water-leg boilers. Fig. 73 illustrates an older double-end type while Fig. 74 shows a new type of single-end soot blower. The manner of introducing the blower into a hollow stay bolt is shown in Fig. 75. The illustration is sufficiently clear to show its application.

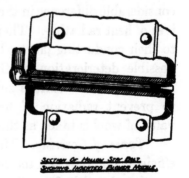

Fig. 75. Diagram Showing Attachment of Blower to Hollow Stay

LAGGING

Necessity for Protection. When steam pipes are exposed to the air, a considerable amount of condensation will collect in them, depending upon the condition of the surface of the pipe, on the differ-

TABLE I
Bare Pipe Data

Heat Losses in Bare Pipes		Variation of Heat Loss with Pressure	
Condition of Pipe	B.t.u. Loss per Sq. Ft. per Minute	Pressure	Heat Loss B.t.u. per Sq. Ft. per Minute
New pipe..............	11.96	340....................	15.97
Painted glossy black.......	12.10	200....................	13.84
Painted glossy white.......	12.02	100....................	8.92
Fair condition	13.84	80....................	8.04
Rusty.................	14.20	60....................	7.00
Coated with cylinder oil....	13.90	40....................	5.74
Painted dull black........	14.40		

ence in temperature between the steam and the surrounding air, and on the velocity of the steam through the pipe. This condensation will cause a large amount of heat to be lost to useful work, and will make the dangers of water hammer possible unless carefully drained. Tests have shown that about 2 B.t.u. are lost per square foot of pipe per hour per degree of difference in temperature. While the loss for a few hours is not likely to be great, yet, if taken for an entire year throughout a considerable length of pipe, the sum total will be very large indeed. Table I* gives some idea of the loss of heat through bare pipe at 200 pounds pressure.

Pipe Coverings. To make this loss from radiation as small as possible, it is customary to cover the pipe or boiler with some material which will prevent loss of heat and which will not burn. There is considerable difference in the value of various substances as preventives of heat radiation. Their value varies nearly in an inverse ratio to their conducting power; but due allowance must be made for the possible deterioration of the pipe covering. Table II gives the relative value of various substances with reference to their ability to prevent radiation of heat. For purposes of comparison, the value of wool is taken as the standard.

Types of Covering. Many of the patented coverings are very efficient, but they are too numerous even to mention. The above-mentioned article from the Proceedings of the American Society of

---

*A full account of some interesting tests can be found in a paper entitled *Protection of Steam-Heating Surfaces*, by C. L. Norton, Vol. XIX, Proceedings of the American Society of Mechanical Engineers, from which Table I has been taken.

TABLE II

Relative Values of Various Preventives of Radiation of Heat

MATERIALS	PER CENT OF VALUE	MATERIALS	PER CENT OF VALUE
Felt; hair, or wool	100	Sawdust.	61–68
Asbestos sponge..........	98	Asbestos paper...........	47
Air-cell asbestos..........	89	Wood.	40–55
Mineral wool.............	68–83	Asbestos, fibrous..........	36
Carbonate of magnesia.....	67–76	Plaster of Paris	34
Charcoal.................	63	Air space (undivided)	22

Mechanical Engineers gives the results of tests of several of these coverings. A good protection is afforded by air confined in minute cells, such as is to be had in the air-cell asbestos board; this is made by cementing together several layers of asbestos paper which have been corrugated or indented by machinery so as to form minute air cells. The more minute the subdivision of these cells, the better the protection is likely to be. Hair felt is one of the most efficient non-conductors, because it is very porous and contains a large number of air cells. It is not one of the best coverings, however, because it is likely to deteriorate, and its life on high-pressure pipes is not likely to be more than four or five years. On low-pressure work it may last for a considerably longer time.

Mineral wool, a fibrous material made from blast-furnace slag, is an efficient and noncombustible covering, but is brittle and liable to fall off.

The coverings most easily applied to pipes are those which can be applied in sectional form. They clasp around the pipe and are fastened by brass bands at convenient intervals. Such coverings are made either of asbestos or magnesia, and are usually about one inch thick for the smaller sizes of pipe.

A good, cheap covering can be made by wrapping several layers of asbestos paper around the pipe, and then putting over this a layer of hair felt three-fourths inch thick, the whole being wrapped in canvas. On low-pressure steam pipes this covering will last ten to fifteen years.

Cork is perhaps one of the most satisfactory coverings from the point of radiation loss, but is somewhat more expensive than asbestos or magnesia.

Cost. It has been the general impression that it is not economical to cover a pipe to more than one inch in thickness. This will depend upon the cost of the covering and the length of time it is likely to last. If it does not last more than five years, one inch is probably the most economical thickness; but if the life of the covering is likely to be ten years or more, a second inch in thickness can be applied to advantage. For instance, in the above-mentioned tests, in the case of Nonpareil cork, increasing the thickness from one to two inches raised the cost from $25 to $30 per 100 square feet, and increased the net saving in five years by $10, and by $30 in ten years. A third inch of covering did not produce saving enough to pay for its cost. In each case with the asbestos fireboard, a second inch in thickness showed a saving of $20 in ten years, while the third inch in thickness showed an actual loss from the dollars-and-cents point of view. It should be remembered that it is of great importance that to keep the pipe covering in repair, for a loose-fitting covering is of little value.

Boiler Coverings. The same may be said with regard to boiler as to pipe covering, except that the covering put on boilers is usually somewhat less efficient and is applied in greater thickness. Probably one of the best coverings for a marine boiler—or, in fact, for any internally-fired boiler—is a layer of air-cell asbestos board, covered with a coating perhaps two inches thick of magnesia or asbestos. This comes in powder form, and when mixed with water can be readily applied with a trowel. Coverings on boilers are best placed directly against the shell without an air space, so that any leak in a joint or rivet will reveal the spot by moistening the covering; otherwise the escaping water may run down through the air space and appear at some remote point, thus making the leak difficult to locate.

An efficient covering for boilers is made of either magnesia or asbestos in the form of blocks of the proper curvature, which can lie directly against the boiler; but this form of covering is rather more expensive than the asbestos or magnesia cement. To secure an extra hard finish a coating of plaster of Paris may be put on outside the magnesia or asbestos. No boiler or pipe covering should contain sulphate of lime, as this is likely to cause corrosion.

Covering for Externally Fired Boiler. If an internally fired boiler is properly lagged, there is little danger that any large amount of heat will be lost, as the heat of the fire must pass through the water before radiating. This is not true with an externally fired boiler, where a considerable amount of heat may radiate through the brick setting of the boiler without coming in contact with the boiler at all.

Many expedients have been tried, most of them with indifferent success, to provide an efficient method of preventing heat radiation from the settings of externally fired boilers. The earlier attempts took the shape of building an air space in the boiler walls; this simple construction is not effective because the air can circulate easily between the walls and, even when the two walls are properly bonded together, the outer wall may be intact while the inner and more important wall may be badly cracked or crumbled. The better form of double or air-space wall divides the air space into noncommunicating cells of, say, 4 square feet of area. It is safe to say that air-space walls are finding less favor as the science of boiler economy is becoming more exact. However, it is quite necessary to apply some better insulation than that afforded by a brick masonry wall for boiler settings. Recent practice is tending to the application of magnesia or asbestos in a layer about 2 inches thick on the whole exterior surface of the usual brickwork, covering this in turn with canvas glued tight to the surface. Several coats of paint are then applied. When work of this kind is properly done, it not only reduces radiation of heat materially but prevents the infiltration of air into the settings, which is of much more importance.

DRAFT APPARATUS

General Classification. The entire subject of draft apparatus is closely linked with both the design and operation of boilers. Primarily, of course, the object of such equipment is to provide air for combustion, but as the manner of application is determined to a large extent upon boiler passages, tube rows, etc., it is thought proper to present the main features here, because the usual situation is that the boiler is located between the draft creator and the place where the effect is to be felt, namely, in the furnace. Even should the apparatus be such as to force the air for combustion through the furnace, the degree of freedom of permitting the gases to move from the furnace is still controlled largely by the boiler or its setting design. The terms used with reference to the way in which the draft force is created are descriptive of the contrivances themselves, namely, *natural*, if brought about by a permanent rigid structure, such as a chimney; *mechanical*, if fans, blowers, stack jets, etc., are used. The second group is divided into *forced* or *induced*, to express whether the air is acted upon mechanically before or after entering the combustion chamber.

CHIMNEYS

Action of Chimney. The proper design of chimneys constitutes one of the most important features to be dealt with in boiler practice, though the factors entering into stack design are so numerous that it has not, thus far, been practicable to evolve a formula including even most of the variables in one statement. Recourse is therefore taken to the results obtained in practice, expressions of which are found in empirical equations which must be very judiciously handled lest grave mistakes result.

The gas leaving a boiler setting, being somewhat hotter than the air surrounding the chimney it enters, weighs less than the same volume of air surrounding the chimney. If the air surrounding the chimney has access to the chimney, or can exert its weight upon the lighter gases within the chimney, even by the devious path through the setting of the boiler and its breeching, there will be a constant tendency to establish a balance between the two. The force tending to establish this balance is termed *draft*.

Determining Factors in Chimney Design. The purpose of providing a draft force at the chimney is to create a force to supply air to the burning fuel and to carry the gases of combustion through the boiler setting and connections to the chimney. The height of the chimney should then be sufficient to perform all the work of overcoming the fuel-bed resistance and the other passage resistances that may be encountered. From this it may be correctly judged that it is the height of a chimney which determines the intensity of draft for a given gas temperature and the maximum probable rate at which the fuel can be burned, while the area of the chimney controls the amount of gas in cubic feet per unit of time the chimney will carry away, considering a given temperature of gas. In further explanation of these two statements, attention need only be called to the fact that the higher a chimney the greater its cubical contents for a given area, and consequently the greater the difference between the interior and exterior gas columns in weight; that the rate at which fuel can be burned is nearly proportional to the difference in draft above and below the fuel bed.

It is true that both the area and the height of a chimney have some influence upon the draft intensity when a gas of a definite temperature is delivered to it, but it is customary to look upon the design of chimneys in the light stated, modifying both dimensions for structural reasons.

Dimensions of Chimneys by Kent's Formula. Many formulas have been advanced for the purpose of arriving at more exact methods for proportioning chimneys than by the unsatisfactory expedient of finding a chimney that has turned out well. Most of them leave so many factors unprovided for that it is now recognized as a mistake to use them except in the simplest cases. Probably the formula advanced by William Kent has received the most favorable consideration in the United States. Table III is computed by using the formula mentioned; a coal consumption of five pounds per horsepower developed is the basis of the computation. The results obtained by the use of this table are satisfactory, as there is a margin allowed for a reasonable overload. It is well to apply an increase to the height figures given in the table when low-grade bituminous coals are dealt with. Many engineers use a uniform increase of 20 per cent for this purpose, but there are circumstances when a much greater increase should be supplied. No definite rule can be given covering these contingencies.

Careful chimney designers make allowances for varying altitudes above the sea level. The reason is easily seen, for the density of air grows less as the height above the sea level is increased.

Influence of Fuel on Draft Required. The draft necessary for burning fuels other than coal is of different intensity than for coal. For a given boiler setting, wood should rarely be provided with as high a draft as for coal; for oil burning less draft is required at the chimney, as there is no fuel bed to offer resistance. In the latter instance the chimney may be of considerable less area also than for coal, because the volume of gas coming from oil economically burned is less than for coal burned at a rate to create the same power or evaporation.

Methods of Construction. Chimneys are usually made of brick, steel, or concrete. If of steel or concrete, they are always circular. When made of brick they are circular, rectangular, or octagonal. For a given area, a circular chimney requires the least material, since a circumference has the least perimeter; it also presents less resistance to wind.

A steel chimney is made up of plates of steel riveted together. The shell is bolted through a foundation ring of cast iron to the concrete foundation. It is sometimes lined with fire brick, with a thickness which varies from 12 to 18 inches at the bottom to about 2 inches to 4 inches at the top. This lining is used to prevent heat being lost through the shell and does not add to the strength of the chimney.

A brick chimney is built in two parts—the outer shell, which resists wind pressure, and a lining. The inner chimney is made separate from the external shell in order that it may expand when the chimney is carrying hot gases.

The interior surfaces of brick chimneys are often of cylindrical shape, while the exterior surface tapers. The taper is about .3 inch to the foot. The brick at the base of the chimney is splayed out to make a large base.

During recent years concrete chimneys have come into much favor, especially since this type of construction has been perfected both in strength and appearance. While the early concrete chimneys had cylindrical shafts they are now quite generally built with tapered shafts which not only reduces the amount of material required for their construction, but improves the appearance.

The concrete is reinforced with vertical steel rods and some form of woven wire mesh made up in rings. When proper concrete mixtures are used with good designs and are placed under the direction of competent construction superintendents, the results are quite satisfactory in concrete chimney work.

As good natural earth should carry from 2000 to 4000 pounds per square foot, the base of the chimney should be large enough so that this pressure will not be exceeded.

TABLE III

Stack Sizes by Kent's Formula

(Assuming 5 Pounds of Coal per Horsepower Hour)

Diameter (inches)	Area (square feet)	HEIGHT OF STACK IN FEET — COMMERCIAL HORSEPOWER								Size of Equivalent Square Stack (inches)	Diameter (inches)
		70	80	90	100	110	125	150	175		
33	5.94	125	133	141	149	156	.....	.....	.....	30	33
36	7.07	152	163	173	182	191	204	.....	.....	32	36
39	8.30	183	196	208	219	229	245	268	.....	35	39
42	9.62	216	231	245	258	271	289	316	342	38	42
48	12.57	.....	311	330	348	365	389	426	460	43	48
54	15.90	.....	.....	427	449	472	503	551	595	48	54
60	19.64	.....	.....	536	565	593	632	692	748	54	60
66	23.76	.....	.....	.....	694	728	776	849	918	59	66
72	28.27	.....	.....	.....	835	876	934	1023	1105	64	72
78	33.18	.....	.....	.....	.....	1038	1107	1212	1310	70	78
84	38.48	.....	.....	.....	.....	1214	1294	1418	1531	75	84

Diameter (inches)	Area (square feet)	HEIGHT OF STACK IN FEET — COMMERCIAL HORSEPOWER						Size of Equivalent Square Stack (inches)	Diameter (inches)
		125	150	175	200	225	250		
90	44.18	1496	1639	1770	1893	2008	2116	80	90
96	50.27	1712	1876	2027	2167	2298	2423	86	96
102	56.75	1944	2130	2300	2459	2609	2750	91	102
108	63.62	2090	2399	2592	2771	2939	3098	98	108
114	70.88	2451	2685	2900	3100	3288	3466	101	114
120	78.54	2726	2986	3226	3448	3657	3855	107	120
132	95.03	3321	3637	3929	4200	4455	4696	117	132
144	113.10	3973	4350	4701	5026	5331	5618	128	144

NOTE: For pounds of coal burned per hour for any given size of chimney, multiply the figures in Table III by 5. For detailed discussion of theory, see Kent's Mechanical Engineers' Pocket Book, ninth edition, 1916.

The external shell is calculated for wind pressure and the weight of brick. This calculation for wind pressure involving higher mathematics will not be treated here. The lining is calculated for compression due to weight. The design, both of the chimney and its foundation, should be made by a competent engineer of experience, on account of disastrous results should a chimney fall.

SYSTEMS OF MECHANICAL DRAFT

Classification of Systems. High chimneys are costly; and it is frequently the practice to build two or three small chimneys in place of the big one, or to supplement them with some form of mechanical draft.

By means of mechanical draft, the rate of fuel combustion can be increased under favorable conditions to 60 pounds of coal per square foot of grate surface per hour. This, of course, greatly increases the capacity of the plant, but may be injurious to the boilers. There are three systems of mechanical draft in common use: (1) closed stokehold (as used in marine work); (2) closed ash pit; and (3) induced draft.

Closed Stokehold. One of the most common forms of forced draft, especially as used on warships, is obtained by closing the stokeholds and blowing a fresh supply of air into the fireroom. This gives an exceedingly good ventilation and keeps the fireroom in good condition; but its chief objection is that, when the furnace doors are opened, there is a tremendous in-flow of cold air, which tends to lower the efficiency of the boiler. If this system is employed, the bulkheads adjacent to the boiler room must be provided with double doors, forming an air lock between. By opening only one door at a time, the pressure in the fireroom is not lost. This system seems to possess but one distinct advantage, and that is coolness and, therefore, comfort for the firemen; but the disadvantage of the inrush of air to the furnaces when firing is sufficient, in some cases, to make the system questionable.

Closed Ash Pit. The essential features of forced draft by this method consist merely in closing the ash pit tight, and blowing the air directly under the grate. When the fires are cleaned, the draft, of course, must be shut off; otherwise the flames will be blown out into the fireroom. The fireroom, under this system, is likely to be hotter than by the other method; but this system would seem to be the better from a mechanical point of view.

As a variation of the ordinary closed ash-pit method of forced draft, the very important class of mechanical stokers, previously described and known as the underfeed type, must be mentioned. In all stokers of this class the success of the underfeeding principle of fuel delivery depends upon the ability of the apparatus to provide the passage of air for combustion through a very thick fuel bed. Any other method than blowing air under pressure into a wind box beneath the fuel bed, in order to overcome the high resistance of the fuel bed, would fail.

There are several patented devices in connection with the forced draft, of which the Howden and the Ellis and Eaves systems may be specially mentioned. It may be worth while to note that if fuel oil is burned, any one of these systems of forced draft will work better than with coal, for the fire can be tended without opening the firedoors.

Induced Draft. Perhaps the most common example of induced draft is to be found in the locomotive, where the exhaust steam is turned into the smokestack. The rush of this steam up the stack, by carrying a large volume of gas with it, induces a tremendous draft. Induced draft may also be obtained in stationary and marine plants by placing a blower in the chimney or stack. In marine work, of course, induced draft by exhaust steam is out of the question. The draft obtained on locomotives is frequently equivalent to a column of five or six inches of water; while a forced draft of two inches is usually considered large, except for torpedo boats, which may have as intense a draft as a locomotive.

Howden System. The Howden system of forced draft with closed ash pit has been used to a considerable extent in both mercantile and naval service. The air supplied to the ash pit is first heated by passing through a heater in the uptake. Waste gases pass through tubes; and the air, passing among them before entering the furnace, is heated to a high temperature. A consumption of 60 pounds of coal per square foot of grate is easily obtained with this system; and care must be taken that the fire is not forced too hard, as there is more danger of burning out the grate than if the air supply is not heated.

Ellis and Eaves System. Heating the air does not necessitate its being forced into the closed ash pit, for it is quite feasible to heat the air in connection with draft induced by an exhaust fan at the base of the funnel. Such is the Ellis and Eaves system. This system was first tried in the boiler shops at the works of the John Brown Company, in Sheffield, England, and was later adopted on many vessels. The Ellis and Eaves heater is fixed on top of the boilers, and is divided into two parts separated at the front by a smoke box and at the back by a funnel. The hot gases, therefore—which pass outside the tubes—have to take a somewhat circuitous course; while the passage of the air to be heated, on the contrary, takes a direct course. The distribution of air to the ash pit is similar to that of the Howden system. The advantages of this system lie in the general convenience of the induced draft and the absence of jets of hot air shooting out into the boiler room. The draft need not be shut off when stoking the fires, unless it is desired to prevent the inrush of air already referred to under the general discussion of "closed stokeholds". The air in the fireroom being of a relatively higher temperature than would obtain with closed stokeholds, and the quantity being much less, this objection has no great weight. With the Howden system it is necessary that the doors should be tight; otherwise hot air will be blown out into the fireroom. With this system a few leaks are of no consequence, and the fireroom will be somewhat cooler than with the Howden system. The objections to the Ellis and Eaves system are those inherent in any system of draft induced by a fan—a poor efficiency of the fan working in heated gases and lost work in drawing air through tortuous passages.

Steam Jets. Steam jets may be used for inducing a draft. They may be placed either in the smokestack, or below or above the grate; but in general they are not so economical as a fan used for the same purpose. In locomotives and fire engines, where the exhaust steam is at high pressure, an intense draft may be induced by exhausting this up the smokestack. In both these cases the saving of weight, due to the use of a small boiler running at high capacity, is of great practical importance; and for such purposes this arrangement is entirely satisfactory. This method of creating draft is becoming more prevalent on the continent of Europe, where many successful installations are operated.

BREECHINGS

General Items to Be Considered. The structure conveying waste or uptake boiler gases to a discharge place, as, for instance, a chimney, is called a *breeching*. These are of such shape and built of such materials as experience seems to justify. They have been and still are located in every conceivable position, both under ground and over head, and the errors in design that have been committed in their construction are in thousands of instances very costly. The following represent the main general items demanding consideration:

1. All turns should be made by long radius bends.

2. All changes in size and shape should be made gradually.

3. No cross-section dimension should ever be greater than twice as large as the dimension at right angles to it.

4. Entrance into chimneys should be made with an upward slant, so as to increase the radius of the gas travel turn at the stack as much as possible.

5. Construct them so as to prevent air infiltration.

6. Unite with other structures so outside air will not enter at the joints.

7. Provide ample air-tight cleanout facilities.

8. If underground, look to the drainage. To be effective, a breeching must be dry.

9. Do not build breechings out of brick.

10. Line steel breechings with an acid-resisting material which also resists heat transmission.

11. Support breechings free of boiler parts.

12. Depend upon individual boiler dampers and not on a breeching or stack damper when more than one boiler is connected with a stack.

13. Never provide two or more paths of travel for gases in a breeching at the same time, as by placing a chimney at each end of a breeching.

14. Do not place dampers in boiler uptakes so as to stand in the way of gases moving in the breechings when opened.

15. Try to avoid the "head-on" movement of gases from two ends of a breeching on their way to a stack.

16. If the breeching *must* be long or tortuous, be sure to allow for these things by additional chimney height to make good for the extra resistance and radiant heat loss.

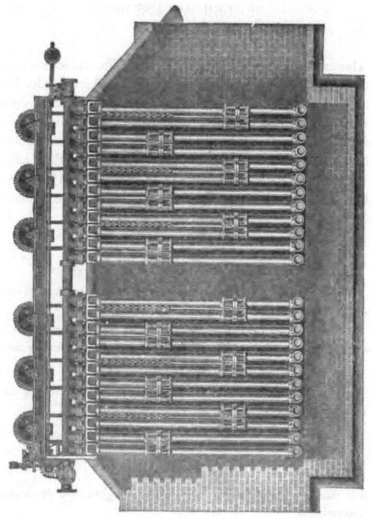

Fig. 76. Side and End Views of Green Economizer
Courtesy of Green Fuel Economizer Company, New York City

FUEL ECONOMIZERS

Many devices have been employed whereby a part of the heat may be extracted from waste gases as they pass from the boiler to the chimney. Most of these devices consist of a tubular arrange-

Fig. 77. Sturtevant Fuel Economizer
Courtesy of B. F. Sturtevant Company, Boston

ment among which the hot gases pass; but, as they are soon covered with a thick deposit of soot, they quickly become inoperative.

Green Economizer. The Green economizer, Fig. 76, solves this difficulty by means of small scrapers which work up and down between the tubes. These scrapers are operated by a small engine, and keep the tubes free from soot. The feed water is pumped through these tubes on its way to the boiler and is heated. An economizer of this sort will extract considerable of the heat from the waste gases; but, by reducing the temperature of these gases, and by the extra mechanical resistance, the draft is somewhat reduced, and either the chimney must be built higher or an exhaust fan must be used. The proper installation of an economizer is a matter requiring judgment and experience, especially in the design of the flue connections and all other gas passages.

Sturtevant Fuel Economizer. In Fig. 77 is shown an economizer manufactured by the B. F. Sturtevant Company. In the illustration the inclosing walls are omitted, thus exposing to view the soot pit, pipe headers, pipes and scrapers, caps, scraper operating mechanism, etc. The casing is made either of brick or of metal-asbestos.

The special features entering into the construction of this economizer are several in number. All joints are made without the use of gaskets, dependence being placed upon metal-to-metal tapered fits. In the case of connecting the tubes to the headers the fit is obtained by hydraulically pressing the tapered ends of the tubes into the tapered holes of the manifolds. This feature does away with the necessity of removing a whole section of tubes when one tube fails, as each tube can be removed by withdrawing it upward if room is available. The tubes are placed "staggered" as a usual thing so that the heated gases more completely envelop the tubes than if they were placed in straight rows.

POWER PLANT ACCESSORIES

Importance of Properly Handling Supplies and Refuse. Distinct from the problems presented in the equipment and operation of boilers, that of providing suitable housing accommodations and facilities for the receipt, storage, moving, and weighing of fuel, and the removal, accumulation, and disposition of refuse constitutes an additional problem of great importance. In fact, the proper handling of these details demands, in most cases, the application of as much ingenuity as the subject of proper boiler setting and equipment. Unlike pure boiler and furnace design, a bad selection of conveying equipment is not reflected in the loss of efficiency in the use of fuel but is strikingly evident in the excessive cost of boiler room labor, shutdowns, and high maintenance.

The investigator of this subject cannot expect to find a complete or correct answer to his inquiries in published works of either the instructional or catalog kinds, as the variables are so numerous and their relative importance so different that it would be only by the merest chance that a proposed installation could find its counterpart in one already existing. However, specialists in the field agree upon certain fundamentals, which it is the purpose of the succeeding paragraphs to set forth.

COAL HANDLING

Systems Employed. There are two principal modes of handling coal, either of which may be adopted without regard to the size of the plant served, namely, (1) A conveying system, the elements of which consist of a coal receiving hopper (as beneath an unloading track); a short elevating conveyor discharging into a coal crusher; a conveyor feeder of an endless bucket conveyor, lifting and distributing the coal to bunkers placed above and in front of the boilers; and chutes leading the coal to stoker hoppers or to a convenient firing space on the boiler room floor. (2) A system consisting of a receiving hopper (as beneath an unloading track); a short conveyor to a coal crusher; a conveyor feeder discharging into a lifting conveyor and delivering crushed coal to a storage hopper; and a traveling larry serving stoker hoppers or the firing space on the boiler room floor.

Variations from the above descriptions are frequently provided especially in the matter of unloading coal cars by means of grab buckets and carrying the coal direct to overhead storage bins.

An excellent illustration of the first class is given by Fig. 78. In the system shown, the ashes are carried by the same conveyor which carries the coal, dumps it into the hopper B, from which it may be loaded directly into the same car, when empty, that brings coal to the plant. It will be noted that the system affords facilities for large storage inside the building and is especially well adapted to large plants. In the second system, distribution is made by a larry traveling the length of the boiler room, as shown in Fig. 79. The larry shown is electrically driven and includes a weighing device. When the weighing feature is desired, together with a long storage bin as in system (1), it is sometimes

advantageous to employ a larry instead of chutes. By this means
the storage bin may have more bottom openings than are required
to serve the stoker hoppers thus affording better bin-emptying
facilities than would occur with chutes alone. The larry of the
type shown may be constructed with movement transverse to its
main translation thus affording greater freedom in the bin construction than when chutes are used alone. It must be kept in
mind that the pitch of the chutes must be ample to allow the
ready flow of coal, consequently, if the horizontal distance between
the furnace hoppers and the discharge pace of the bin is fixed,
the vertical height of the bin above the boiler room floor must

Fig. 78. Coal and Ash Handling System
Courtesy of Link Belt Machinery Company, Chicago

be made to fit, and *vice versa*. Necessarily, any permanent bin
structure in any system of storage must be such as to permit the
renewal of boiler tubes, which adds another element as to position
of bunkers which enters into the problem. Where two rows of
boilers face each other the larry must offer a double spout arrangement or a means for turning the larry discharging device through
an angle of 180 degrees.

The larry system of conveyance overcomes one objection of
the continuous bin type with chutes in that the latter cannot
readily be constructed so as to completely empty themselves by
gravity thus leaving an appreciable quantity of coal constantly in
the bins between the chute openings. Where the coal is conveyed

by a larry the storage bin need not be located in the boiler room nor need the building housing the boilers be as high as for the continuous bin type.

Chutes. Coal chutes should not be of the flaring bottom type, for it is not possible with this shape to obtain a uniform coal size distribution, the tendency being for the larger pieces to

Fig. 79. Weighing Larry Electrically Driven
Courtesy of Brown Hoisting Machinery Company, Chicago

roll to the ends of the flare even if baffling is inserted in the chute. The fires are therefore unevenly charged and poor combustion is the result. The chutes should be cylindrical in section and be capable of a swinging movement along the stoker hopper length.

Coal Storage Bins. Coal storage bins are usually built in the form of what might be termed the continuous pattern, the bottoms constructed in a series of hopper shapes, each terminating below in a coal discharge head leading to a spout or chute. Sometimes a series of cylindrical tanks placed one beside the other takes the place of a continuous construction in which case the bottom of each tank is shaped like an inverted cone. Reinforced concrete bins having a parabolic cross-section are coming into favor because of the protection to the steel afforded by the concrete as well as other features of strength and general adaptability to space economy, etc.

ASH HANDLING

Reason for Handling Coal and Ash Separately. While the quantity of refuse material of a power plant is a great deal less than the amount of coal burned, the moving of it is attended with greater trouble and expense than that of the coal. This is due to the high abrasive quality of ash making it very destructive when used with moving machinery. On this account it has come to be recognized that ash and coal should be separately moved and the tendency is to employ a mechanical conveyor for moving coal and a system of dump cars for the moving of ash, rather than cause the destruction of a very expensive piece of machinery suitable for moving one product because a much lesser quantity of another material is conveyed by it. Again, when a conveyor is used for both materials the fact that ashes are usually wet down before charging to conveyors causes the buckets to become partially filled with a mushy mass which refuses to spill by gravity and the result that either good coal finds its way to the ash heap or ash finds its way back to the coal supply. The corrosive action of wet ashes is very great. Altogether, the problem of ash disposal is always difficult to solve whether having to do with a large plant or a small one.

Types of Systems. Recent developments have brought out two ash systems which appear to have merit within limitations though these limitations have not as yet been fully determined. Both systems use heavy chilled pipe as the conducting machinery; one employs the pneumatic, or suction, principle and the other a steam jet, or ejector, principle. The first has been in commercial existence for a number of years but has not had a wide application.

The steam jet system is a much more recent development though the application has been very marked during the last two or three years.

Pneumatic System. The pneumatic system consists of an air-tight tank connected to the intake of a power-driven fan, exhausting the air from the tank. From the top of the tank the ash line itself is led, with as few turns as possible, to the floor of the boiler room, where it passes in front of the boilers, having intakes leading into the pipes in front of each boiler. The ashes

Fig. 80. Diagram of Steam Jet Ash-Handling Layout
Courtesy of American Steam Conveyor Corporation, Chicago

are raked into the adjacent intake tee and, owing to the vacuum set up in the tank and in the line, they are drawn rapidly into the tank by the column of air set in motion. The actual power consumption per ton of ashes is considerably higher than the ordinary mechanical methods of removing ashes. The initial cost is comparatively high and it is necessary to keep the fan and pipe line in very good condition, so as not to have a resulting drop in the vacuum produced. It is also necessary in this case to inject some water into the ash line before entering the tank in order to kill the fire and thus eliminate the liability of explosion due to inflammable gases, produced by the combustibles, coming in contact with hot ashes as they enter the system.

Steam Jet System. The pipe and fittings employed in the steam and jet system are very much the same as employed in the pneumatic type, but instead of using an air-tight tank and a fan to produce the vacuum, this is done by steam jets inserted at one or more points along the line. The illustration, Fig. 80, shows a typical system in which the ashes are raked into the intake tees from the ash pits and deposited into a tank outside the boiler room for loading into wagons or cars as the case may be. While the power consumption per ton of ash removed is very high, the other items entering into the cost of ash removal are enough lower to make it a paying investment in a great many cases. These items are *initial cost,* including interest on the investment, *depreciation, maintenance,* and *labor.* For the same approximate amount of labor in drawing the ashes from the pit into the conveyor, the initial cost of a steam jet system is a great deal lower than any other type of ash removal conveyor, with a corresponding decrease of interest on the investment. The depreciation and maintenance are considerably smaller than would appear on the face of it. Owing to the recent improvements on the grade of metal used and the proper design of fittings for economical replacement at the points of concentrated wear, the actual maintenance per ton of ashes handled generally comes under two cents. These systems are generally made in 6-inch and 8-inch inside diameters and have a capacity of approximately 3 to 8 tons of ashes per hour. In power plants having an ash production of less than 25 tons per day, one ash system can take care of this amount quite satisfactorily. In plants where there is considerably greater production of ash and particularly those in which large clinkers comprise a considerable amount of the total, these systems are not particularly applicable. One advantage of the steam jet system consists of the dampening effect, due to the condensation of the steam itself, which eliminates any tendency for the bin to catch on fire.

In using the steam jet system, the ashes are usually drawn into a tank, but in some instances are merely deposited in a pile from which they can be removed later. In the latter case the pipe line terminates in a target box which concentrates the pile at one point. The problem of dust prevention is also quite an important one in connection with this scheme. The steam and entrained air naturally carry a good deal of ash dust in suspension, but this is frequently taken care of by the injection of a water spray in the line, effectually abating the dust nuisance. When the ashes are delivered into a tank, it is possible to eliminate a good deal of the dust by a baffle plate and a large vent, but where it is necessary to eliminate this entirely, the vent from the tank can be washed by a series of spray nozzles, thus taking all the dust out together with most of the steam. A great deal of the recent success of these systems is due to the proper study of the system as to location of steam nozzles in relation particularly to the turns and by the proper kind of metal of the greatest wear-resisting properties.

In cold climates steps must be taken to provide for the melting of ice forming masses of ash between times when blowings to or removals from the collecting bin occur.

INSTALLATION OF NEW MODEL RONEY STOKERS FOR THE GERMAN-AMERICAN SUGAR COMPANY, BAY CITY, MICHIGAN

BOILER PRACTICE

INTRODUCTION

Divisions of the Subject. In the volume devoted to Boiler Accessories are described the devices which have to do with the pressure parts of boilers used in conjunction with steam production. In the present paper the allied subjects concerned with the gas side of the heating surface will be treated. Naturally, the two divisions of the subject are very close as to their influence upon the production of steam, and it is possible that some of the material in either paper might, with as good reason, be placed in the other. However, it is well to separate the heat-generating part from the heat-absorbing part of the general subject, with the understanding that a complete treatment of the subject involves both. It will be recognized that in dealing with the subject Boiler Accessories every topic was concerned with something tangible. In the present volume the matter is less definite, and consequently more difficult to grasp. Again, the performance of a given boiler, so far as heat absorption is concerned, is a fairly definite thing and not greatly influenced by the manipulation of the pressure parts. The part here taken up is largely influenced by the way the facilities are manipulated; and, unless fully understood, there is a good likelihood that the over-all performance of the steam-generating equipment may be very unsatisfactory and uneconomical.

HEAT GENERATION

BOILER SETTINGS

Requisites. The setting for a stationary boiler consists of the foundation and as much of the furnace and flues as is external to the boiler shell. Some internally-fired boilers—the Lancashire, for instance—have flues only in the brick setting. The whole furnace, as is the case with the plain cylindrical boiler, may be within the setting. Many vertical boilers have simply a foundation; locomotive boilers have no setting; and marine boilers are usually placed on saddles which are built into the framing of the vessel.

In setting a boiler, there are three principal requisites to be kept in mind: (1) a stable support or foundation, so arranged as to allow for proper expansion of the boiler; (2) properly arranged spaces for both furnace and ash pit; and (3) a structure which will prevent loss of heat by radiation and air infiltration.

SUPPORTING STRUCTURES

Iron Supports. There are two principal methods for support: (1) by brackets riveted to the shell plates, and (2) by suspension from overhead girders by means of hooks, rings, etc. In any case, the supports should be so arranged that each shall bear its proper proportion of the load and at the same time allow for expansion. If the boiler is short, brackets are generally used, while for long boilers the girder method is the more common. If a very long cylindrical boiler is supported only at each end, the great weight between the two supports is likely to cause bending and an excessive stress on the middle plates, tension in the bottom plates, and compression in the top plates.

Foundation. The first requisite for a setting is a good foundation. If the ground is firm and favorable to a solid foundation, the excavation need be only three or four feet below the level. If it is soft, the excavation should be deeper, and the extra depth filled in with concrete; or, for very heavy work, piles may be driven.

Usually all of the setting structure below the boiler-room floor level is built of concrete. In large installations equipped with mechanical stokers, the ash pits are sometimes faced with sheet steel so that the ash will slide to its desired place during the periods between removals.

Area of Bed. In determining the area of the bed, the weight to be put on each square foot should be estimated carefully. With ordinary condition of the soil, this should not exceed 2000 pounds. For greater weights, special construction must be used.

Supporting and Enclosing Walls. The supporting and enclosing walls are built upon the foundation. The outer walls at the sides and rear are sometimes double, the space between—usually about two inches—being an air-space insulation to prevent loss of heat. Projecting bricks, which extend from the outer wall until they just touch the inner wall, allow for expansion without decreasing the strength of the inner wall. As shown in the side and end view of Fig. 1, the side walls are strengthened by buckstays or binders, which are kept in place by long bolts, secured by nuts on each end. The side view shows the supporting brackets. The front brackets rest on iron plates which are built into the walls; the rear brackets, being supported by rollers, are free to move as the shell expands. If designed for anthracite coal, the distance between the shell and the grate bars is about two feet; for volatile coals, this distance should be increased.

Furnace Walls. *Externally-Fired Boilers.* The furnace is lined with fire brick, both front and sides, including the bridge wall; sometimes portions back of the bridge, as well as the bridge itself, should thus be protected. The space between the bridge and the shell is from 6 to 14 inches, which brings the hot gases into close contact with the boiler before they enter the combustion chamber beyond, the rear and side walls being built a little higher than the top row of tubes. The fire line must not be carried above the water line; if it is, the intense heat is likely to injure the shell plates. Never expose any part of the boiler not covered with water to the flames from the furnace. The side walls are built about the same height as the rear walls. The space at the rear is bridged over and stiffened by T-irons or other suitable means.

The smoke box projects over the front end of the boiler, as shown in the side and plan view, Fig 1, and has a rectangular uptake containing a damper.

The front is usually of cast iron, with doors for firing and cleaning, and for access to the tubes. Soot, dirt, etc., are removed through the door in the brickwork at the rear.

The rear end of the boiler should be about two inches lower than the front end, so that the sediment and detached scale will tend to accumulate near the blow-off opening.

Internally-Fired Boilers. Internally-fired boilers may also be enclosed in brickwork. The setting is a support and covering, forming the side flues but not the furnace. Excess of brickwork surface in contact with the shell should be avoided, as brickwork collects moisture, which causes external corrosion.

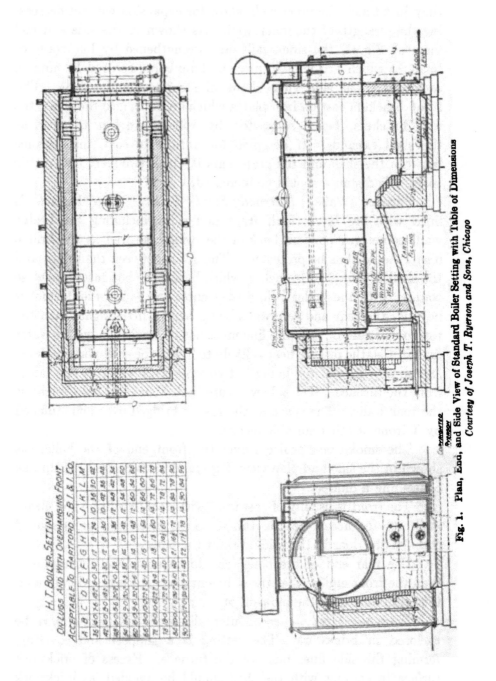

Fig. 1. Plan, End, and Side View of Standard Boiler Setting with Table of Dimensions

Courtesy of Joseph T. Ryerson and Sons, Chicago

Water-Tube Boilers. The settings of water-tube boilers differ from each other in so many ways, and also from the settings of fire-tube boilers, that it is not possible to illustrate them with any degree of completeness. The reader should consult the trade catalogues of the different manufacturers, in which the special features are illustrated. In principle, the settings of water-tube boilers must accomplish the same end that they do for horizontal tubular boilers; that is, properly support and enclose the boiler, allowing expansion space, and prevent radiation and air infiltration.

HAND-FIRED FURNACES

Furnaces and grates should be distinguished from each other in that the former are concerned mainly with providing facilities for the combustion of gas delivered by or distilled from the fuel on the grate, while the latter afford means for bearing fuel and provide means for the removal of ash. It is true that the two are not separable, but for purposes of clearness it is best to keep them separately defined. Certain adjuncts, however, are necessary to both for their successful operation. The furnace, of course, will vary in shape, size, and detail with the type of boiler and the kind of fuel; but certain essentials—such as doors, grate bars, and ash pit—are similar in all furnaces.

Supply of Air. To obtain the maximum efficiency of combustion, there should be a uniform and abundant supply of air to the under side of the grate. This is readily obtained when the boilers are externally fired, but may be somewhat restricted when they are internally fired. If smoky fuels are used, a moderate supply of air is necessary above the surface of the coal to prevent excessive smoke formation; but, as the air thus admitted is usually cold, the quantity should be small to prevent unnecessary cooling of the furnace. This air is generally supplied through a grid in the fire door.

Prevention of Radiation. Of course all possible radiation should be prevented. In the case of internally-fired boilers, this radiation is not likely to be excessive, for most of the heat would have to pass through the water in the boiler before radiating, and it is a comparatively easy matter to encase such a boiler in some sort of lagging which will prevent most of the heat from escaping. The case is somewhat different with an externally-fired boiler, where the furnace is built in a mass of brickwork below the boiler. In such a furnace a considerable amount of heat may radiate directly from the fire without coming in contact with the boiler or water at all.

Complete Combustion. To allow for complete combustion, there should be a sufficient space between the grate and the boiler. In externally-fired boilers, this space may be approximately three feet. If this distance is increased beyond proper limits, some effect of the heat will be lost; and if the distance is small, the plates are likely to be damaged and complete combustion impaired. In the internally-fired boiler, the combustion space is frequently sacrificed in order to obtain a large grate area. If the space between the grate bars and the boiler is too small to allow complete combustion, a combustion chamber must be provided immediately back of the bridge, which will permit of the further combustion of the gases. The ideal place, of course, for the combustion chamber is immediately over the grate. In locomotive boilers, the crown sheet is usually four to six feet above the grate; but such a height is manifestly impossible in marine or other internally-fired boilers, and the combustion chamber behind the bridge wall, in the Scotch boiler, partly compensates for the loss of space immediately over the grate.

The incandescent fuel and unconsumed gases should not come in contact with the cold surfaces of the boiler, if the most efficient combustion is desired. This condition is violated in internally-fired boilers, where the fire comes directly against metal having water on one side of it. If the flame is chilled by contact with cold surfaces before the gases are completely burned, a considerable amount of smoke is likely to result.

Dimensions of Grate. The grate should be of such dimensions that the fireman may be able to work it efficiently. A grate more than six feet long cannot be properly taken care of at the farther end; and if the grate is more than four feet wide, two or more fire doors should be provided. The height of the grate should be laid out with proper reference to the floor, two feet above the floor being about right. If the grate is high, it is difficult, if not impossible, to tend the fire properly. These conditions are dependent, not so much upon the boiler as upon the physical limitations of the fireman, and are eliminated by using the mechanical stoker.

Fireroom Temperature. To the above conditions may be added a suitable temperature in the fireroom. No man can tend a fire properly in excessive heat. In stationary work it is not difficult to maintain proper conditions in the fireroom; but at sea, where the supply of air is necessarily limited to what can come in through small openings, it is a different problem. The firing space on board ship is small, and the air coming through the ventilating ducts usually makes an exceedingly cold spot immediately under the duct without producing much effect in other parts of the room.

Furnace Doors. The furnace door is usually made of cast iron, and is supplied with a circular or sliding draft plate or grid, which admits air to the top of the fire as needed. It is usually protected by a perforated cast-iron baffle plate bolted to the door casting inside, with an air space of two or three inches between. This not only protects the cast iron of the door from the direct action of the flame, but it forms a chamber for the proper distribution of the air supply, and also helps to heat it somewhat before reaching the furnace.

In many of the French torpedo boats, a patent swinging door is provided, set on horizontal hinges swinging inward. The door, of course, must be held open while the stoker is tending the fire; but in case a tube blows out, it prevents the rapid escape of steam into the fireroom. This is a matter of much more importance in the restricted fireroom commonly found on a vessel than it would be on land. Doors of this kind are gradually finding greater favor in land practice, especially in those cities where the making of excessive smoke is prohibited by ordinance.

HAND-FIRED GRATES

Size. The size of grate will depend upon the quantity of coal likely to be burned. For ordinary draft, this may be 15 pounds or upward per square foot of grate surface per hour; for forced draft, 40 to 60 pounds; and in some cases as much as 100 pounds per square foot of grate surface has been burned. If the grates are long, they are usually inclined slightly downwards, say $\frac{3}{4}$ inch to the foot, which is of great assistance in firing and makes it easier to keep fire on the farther end of the grate.*

---

*The grates have an incline of a few inches, so that the bed of coal will be thicker at the rear than at the front; this allows a more even consumption of fuel, as the draft intensity at the rear is greater than in front.

Grate Bars. The grate bars are always made of cast iron. The bars are made in various forms, according to the fuel burned and the shape of the fire box. For large grates, the bars are made singly or in pairs. For smaller grates, they are made in larger groups. Grate bars should not be more than three feet in length. The length of grate can easily be a multiple of the length of these bars. The bars have distance pieces at the ends, and perhaps in the middle, to prevent distortion. They are usually 3 inches or more in depth at the middle, tapering to perhaps an inch or two at the ends; and the cross section is slightly tapered from top to bot-

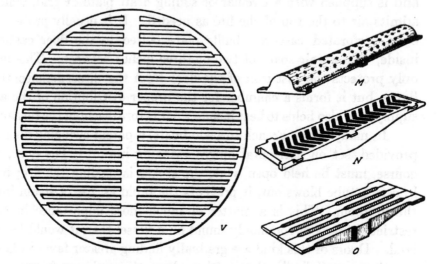

Fig. 2. Types of Grates for Boilers. *V*, Circular Grate for Vertical Boiler; *M*, Grate for Sawdust and Shavings; *N*, Herringbone Grate; *O*, Group of Grate Bars of Ordinary Form

tom, so that the pattern can easily be withdrawn from the sand after casting. They are usually made a trifle shorter than the place into which they fit, to allow for expansion, 2 per cent of the length of the bar usually being sufficient for this purpose. The air spaces between the bars are usually about one-half inch in width. For burning pea coal or screenings, narrower air spaces must be used. For anthracite coal, the space may be a little larger. Bituminous coal, which readily cakes, can have considerable space between the bars—and this, indeed, is essential for a proper supply of air.

In Fig. 2, *V* shows a circular grate, such as is placed in a vertical boiler. *M* shows the style of grate bar used in burning sawdust or shavings; N is what is known as the herringbone grate; and O is a group of bars of the ordinary form.

Grates have been made of hollow bars, through which water is caused to circulate. By this method their durability is increased. This type of grate, however, is expensive.

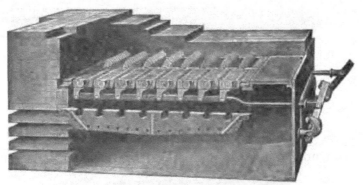

Fig. 3. Standard Rocking and Dumping Grate
Courtesy of Kelley Foundry and Machine Company, Goshen, Indiana

Rocking Grates. The labor of breaking the clinkers is considerable when the ordinary fixed grate bars are used, and, to economize this labor, various forms of rocking grates or shaking grates

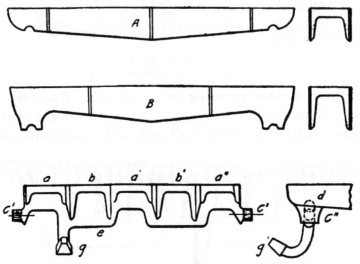

Fig. 4. Rocking Grate Consisting of Alternate Bars with Ends of Different Depths Resting on Crankshaft, Oscillated by a Lever

have been devised. In locomotives, rocking grates are essential; and, since the rate of combustion is high, the fire must always be kept in good condition; and the grate, being below the cab floor, cannot easily be reached.

Fig. 5. Twentieth Century Rocking Grate
Courtesy of Water Arch Furnace Company

Types.   Fig. 3 shows the Kelley Standard rocking grate.   Each bar is made up of a number of separate leaves, which can be removed

Fig. 6.   Martin Shaking Grate
Courtesy of Martin Grate Company, Chicago

and replaced without renewing the whole bar.   When the bar is moved back and forth by means of a lever outside the brickwork, the leaves oscillate through a small angle and break up the clinkers.

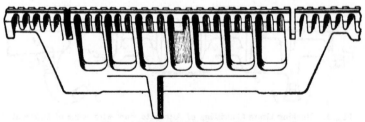

Fig. 7.   Single Bar of Martin Grate

Another form of bar, shown in Fig. 4, has proved very satisfactory.   *A* and *B* are two bars, the ends of which are of different depths. These rest at each end on a crankshaft C. As this is oscillated by the lever G, the alternate bars move up and down, and the clinkers are shaken out.

Still another example of rocking grate is shown in Fig. 5. In this grate the rocking and stationary bars alternate; when the rocking lever is removed from its socket, the grate must be in its neutral position, thus insuring against burning off grate fingers. It is known as the Twentieth Century rocking grate.

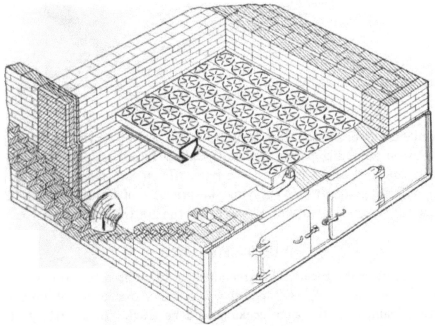

Fig. 8. Sectional View of a Furnace Showing Nicholson Grate Bars Assembled
Courtesy of Improved Combustion Company, Chicago

Dumping Devices. Opinions differ as to whether or not the grate should have a dumping feature. Consequently, there are all types in the complete list—those going to extremes in providing dumping facilities; and those having shaking grates which, instead of dumping, depend upon frequent shaking to remove the ash before it has time to fuse into clinker. Figs. 6 and 7 illustrate the Martin grate, clearly showing that the lift of the grate can only be very small.

Forced-Draft Arrangement. For the burning of some kinds of fuel, and sometimes for the more rapid burning of fuel, forced-draft equipment is provided with hand-fired grates. Such an arrangement is illustrated in Fig. 8, which is known as the Nicholson furnace. The air is delivered beneath the grate under pressure and is discharged through slots in the bars, Fig. 9, which bear the fuel. The slots are cast at a slant, so that the air does not blow vertically;

Fig. 9. View of Single Nicholson Grate Bar
Courtesy of Improved Combustion Company, Chicago

while the bars are set close together and a seal of cement is placed between adjoining pairs, so that the air is forced to pass through the slots instead of between the bars. There are many forms of hand-fired grates in use applying the principle of forced draft, but the one shown is typical of all except for the grate-bar details.

FIRING BY HAND

Starting the Fire. The fireman should first ascertain the water level. As the gage glass is not always reliable, on account of impurities, foam, etc., the gage cocks should be tried. In a battery of boilers, the gage cocks of each should be opened, for the water may not stand at the same level in each. The safety valve should be raised slightly from its seat. If the fire has been banked over night, open the dampers, and remove the ashes and clinkers from the grate. In case the fire has been allowed to go out, a new one may be started if the gage glass shows the proper amount of water and the valves work well.

If anthracite coal is used, first throw a thin layer of coal all over the grate, then place a piece of wood across the mouth of the furnace just inside the door and lay other pieces of wood at right angles to the crosspiece with the ends resting on it. This allows a space under the wood for air. Now throw on coal until the wood is covered.

The fire may be started with oily cotton waste, shavings, or any combustible material.

Keep the furnace door open and the damper almost closed until the wood is burning freely, which causes the flame to pass over and through the coal and to ignite it. The fire is then spread or pushed back evenly over the furnace bars; the furnace door is closed, and the ash-pit door opened; more coal is added when necessary. If bituminous coal is used the same process is serviceable.

The fire at the start should be slow, to cause gradual, uniform heating of the water and various parts of the boiler. If steam is raised too rapidly, enormous stresses are set up, due to unequal expansion, thereby causing leakage at seams, and perhaps rupture.

If the boiler is of the water-tube type, steam may be raised more rapidly, because the amount of water is less and the seams are usually placed at some distance from the intense heat of the fire.

Methods of Adding Fuel. The fire being started, the method of adding coal depends upon the fireman, the kind of coal, the type of boiler, and the rate of combustion. There are three general methods of firing—spreading, alternate or side firing, and coking.

Spreading. Spreading is accomplished by placing small quantities of coal uniformly over the entire surface of the grate at short intervals. By this method, the coal is thrown just where it is wanted and then not disturbed. Good results are obtained from this method, since the fire can be kept in the right condition at all times, if the coal is of the right sort. During the operation of firing, the door should be kept open as little as possible, or the fire will be cooled by the entrance of cold air. For a short time, while the coal is giving off gas, the draft plate of the furnace door should be opened, in order that sufficient air may be admitted above the coal to burn the gas. The spreading method is especially effective for high rates of combustion.

Alternate or Side Firing. When the alternate or side-firing method is used, coal is spread so as to cover one side of the fire completely at one firing, leaving the other side bright. At the next firing, the bright side is covered. The gases given off by the fresh coal are assisted in burning by the hot gases coming from the incandescent coal. This method is superior to spreading, because the entire furnace is not cooled off by the addition of fresh fuel.

Side firing is very advantageous when two furnaces lead to a common combustion chamber. The furnaces are fired at regular intervals with moderate charges of coal, and the draft plates in the firing doors are opened while the coal is giving off gas.

The two systems described above are also adapted to anthracite coal, since it burns with comparatively little smoke.

Coking. With semibituminous coal, which is volatile and burns with considerable smoke, the coking method is used. The coal is piled on the grate just inside the door, and allowed to coke from 15 to 30 minutes. During this time, the hydrocarbons are driven off and burned while passing over the more intense fuel bed behind. In order to accomplish this fully, air must be admitted in small quantities above the grate through the draft plates of the furnace doors. The coke is next pushed backward over the fire, and a new supply placed on the front of the grate. It is very important that the air admitted over the fire be enough but not excessive, for, in the latter case, economy is reduced, the furnace cools somewhat, and the rate of evaporation is reduced. This last objection is not serious unless the boiler must be worked to its maximum capacity in order to furnish the required amount of steam. The available draft over the fire is the main factor determining the rate at which a given fuel can be burned, while the temperature of the furnace above the grate also has an influence.

Thickness of Fuel Bed. The thickness of the fuel bed can be determined only by experiment. As a general thing, the thickness is changed according to the steam requirements, for the rate of combustion is large or small as the amount of air passing through the grate and fuel bed is large or small. By thickening the fuel bed, and consequently the fuel-bed resistance, the amount of air is reduced, and *vice versa*. The economical thickness at which to burn fuel is an entirely different matter than the amount which *can* be burned. In general, speaking of bituminous and semibituminous coals only, the better coking coals are best burned with thick fires and the free-burning non-coking coals with thin fires. A fire fifteen inches thick is considered about right for a good coking coal, while a fire five inches thick is about right for a free-burning bituminous coal. Should the rate of combustion, using a desirable thickness of fuel bed, be wrong in the production of the desired amount of steam, the grate area should be changed so that both conditions are approximately right. The secret of success in the burning of fuel is one concerned almost altogether with the selection of a proper grate area within the possibilities presented by the available draft over the fire for the fuel to be burned.

After finding from experiment the best thickness for the bed, keep it at that thickness. Always keep the bed of uniform thickness, and never let the fire burn holes in the bed, and *do not let the rear of the grate become bare.* If a larger amount of steam is required, fire smaller quantities at more frequent intervals. Do not fire a large amount of coal, and then wait for the pressure to rise. The firing of fresh coal chills the furnace and temporarily retards combustion. The coal should be fired in small quantities and as quickly as possible. Keep the fire free from ashes and clinkers, but do not clean the fires oftener than is necessary.

Cleaning the Fire. *Tools.* Four tools are used for cleaning the fire—the slice bar, the prick bar, the clinker hook—sometimes called the devil's claw—and the hoe or rake.

The slice bar is a long, straight bar, with the end flattened. It is used to break up clinkers by thrusting it between the grate and the fire. It is also used to break up caking coal. The prick bar is similar to the slice bar, except that the end is bent at right angles like a hook. To remove ashes, the prick bar is run along from underneath up between the grate bars. This bar is often made with detachable hook, so that the end may be replaced when burned off. The clinker hook, or devil's claw, is used to haul the fire forward. The hoe, or rake, is used to draw out cinders, to haul the fire forward, to level the fuel bed, etc.

Cleaning Methods. In cleaning the fire, the fireman first looks to the water and steam. There should be enough water and sufficient steam pressure to last during cleaning. Then he breaks up the clinkers with the slice bar, and removes the ashes with the prick bar. If necessary, he pushes the fire to the rear, thoroughly cleans the front of the grate bars, and then hauls it forward and cleans the back of the furnace bars. Some firemen clean one side at a time, instead of first the front and then the rear. The fire should be allowed to burn down before cleaning, but sufficient fuel should be left to start the fire quickly. Before cleaning, partly close the dampers, so that the amount of cold air admitted will be small. For this reason, and to prevent loss of pressure, clean as rapidly as possible.

When the demand for steam requires the most that can be made at all times, and more than one boiler is in service, one portion of the grate of one boiler is cleaned first; a similar portion of the adjoining grate next; and so on down the whole line before returning to the first fire to finish. Skill is required in carrying out such a program.

Banking the Fire. Banking the fire depends upon the condition of the fire, the fireman himself, and the length of time it is to remain banked. First clean the fire and place all the coal in a small space at the bridge; then cover it with fresh coal to a depth depending on the length of time the fire is to remain banked. Then almost close the dampers and open the firing doors slightly. Some firemen cover the front of the grate bars with ashes.

To start from a banked fire, first examine the condition of the water level, steam pressure, safety valves, etc. Then clean the fire with the slice bar and shake the ashes down with the prick bar. After spreading the live coal evenly over the grate, cover with a thin layer of green coal and open the dampers.

SPECIAL HAND-FIRED FURNACES

There are a great many forms of settings for stationary boilers different from the standards manufactured by the boiler builders, and only a few can be touched upon here. From a plain hand-fired setting—where no special provisions for combustion are made—to the most elaborate mechanical stokers, there is an endless variety of furnaces.

Horizontal Tubular Boilers. For horizontal tubular boilers it is usual to retain hand firing because the size of the unit is not large enough to justify the use of a more efficient, and possibly more complicated, firing arrangement. The men who are hired to operate horizontal tubular boilers are frequently not as well informed and as capable as those who operate larger units; and this has something to do with the matter also.

Steam Jets, Fire-Brick Arches, etc. Where the attempt is made to improve the combustion conditions under horizontal tubular boilers, the first thought is usually to supply steam jets, either manually or automatically operated; fire-brick arches and piers are next added and, when further progress is wanted, one of the special furnaces described later may be adopted. In principle, the advantages of the several forms of fire-brick furnace constructions are identical. They all aim to provide a chamber in which the mixture of unburned gas with air can be carried on for a sufficient length of time to permit the complete combustion of the gas evolved from the

Fig. 10. Down-Draft Grate Fitted to Fire-Tube Boiler
Courtesy of Hawley Down-Draft Furnace Company, Easton, Pennsylvania

fuel bed. During the time the combustion process is taking place, it is aimed to prevent contact between partly burned gas and the boiler-heating surface lest the temperature of the burning gas be reduced to a point not favorable to combustion.

Semi-Automatic Furnaces. In order to overcome to some degree the human operating element in firing, furnace constructions are sold which are more or less independent of the manner in which the fireman supplies the coal or other fuel to the chamber or hopper leading to the furnace or grate.

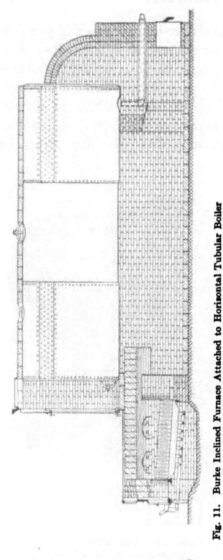

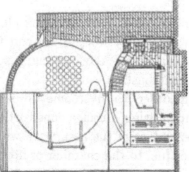

Fig. 11. Burke Inclined Furnace Attached to Horizontal Tubular Boiler
Courtesy of Burke Furnace Company, Chicago

Down-Draft Furnaces. In order to increase economy and capacity, or to prevent smoke, a down-draft furnace is sometimes used. In this type of furnace, there are two grates, one a foot or more above the other. Fresh coal is fed to the upper grate, and, as it becomes partly consumed, falls through to the grate below, where the combustion is continued. The draft is downward through the upper grate, and upward through the lower, because the connection to the chimney is from the space between the grates. The volatile gases are carried down through the bed on the upper grate, and are burned in the space below it, where they meet the hot air drawn upward from the lower grate. Most of the air for combustion enters the door at the upper grate.

In the furnace made by the Hawley Down-Draft Boiler Company, the grates are formed of a series of water tubes opening at the ends into steel drums, which are connected with the boiler. Fig. 10 shows this furnace attached to a horizontal tubular boiler. It may be applied to both tubular and

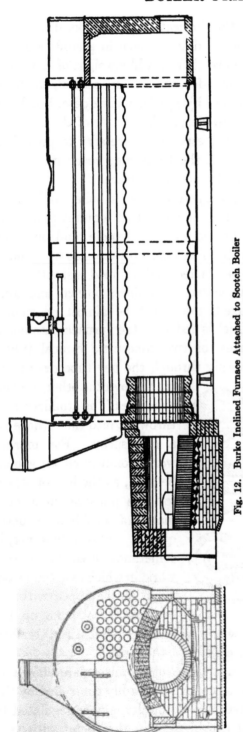

Fig. 12. Burke Inclined Furnace Attached to Scotch Boiler
Courtesy of Burke Furnace Company, Chicago

water-tube boilers with good results. It is claimed that this attachment insures complete combustion, small amount of ashes on account of the second grate, good water circulation, and increased economy.

Gravity Feed Furnaces. The difficulty in getting firemen to carry out good firing methods has brought about the construction of a class of furnaces into which the fuel is charged by gravity. The Burke gravity feed furnace is illustrated in Fig. 11, which shows this furnace applied to a horizontal tubular boiler. The fuel is placed upon the furnace arch and allowed to enter the furnace by running down through the holes or "pockets" on each side of the grate. By keeping the hopper (not shown in the illustration) filled as the fuel burns away in the furnace, additional new fuel finds its way into the furnace.

In Fig. 12 is shown the same furnace applied to a Scotch boiler. This is particularly effective as it tends to overcome some of the inherent defects of an internally-fired Scotch boiler.

Oil-Burning Furnaces. *Requirements.* In some localities oil is the fuel most readily available, and since, even in a crude state, it has a heat value somewhat above that of a like weight of coal, it is quite essential to make provisions for its use. In general, the oil is sprayed into the furnace chamber by special means described hereafter. Of great importance, however, is the matter of the chamber in which the oil is burned. It is especially necessary to provide a chamber sufficiently large so that the flame may reach its natural limits without encountering boiler-heating surface.

Advantages. Oil has many advantages as a boiler fuel. It is clean, gives a uniform heat, is economical, and requires much less attention than coal. There are no ashes to handle, and one man can easily tend two or three times as many furnaces as he could if burning coal. The fire can be started and stopped instantly; and the supply of air can be so regulated that, unless burners and combustion chamber are overtaxed, there will be almost no smoke.

Method of Action. Oil fuel is fed into the furnace through a sprayer formed, in some cases, of two concentric conical tubes. Compressed air or steam entering through the one tube draws the oil through the other, on the principle of the atomizer, and throws it into the furnace in a fine spray. For marine work, compressed air should be used, as the loss of steam for this purpose would be a matter of considerable consequence. Steam, however, is sometimes used in marine work, in which case the vessel must be equipped with an evaporator to make up the steam thus lost. On land, where fresh water is plentiful, steam is usually preferred and is less expensive than air.

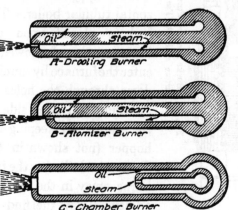

Fig. 13. Types of Atomizers for Liquid Fuel

Types of Sprayers. Several types of atomizers are shown in Fig. 13. The use of the oil as a fuel can be readily controlled by the simple manipulation of a valve; and if the fire is once regulated to produce the required heat, it can be kept at that point with very little care. The fire can be started with slight trouble, and can be extinguished instantly. The evaporative capacity of oil is much greater than that of coal; and on the Pacific Coast, where oil can be readily obtained, it is a much more economical fuel. If burned properly, without too heavy an air blast, there should be no production of smoke. A considerable saving may be effected in the fireroom force, one man being able to operate several burners. There is, of course, danger from explosion, on account of the vapor which rises from the fuel; but if the fuel tank is thoroughly ventilated, there should be little danger from this source.

Oil fuel may be used to advantage in what is called mixed firing; that is, the oil may be sprayed on to the bed of burning coal. This has been condemned by many engineers, but it has nevertheless gained considerable headway and, under proper conditions, has given satisfactory results. It is beyond the scope of this work to go minutely into the subject of oil fuel; but for further information the student is referred to the reports of the Oil Fuel Boards of the United States Navy and of the British Admiralty.

MECHANICAL STOKERS

Function. A mechanical stoker is a device having two functions; namely, to introduce fuel into a furnace, and to remove the resulting refuse. If the stoker introduces the fuel at a uniform rate, and removes the refuse at the rate at which it is formed, without manual assistance, it accomplishes every possible service that can be expected of it. The facilities which must be provided in addition for the combustion of the gases rising from the fuel bed are properly known as furnaces. It is true, however, that some forms of stokers lend themselves by their construction and shape to good furnace construction, while others do not. This feature of the subject will become clearer when the several forms of stokers are described.

Classification. There are five principal types of mechanical stokers. They are:

    (1) Mechanical fuel spreaders or firemen
    (2) Traveling grates
    (3) Inclined grates
    (4) Underfeed stokers
    (5) Combinations of the above

The devices of the first group accomplish little beyond that performed by a careful fireman except that the fuel may be more uniformly charged, though it is likely that the fuel bed may not be so evenly charged as by a competent fireman. This class of stoker fails to remove the ash and refuse from the grate, and in this particular is quite deficient.

All of the other types mentioned aim to introduce the fuel steadily by bringing it into the hottest zones of the furnace at a uniform rate. The result is that the volatile gases are driven from

Fig. 14. Chain Grate Mechanical Stoker
Courtesy of Babcock and Wilcox Company, New York City

the fuel at a nearly uniform rate, and consequently the furnace can be constructed of such a shape and size as to provide an adequate chamber in which to facilitate combustion.

Fuel Used Determines Type of Stoker. The character of fuel burned should determine the kind of stoker selected, as some forms are very efficient with one grade of fuel and wholly inefficient with other grades. The leading coal characteristic needing consideration is its ability to coke or cake, which, of course, is largely influenced by the percentage of refuse, and its kind, in the natural fuel. To illustrate the point just made, attention need only be called to the fact that a traveling grate without special facilities for handling coked fuel is not at all successfully used with the high-grade coking coals mined in Virginia and Pennsylvania. This type of stoker is especially adapted for use with the free-burning, highly volatile coals found in Illinois and Iowa. On the other hand, some types of stokers require, for their successful use, the coal to have caking qualities. As an example, the Murphy double-inclined grate may be mentioned.

Traveling Grate Stokers. Among the various makes of traveling grates, probably the best known are the Babcock and Wilcox, the Green, the Playford, the La Clede, and the Illinois. These all operate on the same principle, differing only in details of construction.

The Babcock and Wilcox chain grate which is typical of the rest, Fig. 14, consists of an endless chain of short grate bars or links moving over sprocket wheels at the front and rear end. These sprocket wheels are driven by a mechanism consisting of a gear train actuated by pawls and a ratchet, the arms carrying the latter being given a reciprocating motion by a rod and eccentric mounted on a shaft. This shaft may be operated by any type of motor or engine, and the speed of the grate is regulated by varying the stroke of the arm carrying the pawls. The fuel is fed to the traveling grate through a hopper, which extends the full width of the grate and is mounted on the front end of the frame. The depth of the layer is regulated by a gate in the hopper, which can be raised or lowered. The coal is ignited at the front end and carried slowly toward the rear, the speed of the grate and the thickness of the fire being so regulated that the fuel shall be completely burned by the time it reaches the back end, nothing but ashes being discharged into the pit. A flat firebrick arch in the front end aids combustion by igniting the fresh fuel as it enters and keeping up the temperature of the burning volatile gases. The entire hopper, grate, and driving mechanism are mounted on a truck running on rails and thus may be withdrawn from beneath the boiler when repairs to grate or furnace are necessary.

Inclined Grate Stokers. *Front Feed.* Some of the types of this form of stoker are the Roney, Wilkinson, and Acme. The Roney stoker, Fig. 15, consists of a hopper for receiving the coal, a set of rocking stepped grates inclined at an angle from the horizontal, and a dumping grate at the bottom of the incline for receiving and discharging ash and clinkers. This grate is divided into several sections for convenience in handling. The coal is fed to the inclined grates from the hopper by a reciprocating pusher. The grate bars rock through an angle of 30 degrees, assuming alternately the stepped and inclined position. These also receive their motion from the agitator, which receives its motion from an eccentric on a

shaft attached to the stoker front under the hopper. The range of
motion of the pusher is regulated by the feed wheel and the range of
motion of the grate bars is regulated by the position of the nuts on
the connecting rod. Each grate bar consists of two parts: the
vertical web carrying trunnions at each end; and the horizontal part,
or fuel plate, which is detachable. A flat fire-brick arch is sprung
across the front of the furnace. This ignites the fresh fuel as it

Fig. 15.   Roney Step-Grate Mechanical Stoker
Courtesy of Westinghouse Machine Company

enters and aids in keeping up the temperature of the volatile gases
until they are burned.

The Wilkinson stoker, Fig. 16, consists of a hopper, a set of
inclined grate bars having every other bar movable, and the operating mechanism. When in operation there is a constant sawing
action of the grate bars, causing the fuel to be fed forward continuously. The grate bars are hollow and have a succession of steps
cast on them throughout their length. Through the rise of each
step is an opening of about ⅛ inch by 3 inches. A small steam jet

Fig. 16. Wilkinson Step-Grate Mechanical Stoker
Courtesy of Wilkinson Manufacturing Company

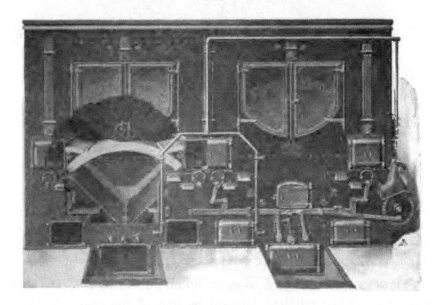

Fig. 17. Front View Murphy Mechanical Stoker
Courtesy of Murphy Iron Works

with about $\frac{1}{16}$-inch opening is introduced into the end of each **grate** bar, and this induces an air supply through the openings in **the** steps. The motor for operating these stokers may be either **steam** or electric and is attached to the front of the stoker.

Side Feed. The best known stokers of this type are the Murphy, the Detroit, and the Model. The Murphy stoker, Figs. 17 and 18, consists of two hoppers, or magazines, one on each side **of**

Fig. 18. Side Section Murphy Mechanical Stoker
Courtesy of Murphy Iron Works

the furnace, two sets of grates inclined downward from the sides of the furnace, and the operating mechanism. Coal is introduced into the hopper and falls upon the coking plate, Fig. 17. Here the reciprocating pushers feed the coal out upon the inclined grate bars. Alternate grate bars are movable and pivoted at the upper ends. The lower ends are caused to move up and down by a rocker shaft, thus causing the required forward feeding of the coal. A device, Fig. 18, consisting of a hollow bar provided with teeth, is placed at the lower ends of the grates, and serves to grind up clinkers and ash. Air is supplied through flues passing under the coking plate, and the speed of the grate bars and pusher is regulated to suit the desired rate of combustion. A small motor or engine operates the driving mechanism of the stoker.

Underfeed Stokers. Among the various stokers of this class will be found the Jones, the American, the Taylor, the Riley, and the Westinghouse.

Jones Type. The Jones stoker, shown in Fig. 19, consists of a steam-actuated ram and a hopper outside of the furnace and a retort or fuel magazine and auxiliary ram or pusher rod within. Fuel is forced underneath the fire by the ram and its auxiliary,

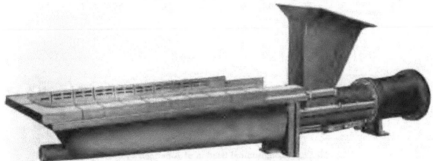

Fig. 19. Jones Underfeed Mechanical Stoker
Courtesy of Underfeed Stoker Company of America

and this forces the incandescent fuel and ash back and up over the sides of the retort upon the dead plates. As there is no ash pit, the ashes are raked from the dead plate by hand. Air supplied by a blower is admitted through openings in heavy cast-iron tuyère blocks placed on either side of the retort. These are at a point above the green fuel in the retort but below the fire, and the air moving upward keeps the retort cool.

American Type. The American Underfeed Stoker is illustrated in the two sections given by Figs. 20 and 21. Its principle of fuel introduction is practically identical with the Jones, just described. The device differs from the Jones in that side grates are added both for the further supply of air, and consequent greater range of combustion, and in the facilities for the removal of refuse by means of dumping grates on the sides of the grate. In both of these particulars the American comes more nearly fulfilling the functions of a stoker than a retort stoker requiring cleaning by hand altogether.

In this stoker the attempt is also made to introduce preheated air by taking air which has previously passed through the grate bars as the supply for the grates bordering the retort.

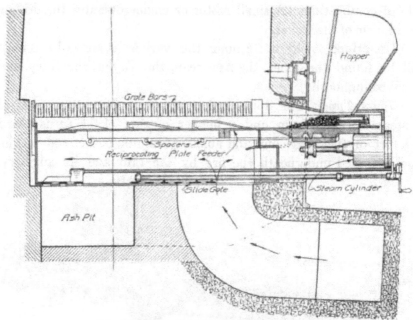

Fig. 20. Longitudinal Section of American Stoker
Courtesy of Combustion Engineering Corporation, New York City

Inclined Underfeed Type. The principle of underfeeding has for many years been recognized as excellent, but the difficulties

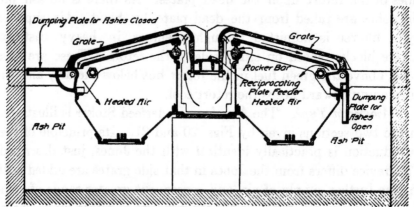

Fig. 21. Cross Section of American Stoker
Courtesy of Combustion Engineering Corporation, New York City

encountered when removing the ash and refuse have made its application less attractive than would otherwise obtain. To overcome

these difficulties and others of a similar nature, the gravity underfeed stoker has been evolved. There are three principal makes: the
Taylor, which was the pioneer of the type; the Westinghouse; and
the Riley. All of them use the underfeed scheme and forced draft,

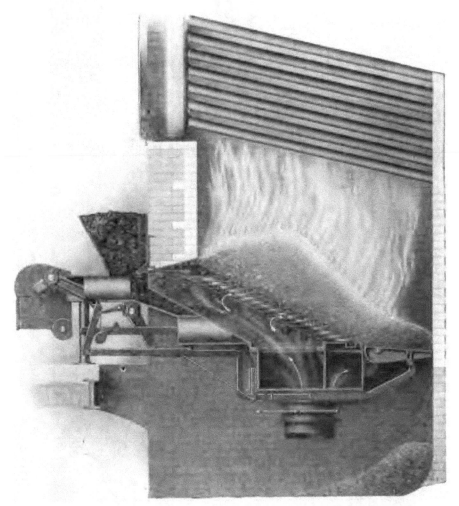

Fig. 22. Section of Taylor Stoker Through the Fire
Courtesy of American Engineering Company, Philadelphia

but their details of construction are in many particulars essentially
different. This type has, in recent years, been given wide application in plants, especially where steam demands are large enough
to warrant the employment of technical knowledge and skill.

Taylor Underfeed Stoker. In Fig. 22 is illustrated the **Taylor** type of stoker applied to a horizontal water-tube boiler, the view

FIG. 23. Westinghouse Underfeed Stoker Applied to Horizontal Water-Tube Boiler
Courtesy of Westinghouse Electric and Manufacturing Company, East Pittsburgh, Pennsylvania

being taken through one retort so as to show the manner of feeding coal by the upper reciprocating cylindrical plunger, its enforced movement to the lower portion of the grate by means of a second plunger, the location of the wind box, and the path taken by the air under pressure to and through the tuyères. The width of the furnace space is made up of retorts spaced about 22 inches apart, each being served with a complete plunger system. The expectation is that by the time the fuel has moved to the dumping plate, practically all of it that is combustible has been consumed, thus permitting its removal into the ash pit without appreciable fuel wastage. The illustration represents one of the earlier applications of the gravity underfeed idea not complicated by refinements to meet the requirements of all grades of bituminous fuels. Modifications take the form of plunger extensions, greater retort lengths, and better refuse dumping facilities. The ash pit construction, Fig. 22, would not be considered good practice, being wholly inadequate according to modern requirements.

Westinghouse Underfeed Stoker. Like other stokers of the underfeed type, the Westinghouse, shown applied to a horizontal water-tube boiler in Fig. 23, is made up of a series of retorts, each retort consisting of a fuel trough and two parallel tuyère boxes. Cylindrical rams push the new fuel into the furnace beneath a bed of incandescent fuel. By means of an adjustable feeding motion of secondary rams the travel of the fuel toward the rear of the furnace is continued, finally passing out over the rearmost grate section which acts as an overfeed with incandescent coke as the fuel. In this stoker the dumping section becomes active grate area by reason of air supply. The air-regulating facilities constitute one of its distinctive features, making possible the adjustment of the supply as desired at the several grate zones independent of and without impairment to the air supply of other zones.

This stoker is manufactured with a variety of dumping grates and lengths so as to permit selection to meet variations in fuel behavior as encountered in the several fuel districts of the country.

Riley Underfeed Stoker. In Figs. 24 and 25 are shown views of the Riley stoker mechanism, which, like others of its class, consists of multiple retorts placed side by side. Its distinctive feature is that the reciprocating retort sides move relative to the retort bottoms. This feature provides a means for flooding the coal over the grates and also for carrying it down toward the bottom rear of the furnace chamber. At the ends of the retorts, overfeed grate bars extend across the width of the furnace, while beyond these are rocker dump plates which are continuously

Fig. 24. Perspective View of Riley Nine-Retort Underfeed Stoker Partially Assembled
Courtesy of Sanford Riley Stoker Company, Ltd., Worcester, Massachusetts

agitated, thus breaking up caked refuse. Unlike other underfeed stokers only one plunger per retort is required, which feature offers the advantage of a free space beneath the grate. The air chamber

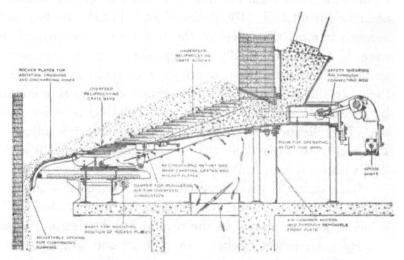

Fig. 25. Sectional View of Riley Stoker Applied to Boiler Setting
Courtesy of Sanford Riley Stoker Company, Ltd., Worcester, Massachusetts

is formed by the boiler side walls, floor, and front, thus inclosing the space beneath the entire grate area with the exception of the rocker dump plates. The fuel and air supply are so controlled that a change in the rate of feeding the former is accompanied by a corresponding change in the latter. This stoker is capable of change in construction details to meet the requirements of variations appearing in different grades of bituminous coals.

MANIPULATION OF SPECIAL FURNACES AND MECHANICAL STOKERS

Assumptions. In the material which follows it is presumed that the important conditions requisite for the use of mechanical contrivances for feeding fuel and removing refuse have been properly provided, namely, good draft, correct furnace construction, and accessibility for suitable inspection and operation. In some instances it is also presumed that certain indicating instruments are provided, such as draft gages, without which the particular contrivances in question cannot be effectively manipulated. It is likewise expected that the operators have sufficient knowledge of boiler room practice to be able to understand the elementary methods employed in connection with the contrivances given into their charge and that the plant design is such as to represent good judgment, taking into account the character of labor available, the size of the units, and the total rated capacity of the plant as a whole. It is impossible in an article of this scope to consider all the details to be observed in every contingency, but the aim is to supply the fundamentals which must be observed to gain success.

General Features of Fuel Burning. The reader can gain the best and quickest grasp of the subject by learning a few but all-important facts respecting combustion, which are universally applicable whether dealing with hand firing or mechanical firing according to the several systems previously described. Stated briefly these facts are as follows:

(1) Only such air as enters into the combustion process is useful; any other air, wherever admitted, acts as a diluent, tends to lower temperatures and thus decreases the range of temperature through which the heat absorber (boiler) may act, and provides a larger vehicle for carrying away as waste the heat rejected into the chimney.

(2) It follows from item (1) that the less the amount of air employed in the combustion process without impairing the com-

pleteness of the process, the higher the resulting initial temperature and the larger the probable percentage of heat absorbed.

(3) The rate at which fuel will burn is dependent solely upon the amount of air which passes through the fuel bed, other conditions remaining the same. Difference in the draft above and below the fuel bed, combined with fuel-bed resistance, fixes the rate at which the fuel will liberate gases, furnace temperature remaining the same.

(4) A uniform rate of fuel feeding and, corresponding uniformity of refuse removal afford the best opportunity for completeness of combustion with a minimum air supply for a given furnace space and shape.

(5) It is not possible to burn fuel with an air supply closely approximating the amount theoretically required for complete combustion without encountering incomplete combustion because the chemical avidity of carbon (the main combustible constituent of coal) for oxygen (the combustion agent in air) is not sufficiently great to cause these elements to seek each other out when widely separated. Furnace constructions imposing mixing action tend to reduce the quantity of needed excess air and are serviceable unless available draft above the fuel bed is impaired by their use.

(6) Moisture is not a combustible material. It may be useful, in some instances, in retarding the rate of combustion, thus compelling a more uniform distillation of volatile gases, or in holding coal particles in mechanical union, thus preventing sifting through grates, as is sometimes important with traveling chain grates. The use of extra or added moisture is usually attended with loss.

(7) Clinkers are the result of fusion of ash or refuse. Any cause that places refuse into zones of a higher temperature than that of fusion will cause clinkers. Disturbances to natural fuel beds by the use of slice bars, etc., puddling refuse with burning fuel will cause clinkers where they might otherwise be avoided. Where it is not possible to obtain a satisfactory rate of burning without resorting to much slicing, the furnace most probably is operating under deficient draft.

(8) High furnace temperatures without correspondingly high rates of combustion are due to "bottled-up" furnace conditions caused by too slow gas movement from the furnace because either there is too little draft to carry the gases out of the furnace or the fuel bed resistance is too great to allow the air to pass through the fuel bed in sufficient quantities.

It will thus be seen that air—its manner and rate of supply— is the one item of importance in addition to the fuel itself that determines the capacity and the economy of performance in combustion processes. Let the student apply to his problem the thought that the expensive article employed is air and that the fuel is merely incidental to the use of it and he will gain a valuable point of view.

Gravity Furnaces

General Instructions. When operating at capacities near or above full load the center and side ash-pit doors should be wide open, permitting the free access of air to both the side grates and the center grates. Under light load conditions, which might permit the center grates to be bare of fire or large holes to be present in the center grates, the most economical way to run is to close the center ash-pit doors to keep the cold air from going through the center grates. If the furnace under these conditions still causes too much steam to be made, regulate the air supply entering by means of the side ash-pit doors by partially closing them. When the load is so light that the entire grate is not required, success is sometimes obtained by closing off one whole side, doing all the firing through the coal pockets on the other side.

When burning a high volatile coal the center ash-pit doors should be left open a minute or two when poking the coal down the pockets, in order to admit an extra supply of air through the center grates.

Siftings which fall through the side grates should be placed with other new coal; this is good fuel and need not be wasted.

Mechanical Fuel Spreaders. If it is known how to fire the available fuel on a hand-fired grate, then nothing further need be said here, as mechanical fuel spreaders at their best can only duplicate hand firing. The difficulties that arise with this class of equipment are due to the fact that those in charge assume that because the coal is fed mechanically, it is necessarily fed correctly, and mistakes in firing which would not be permitted in hand firing are allowed to go unchecked when made by the machine. Nothing could be farther from good judgment. If the character of fuel when fired by hand demands a fuel thickness, say, of 7 inches uniformly distributed over the grate, the mechanical fuel spreader should be adjusted to perform the same service. In a like manner all other features need to be looked after.

Traveling Grates

General Instructions. The first principle of firing coal on traveling grates is that the fuel bed must not be disturbed by hand manipulation. If the fire is not burning properly, recourse should be taken to the adjustable features of the installation which are: dampers, grate speed, and feed-grate height. The sole guide in judging of fire conditions by eye inspection is whether the entire grate surface from the feed gate back to the bridge wall is covered with active fuel. If the fuel fails to ignite quickly at the feed gate, the ignition may be improved by draft regulation or by altering the gate height. If the fire does not extend to the bridge, a needless excess of air is admitted to the furnace unless special dampering devices make a corresponding reduction of grate possible. If the fuel passes over the inner end of the grate unburned the ash pit losses become excessive.

Thickness of Feed. Fire thickness at the feed gate may vary from 3 to $7\frac{1}{2}$ inches, but for a given mechanical condition of coal and chemical composition a definite thickness within this range will be found by experiment to be satisfactory, after which determination the variables are reduced to damper and grate speed manipulation. Manifestly, the available draft in the furnace chamber influences the thickness of fire that may be employed, the greater the draft intensity the thicker the fuel bed. The rate at which the air passes through determines the rate at which the fuel will burn; consequently, a thick fire, with a given draft, tends to *reduce* the rate of combustion.

The coarser the coal the thicker should be the fuel bed and the slower the speed of grate for a given capacity. As to grate speeds, the only guide is to run the grate just fast enough to keep the active coal right up to the bridge wall but not fast enough to allow unburned coal to be carried into the ash pit. The load conditions have no direct bearing on the speed of the stoker.

Load Variations. If a load variation occurs it is met by a change of damper position. Thus a larger steam demand requires greater furnace draft. Necessarily, with greater furnace draft the coal will be burned more quickly, which calls for a greater grate speed if the grate is to be kept covered. From these facts is gathered the reason why automatic damper regulation alone will not work successfully; the coal-feeding speed must be connected with the automatic damper-moving mechanism to gain success.

Importance of Furnace Draft. The rate of burning and the degree of elasticity of the rate of burning coal on traveling grates is then a function solely of the available draft in the furnace chamber when once a furnace construction has been installed. To afford certainty of quick ignition and the use of a minimum quantity of air, the design of the furnace construction is highly important and the best guide is the experience of manufacturers of this type of stoking equipment.

From the foregoing discussion it will be gathered that it is highly important that the draft facilities should not only be ample but capable of close adjustment. The controlling damper rods or chains should be within easy reach of the fireman, and the effects of damper position should be indicated on a differential draft gage for each fire.[*]

Starting New Fires. To start a fire under a cold boiler, set the feed gate at about 6 inches and run in enough coal at this depth to cover about half the length of the grate. The grate can be moved in by hand, with the aid of a hand-crank provided for that purpose, if no motive power is available. After this much coal is fed in, stop the travel of the grate by throwing the stoker out of gear and then raise the feed gate to full height. Next lay a sufficient quantity of wood on top of the bed of coal clear across the entire furnace width. Before lighting the fire the stack damper should be only partially opened and the wood then lighted by lighting oily waste or the like placed just inside the feed gate. When the fire is burning briskly over the full width of the grate, the feed gate can then be let down to operating conditions and the hopper filled with coal. In time the coal underneath the wood fire will begin to ignite, and, as the burning becomes more brisk, the damper can gradually be opened. As soon as the coal begins to burn the grate can be started ahead slowly, the ignition of the coal being watched through the inspection door all the while to see that the fire does not leave the feed gate. The damper should not be opened wide until the burning coal has completely

---

[*]An excellent treatise on traveling grate operation is published by the LaClede Christy Clay Products Company, St. Louis, Missouri.

covered the grate, after which the damper can be opened quite rapidly.

Banking Fires. The load usually drops off gradually just before banking takes place, and during this time the stack damper should gradually be closed and the stoker swinging damper closed. The feed gate can then be run up to a height of about 9 or 10 inches. Retard the stoker speed, allowing the fire to burn short gradually and, as the furnace cools down, continue closing the boiler damper. The speed of the stoker and the condition of *burning short*, together with the gradual closing of the dampers, should be such that by the time the grate is half covered with dead, ash, the 10-inch fuel bed will have covered the front half of the grate surface. When this condition is reached the boiler damper should be nearly closed or at least just to the point where the gases from the fire all but come out into the boiler room. The stoker is then turned out of gear. If this changing to a banked condition has been gradual, the furnace brickwork, etc., will have cooled down sufficiently to allow this 10-inch bank of coal to hold fire ten or twelve hours. If, however, the load has dropped off so quickly as to leave an extremely hot furnace at the beginning of the banking period, the first bank laid may last only a few hours, and it will be necessary at the end of that period to crank-in briskly by hand another 4 or 5 feet of green fuel, which bank will be found to hold fire twelve or fourteen hours without being disturbed. Should operating conditions be such as to make it inconvenient to lay in the second bank of fuel, the first bank can be laid with the drippage from the tailing pan underneath the stoker, and if this drippage is wet down before being fed to the hopper, it will be a further aid in causing the bank to hold fire for a long period. Just prior to banking, no more coal should be fed to the hopper than is just required for laying the bank. During the period of banking the hopper should be entirely empty, the coal in the furnace on the grates extending just to the feed gate. There should be a space of about 1 inch between the underside of the feed grate and the fuel bed. Such a space allows air to sweep above the fire, preventing smoke and slowing down the burning of the fuel. Allowing the hopper to burn dry before banking and keeping the 1-inch space between the feed gate and the fuel bed will prevent the fire from burning back into the hopper, thus preventing burning the feed-gate shoes and the cheek plates of the hopper frame.

Starting with Banked Fire. To start the boiler steaming from a banked fire, it is only necessary to take a light firing tool and break up the bank of coal, lower the feed grate to its normal position, and fill the coal hopper, after which the stack damper can gradually be opened. Care should be used that the stoker is not speeded up so fast as to carry the fire away from the feed gate, and the draft should gradually be increased, as too much draft might, after breaking up the bank, retard the burning rather than accelerate it.

Preserving Furnace Brickwork. If, when letting down the boiler, the damper is allowed to remain open while the fires are burning out, the cold air that comes in through the grates sweeps over the underneath surface of the ignition arch, chilling just the outside inch or two of the tile. This tile has a large capacity for heat and the body, or inside, of the tile retains its temperature for some time. The rapid cooling of the outside surface causes the tile to spall off; hence spalling can be prevented by gradually closing the boiler damper as the fire begins to cool down. If the dampers are left wide open after the fire begins to burn briskly, the lower surface of the tile will heat quickly while the center, or interior, of the tile will remain cool, and this quick heating may cause the bottom of the tile to drop off, or at least to crack.

The greatest enemy of an ignition arch is water, and every precaution should be taken when washing out the boiler to see that none of the water reaches the arch. Arch tiles that are kept on hand for repairs should by all means be kept under cover.

Chain Tension. It is important to keep the chain at the proper tension. An experienced operator can determine the proper amount of tension by watching the grate as it leaves the front driving sprockets. If the chain dips down and the ends of the links show prominently as the chain leaves the sprockets, the tension bolts should be tightened until the chain is straight at this point.

Wetting Coal. Some advantage is obtained by wetting the coal because it is easier to keep the fire in good condition when

the coal is moist. This wetness should be just sufficient that
the coal will tend to stay together when squeezed tightly in the
hand but not to drip or be mushy. Under no circumstances
should the water be sprayed at the hoppers; all extra moisture
should be supplied before the coal is placed in the storage bins.
If the spraying is done in the stoker hoppers, the water trickles
through to the links and is evaporated by the furnace heat and
the solid residue forms scale deposits on the chain rods, rollers,
and links.

Coal Siftings. When the amount of coal which sifts down
through the grates becomes excessive, it produces a very annoying
condition. It should in no instance exceed 5 per cent of the coal
fed to the stoker, and 3 per cent is a more common performance.
The drippage pits should be cleaned regularly—say once or twice
on each watch—and it is important that they be cleaned clear to
the back end. Should the drippage become excessive it can be
remedied by thickening up the fire, or wetting the coal, and by
making sure that the proper chain tension is obtained.

Burning Refuse. Sweepings about a building containing
metal clippings, nails, or other small hard metallic parts should
not be burned on the chain grate stoker, as these iron parts work
into the moving parts of the chain and cause trouble.

Inclined Grates

Front-Feed Type. The success of the front-feed inclined grate
type of stoker depends altogether upon maintaining an active bed
of fuel spread over the entire grate surface or, at least, a part of it
large enough to allow sufficient coal to be burned to make the
required steam within the draft facilities afforded.

The motion of the grate bars is expected to be such that
there will be a progressive movement of burning fuel down the
grate incline, so that when the lower dump grate is reached
practically all the combustible matter has been burned out. Any
act on the part of the fireman which disturbs such a progressive
movement of fuel defeats the purpose of the stoker. He may
interfere on occasions when the stoker fails to carry the fuel down
the grate as a result of a lack of sufficient movement of the bars
caused by the clinkering of the refuse. If the fuel sticks so badly

that it has to be dislodged, it is a mistake to dislodge it to such a degree that large areas of fuel avalanche to the bottom. Whenever avalanching occurs and the coal has the slightest tendency to clinker, the refuse will fuse and a great deal of trouble will be experienced in getting the clinkers out. Demands for more steam are usually met by assisting the fuel in traveling down the grate and gradually introducing new fuel at the upper end. When the steam demand becomes less, recourse is taken to partially closing the boiler damper and closing the furnace doors so as to admit a less amount of air through the fuel bed.

Side-Feed Type. There is no essential difference between operating the side-feed type and the front-feed type just dealt with. There is a difference, however, in the facilities for inspecting the condition of the fire and the degree of freedom in getting at the fuel bed. The gases when leaving the fuel surface travel across the face of the fuel bed, with the result that the furnaces tend to burn out at the upper rear grate portions and require particular attention there and at the corresponding front portions, where the progressive movement of coal down the grates may be disturbed because of clinkers lodged on the front furnace wall. The mistakes in operating this type of stoker are, viz, failure to keep the hoppers filled with coal; puddling the fire with pokers and slice bars; and failure to employ the stack damper properly.

Starting Fires. To start a fire, fill the magazines and, after covering the clinker bar with wood to prevent the fuel running through into the ash pit, feed just enough coal by hand from each magazine to cover the grates. Place a small amount of kindling on top of this coal and ignite. After the fire is well started, feed coal, as required, onto the grates from the magazines by hand until the steam pressure is high enough to operate the furnace driving engine. Before starting this engine, open the cylinder drain cocks until the condensation in the steam pipe leading to the same is discharged. Also open the valve connecting the exhaust with the grate bearer of the furnace.

It will not be necessary to revolve the clinker bar for some little time after the furnace is started, but the stoker arms and the grate rocker arms should be connected to and operated by the driving bar of the furnace at a speed sufficient to keep the grates covered with coal. When refuse accumulates sufficiently at the lower ends of the grates, connect the clinker bar to the operating mechanism by dropping the driving pawl into the clinker bar ratchet gear. To prevent breakage, the stoker shafts and clinker bar should be moved by hand before they are connected to the driving bar of the stoker.

When starting after the fire has been banked, spread the coke from the banked fire along the lower ends of the grates, feed sufficient coal from the magazines to cover the grates, open the drafts, and start the driving engine.

Stopping Furnaces. To stop the furnace, see that all the coal in the magazines is fed out. If the fire is to be banked, pull the coke to the bottom of the grates and cover well with coal. The fine coal from the sifting pits is very suitable for this purpose. The ash and sifting pit doors should be closed tight and the damper opened only sufficiently to allow the gas from the fresh coal to escape. The fire door should be left open for a short time if the furnace arch is very hot when the fire is banked. The clinker bar ratchet pawl should always be raised and the grate rocker arms disconnected when the furnace is shut down.

Load Variations. When there is a sudden reduction in the demand for steam, close all doors admitting air under the grates. Leave the boiler damper open and, if the steam pressure still rises, open the fire door.

Magazine Condition. To insure an even feed of coal from front to rear, the magazines should be kept full of coal. When filling the magazines with a shovel, throw the coal well to the rear end. When feeding through the magazine top occasionally shut the slides and push the coal to the rear with a hoe, as the feed is faster at this point. Never let the magazines run so empty that light from the fire can be seen in them. Feed the coal into the furnace continuously. If it is necessary to shut down the furnace engine for a considerable time, do not let the stoker boxes stand still with coal in the magazines but give the stoker shaft one motion with the wrench every fifteen minutes. This will prevent the coal in the magazines taking fire. If coal in the magazines should take fire, do not recharge until the ignited coal is all fed out.

Fuel Bed Thickness. A V-shaped fire a little thicker over the clinker bar than on the grates will give the best results. The thickness of the fuel bed should be from 3 to 8 inches, according to the character of the coal, the draft, and the rate of duty. For fine coal or a low draft the fire should be thinner than for coarser coal or a good draft. For a fluctuating load it is good practice to work with a fairly thick fire. Should the fire on one side of the furnace get heavier than on the other, disengage the link from the stoker arm for a few minutes. If the fire is thinner than it should be, a stroke or two of the stoker shaft by hand will correct the feed.

When the furnace is in operation always keep the driving engine running with the grates in motion. If necessary to stop the feed, disengage the stoker arm links. To stop the clinker bar, raise the pawl.

Clinker Bar Speed. The speed of the clinker bar should be regulated to the ash in the coal. It is better to have it revolve at a slightly slower speed than will discharge all the ash, using the wrench occasionally to remove the refuse which accumulates, thus avoiding unnecessary waste of coke. When using coal having a large percentage of ash, take out the loose pieces alongside the clinker bar, if increasing the speed by lowering the clinker bar ratchet connection does not give the desired result. If the coal which is burned shows a tendency to clinker badly, discharge a little more steam to the fire through the grate bearer. This will prevent the clinker welding together in masses which cannot easily be removed by the clinker bar.

Draft. As a general rule, all the air to the grates should be admitted through the sifting-pit doors. With some varieties of coal, however, it is noticed that the fire at the bottom of the V gradually thickens unless a proportion of the air is admitted through the ash-pit doors. Occasionally the best results are produced by admitting most of the air in this manner. Under no circumstances, however, should the sifting-pit doors be entirely closed when the furnace is in operation.

Underfeed Stokers

Horizontal Feed. All underfeed stokers depend upon forced draft for air supply through the fuel bed and upon natural draft to carry the burning gases out of the furnace and through the boiler setting.

Starting Fires. When starting fires with steam to operate the stoker, fill the retort by means of the ram so that the tuyère blocks are covered with green coal. Scatter fire along each side and the center of the retort on top of the green coal and then start the blower, slowly increasing the speed as the fire builds up. If without steam to operate the stoker, shovel coal through the fire doors till the retort is full and the tuyère blocks are completely covered. Build a wood fire on top of the green coal, leaving the fire doors open for draft. Fire with wood until sufficient steam has been raised to operate the blower; start the blower slowly, increasing the speed as the fire builds up; then discontinue the wood and fire by hand through the fire doors in the usual manner until sufficient steam pressure is obtained to operate the ram.

Cleaning Fires. Fires must be cleaned when the accumulation of noncombustible matter in the furnace interferes with combustion. The greater portion of refuse forms in a vitrified clinker on the side grates. Lift this clinker with a slice bar and remove only the clinker with a hook. Never clean so as to expose the side grates to the intense heat of the fires. Let the ash and unconsumed coke remain on side plates; clean on dead plates and top of tuyère blocks only. The retort will keep itself clean. Shut off the forced draft when cleaning. Do not burn the fire down too thin before cleaning.

Banking Fires. To bank fires, introduce several charges of coal by means of the ram, shut off the forced draft, and close the fire doors and the damper. If the fires are banked for a long period, clinker and coke may form in the retort. The clinker should be removed and the coke broken up before attempting to operate the ram.

Inclined Underfeed. Stokers of the inclined underfeed type are dependent for their economical operation more on the indications of draft instruments and gas determinations than on judgment of fire conditions by eye inspection. It is true that when a particularly bad condition of fire exists it is possible to see that the results are bound to be economically bad, but there are conditions of bad operation, especially in the direction of supplying useless air, that are not visible and can be determined by gas analyses only. The proper manipulation of this class of stoking equipment can therefore be best accomplished under the direction of competent technical skill. The best method to pursue is to co-operate with the engineers of the companies manufacturing the equipment in determining the best way to operate, later using as a guide the draft indications observed during good trial running, occasionally checking the result by gas analyses.

The best usual operating conditions are those which prevail when almost balanced draft in the furnace is employed. If an automatic draft control to bring this about is available, so much the better, but in any case the balanced condition should be striven for.

OPERATING COMBINATIONS OF UNITS

Plant Economy vs. Boiler Economy. The discussions preceding this have been devoted to the considerations entering into the economical burning of fuel, with particular reference to the character of the equipment connected with the boiler treated as a single unit but not especially with reference to the fact that several such units are usually operated as a plant. In a measure, the matters of plant load and of its variation, which are both frequently large, were intentionally neglected so as to give more emphasis to the immediate problem of presenting the main features of boiler and furnace unit operation uninfluenced by complications set up when a battery of boilers is operated. It is wrong to conclude, offhand, that if every unit makes good use of the fuel supplied to it, the plant as a whole must necessarily be economically run, for fuel is not the only item entering into the cost of boiler operation. Mention only need be made of plant investment, labor, and maintenance costs of furnaces and boilers to justify the foregoing statement, and all of these enter into the question. More striking than any of these considerations is the fact that, whatever conclusion may be drawn from a carefully conducted series of tests over a considerable range of boiler capacity, actual running conditions show that unless the operators are compelled to busy themselves continuously either manually or mentally, in order to maintain steam pressure, attention becomes lax and as a result fuel-burning economy suffers.

Few Units with High Boiler Rating. Where there is a choice as to number of units for operating service, the tendency on the part of the directing authority should be to reduce that number to a workable minimum rather than permit a lazy performance on the part either of the equipment or the men. It does not follow' however, that the highest available unit operation is necessarily the best practice; to explain how to determine the reasonable stopping place in applying the higher capacity policy is the purpose of the succeeding paragraphs.

Analysis of Method. Let us assume that good daily operating performances of the boiler units of two plants are as shown in Fig. 26, in which A–A represents the efficiency of one and A'–A' that of the other over the range of capacity indicated. These lines are intended to show the average results of the units, not the possible test performances represented by A_1–A_1, which might be several per cent higher throughout the capacity range. Consider first plant A; it will be noted that it does not make a great deal of difference at what point between 80 per cent and 140 per cent of boiler rating the boiler units are operated, provided the operators obtain the realizable results as shown by the curve A–A. As a matter of fact the probabilities are that they will get, instead of A–A of Fig. 26, the curve A''–A'' of Fig. 27, which indicates departures from A–A. (Curve A–A, Fig. 27, is simply a duplication of curve A–A, Fig. 26.) The reason why the curves converge at the higher capacities is because carelessness in firing is not attended by loss of pressure when there are enough units in service to carry the plant load anyway.

Out of considerations like these comes the conclusion that it is best all around to tend to higher running rates, but to do so intelligently and with a full realization that the effects in particulars besides heat evolution and absorbtion efficiency must be weighed also.

Referring again to Fig. 26, note that the curve A'–A' for plant A' has a different position on the chart than A–A. This may be due to a variety of causes, among which may be mentioned difference in size and character of boiler units, character of furnaces, drafts, fuels, etc. Let us consider the plants to be of equal steam demand. Manifestly it would be wise to operate the units of $A'-A'$ at a higher percentage of boiler rating than those of $A-A$. So it is important to know what sort of a performance with reference to capacity may be expected from the equipment dealt with. This knowledge can be gained only by obtaining evaporation and fuel figures by reliable means, preferably through

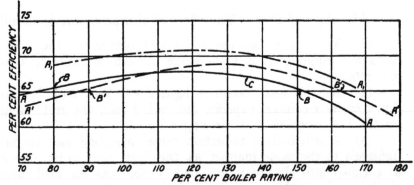

Fig. 26. Theoretical Boiler Curves Showing Variation of Efficiency with Boiler Rating

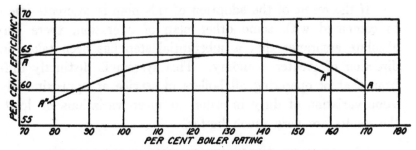

Fig. 27. Actual Boiler Efficiency Curve Compared with Theoretical Curve

the compilation of test data taken during daily operation over extended periods.

Assuming that information such as given by the curve $A-A$ is available and that it is known by equally reliable means what the probable steam demand will be, the method most likely to gain economical results is as follows:

(1) Estimate the likely *maximum* boiler horsepower demand for one hour, using accumulated data and experience, etc.

(2) Divide this figure by the boiler horsepower created when running a little less capacity than the *maximum capacity economical rate* as shown by compiled or plotted data. The dividend for

plant A-A, Fig. 26, would be 135 per cent of the boiler rating as shown by point C, which is a little less than B on the right, the latter being still within the range of economical performance. The quotient increased to the next larger whole number represents the total number of units to be in service.

(3)   According to the load operate as many of these units as possible at the C-rating so long as none of the rest is compelled to operate below its lower capacity efficient basis as shown by point B on the left, Fig. 26.

Advantages of Plan.   The effect of this procedure is as follows:

(1)   When the maximum demand occurs all the operating units are running at a little below maximum capacity economical rate.

(2)   As the load becomes lighter *one unit only* is brought down to its *minimum capacity economical rate*, the rest remaining on the line working at their upper limits.

(3)   A still further reduction causes a second unit to be load lightened in the same manner as the first; and so on, one boiler at a time, until the minimum load is met.   As the load increases the lower operated units are brought into maximum service in turn.

If the result of the adoption of this plan is to create idle units as compared with some other plan of operation, there may be absolute assurance that a substantial step has been taken in the direction of greater economy.   This system is distinctly different from that of operating all boilers in service at approximately the same variation of duty in order to meet variations of load, but the results are very much better.

BOILER ROOM MEASURING INSTRUMENTS

Function of Instruments.   It is so obvious that measuring instruments are essential to good boiler room performance that one is tempted to agree that the use of instruments of all kinds is justified in every instance, provided they are reliable and accurate.   However, the matter is not so simple as this, for in the generation of steam as in all other mechanic arts, the character of the operating processes involved is limited by the human capabilities of the operators.   It is therefore well to investigate the subject from this standpoint and state its main principles at least.

The function of instruments is to supply information—(1) to permit operators to judge of the performance while the operation is actually going on, thus permitting an intelligent adjustment if adjustment is desirable; (2) to provide responsible managers, foremen, or chiefs, with permanent records of past performances, thus supplying evidence on which to base operating reforms; and (3) to provide the basis for cost accounting, or charges for service to departments, according to service rendered.

Limits of Usefulness. Manifestly, in order for instruments to be useful under the first head, the operators must be capable of interpreting the instrument indications and be able to apply the remedies when unsatisfactory conditions exist. Under the second head the responsibility rests with the managers as well as the operators and, in addition, the records must be regularly and thoroughly digested if they are to be of any real service. Unless a genuine cost distribution system exists it is needless to provide the devices that make possible such a distribution. Experience teaches that, however desirable it may appear to be to have available the several kinds of instruments that the market affords, it is actually worth while to supply only the minimum number. However, it is highly important to have and use this minimum and the highest grade of each particular type is always justified, as is the most painstaking care in preservation and use. In other words, it is easy to overequip a plant with measuring instruments, creating a condition similar to that sometimes proposed in other branches of business where the system is so complicated that it requires another system to run it.

Types of Instruments. The measuring instruments and devices employed in boiler rooms are, viz, draft gages—indicating and recording; thermometers—indicating and recording; gas analyzing apparatus—indicating and recording; smoke gages—indicating and recording; coal weighers; water measuring or weighing devices—indicating, recording, and integrating; and steam meters—indicating, recording, and integrating.

Draft Gages. Draft obtained by the use of chimneys is the difference in pressure created by a heavier column of gas overcoming an equal volume of gas of a lighter weight per unit of volume. It should be distinguished from the air and gas itself which are mass quantities, and it should always be recognized as an intensity factor. We, therefore, speak of draft in terms of the pressure exerted by a column of water, as, for instance, .5 of an inch of water, by which is meant that the draft intensity is such as to sustain, when exerted upon a water surface, a column .5 of an inch high against gravity.

An instrument for measuring draft intensity is called a *draft gage*. There are various forms of such instruments, all of which are based upon the same principle. Where the intensities of draft are large, sufficient accuracy may be obtained by the use of a simple glass U-tube containing water, one tube end of which is in communication with the chamber or conduit of which the draft intensity is to be determined. If a suitable scale is attached, the instrument can easily be read by noting the difference in height of water level in the two legs of the tube.

A much more sensitive and, if intelligently used, more accurate instrument is that shown in Fig. 28. The glass contains a

Fig. 28. Differential Draft Gage
Courtesy of Lewis M. Ellison, Chicago, Illinois

colored oil of known specific gravity. As the inclination of the tube portion determines the sensitiveness of the instrument, to obtain accuracy, the bubble vial for leveling and its position with respect to the glass portion of the gage within its working range should be carefully adjusted by the manufacturer. There is no greater difficulty in using a differential draft gage than any other less sensitive kind.

Of all instruments, the draft gage is the simplest and most useful in the steam generating art. It is no exaggeration to say that every change of condition of fuel, furnace, boiler setting, cleanliness of heating surface, or the manner of operation is reflected by the draft difference indication. To be sure, some of these draft indication changes are submerged in changes of a wider scope and, consequently, it is not to be expected that the draft gage alone will tell a complete story of boiler operation.

There is no plant, however small, that does not warrant the employment of one well-made differential draft gage, and in most instances there is needed at least one draft gage for each boiler

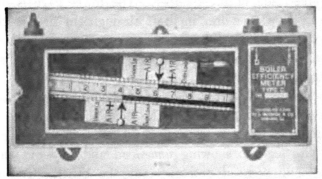

Fig. 29. View of Face of Blonck Efficiency Meter
Courtesy of W. A. Blonck & Company, Chicago, Illinois

unit, connected and located in a cool protected position so as to permit the ready determination, in turn, of the draft in the furnace region and in the boiler uptake.

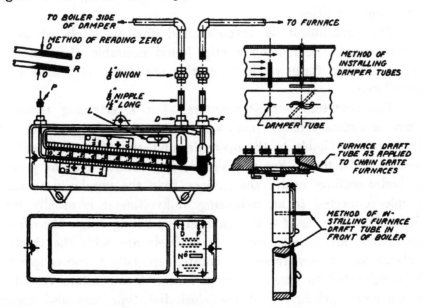

Fig. 30. Layout Showing Method of Installing Blonck Meters

Efficiency Meter by Draft Method. An interesting and valuable adaptation of the differential draft gages for judging of furnace operating efficiency is found in the Blonck efficiency meter illustrated in Figs. 29 and 30. This meter is the pioneer of several instruments of the same type. It consists essentially of two sensitive draft gages, one connected to the furnace and the other to the boiler side of the damper. The lower gage is filled with *red oil* and shows the drop in draft through the fire, or the resistance of the fuel bed; the upper gage is filled with *blue oil* and registers the drop in draft between the furnace and the damper, or the resistance of the boiler.

Two sliding indicators are arranged so they can be set at the point of *perfect firing*, that is, the point at which the boiler is operating at its highest efficiency. These indicators are plainly marked with legends showing *underload* and *air+* at one side of the arrow and *overload* and *air−* at the other. To locate the point of perfect firing, it is necessary to determine what conditions exist when the boiler is operating at its best efficiency. The indicators should be so set that any departure from these conditions is registered. Thereafter the problem is to interpret the indications and thus make possible the remedying of a faulty operating condition.

This instrument is manufactured for all kinds of boiler furnace service and many niceties found desirable when encountering different forms of draft creating apparatus, etc., have been introduced.

Thermometers and Pyrometers. For ascertaining temperatures in ordinary boiler room work a mercury thermometer will be found intelligible to the operators and the indications will be readily understood. For the higher temperatures, such as prevail in boiler settings nearer the furnace than the uptake, a thermocouple connected to an indicating millivoltmeter is usually very desirable. When used well within safe operating ranges the *relative* indications are usually found to be fairly accurate; the absolute indications are sometimes inaccurate, especially if the couple has been subjected to excessive temperature. Temperature recording instruments, principally of the clock-dial type, are also manufactured.

Flue Gas Analyzing Apparatus.* *Description of Orsat Type.* The Orsat apparatus, illustrated in Fig. 31, is generally used for

---

*Courtesy of The Babcock & Wilcox Company, New York City.

analyzing flue gases. The burette A is graduated in cubic centimeters up to 100 and is surrounded by a water jacket to prevent any change in temperature from affecting the density of the gas being analyzed.

For accurate work it is advisable to use four pipettes B, C, D, and E, the first containing a solution of caustic potash for the absorption of carbon dioxide, the second an alkaline solution of pyrogallol for the absorption of oxygen, and the remaining two an acid solution of cuprous chloride for absorbing the carbon monoxide. Each pipette contains a number of glass tubes, to which some of the solution clings, thus facilitating the absorption of the gas. In the pipettes D and E copper wire is placed in these tubes to re-energize the solution as it becomes weakened. The rear half of each pipette is fitted with a rubber bag, one of which is shown at K, to protect the solution from the action of the air. The solution in each pipette should be drawn up to the mark on the capillary tube.

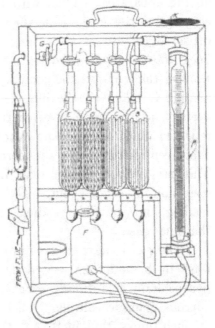

Fig. 31. Diagram of Orsat Apparatus for Analyzing Flue Gas
Courtesy of The Babcock & Wilcox Company, New York City

Method of Use. The gas is drawn into the burette through the U-tube H, which is filled with spun glass, or similar material, to clean the gas. To discharge any air or gas in the apparatus, the cock G is opened to the air and the bottle F is raised until the water in the burette reaches the 100 cubic centimeter mark. The cock G is then turned so as to close the air opening and allow gas to be drawn through H, the bottle F being lowered for this purpose. The gas is drawn into the burette to a point below the zero mark, the cock G is then opened to the air, and the excess gas is expelled until the levels of the water in F and in A are at the zero mark. This operation is necessary in order to obtain the zero reading at atmospheric pressure.

The apparatus and all connections leading thereto should be carefully tested for leakage. Simple tests can be made; for example, if, after the cock G is closed, when the bottle F is placed on top of the frame for a short time and again brought to the zero mark, the level of the water in A is above the zero mark, a leak is indicated.

Before taking a final sample for analysis, the burette A should be filled with gas and emptied once or twice, to make sure that all the apparatus is filled with the new gas. The cock G is then closed and the cock I in the pipette B is opened and the gas driven over into B by raising the bottle F. The gas is drawn back into A by lowering F, and when the solution in B has reached the mark in the capillary tube, the cock I is closed and a reading is taken on the burette, the water in the bottle F being brought to the same level as the water in A. The operation is repeated until a constant reading is obtained, the number of cubic centimeters being the percentage of CO_2 in the flue gases. The gas is then driven over into the pipette C and a similar operation is carried out. The difference between the resulting reading and the first reading gives the percentage of oxygen in the flue gases.

The gas is next driven into the pipette D, then given a final wash in E, and then passed into the pipette C to neutralize any hydrochloric acid fumes which may have been given off by the cuprous chloride solution, which, especially if it be old, may give off such fumes, thus increasing the volume of the gases and making the reading on the burette less than the true amount.

The steps in the process must be performed in the order named, as the pyrogallol solution will also absorb carbon dioxide, while the cuprous chloride solution will also absorb oxygen.

As the pressure of the gases in the flue is less than atmospheric pressure, they will not of themselves flow through the pipe connecting the flue to the apparatus. The gas may be drawn into the pipe in the way already described for filling the apparatus, but this is a tedious method. For rapid work a rubber bulb aspirator connected to the air outlet of the cock G will enable a new supply of gas to be drawn into the pipe, the apparatus then being filled as already described. Another form of aspirator draws the gas from the flue in a constant stream, thus insuring a fresh supply for each sample.

The analysis made by the Orsat apparatus is volumetric; if an analysis by weight is required, it can be found from the volumetric analysis by computation based on the molecular weights of the gases involved.

Other Types. There are forms of manually operated gas analyzing apparatus other than the one described above, but they are all based on the Orsat principle. Many ingenious forms have been developed with a view toward making the instrument less liable to breakage and more portable. Many attempts have been made to evolve recording or continuous CO_2 instruments by far the most of which have been failures, especially when placed in the hands of boiler room engineers. Certainly there has been no recording CO_2 instrument constructed that, considered in connection with boiler furnace practice, warrants the employment for its own sake of the necessary skill to keep it working.

Smoke Indicators and Recorders. Smoke indicators and recorders are gradually coming more into favor as their importance is appreciated. Where an indicator is wisely employed the results are gratifying. The smoke recorder has the added advantage of providing evidence of failure of operators to carry out instructions in case the record shows avoidable smoke.

Smoke Indicators. Smoke indicators are constructed on the simple principle of so placing an artificial light opposite an opening in the boiler stack connection that it shines into the breeching. When the flue gases are clear, the light will shine across the breeching into a tube connection fitted with mirrors and reflectors so as to project light rays upon a ground-glass disk, or *moon.* An obstruction to light passage by smoke will cause this moon to darken corresponding to the density of the smoke. The fireman may thus have a fair conception of the exhalation coming from the top of the stack without looking at the stack at all and can act to remove the cause of the smoke at once.

Smoke Recorders. Smoke recorders are constructed on the principle of taking minute samples of flue gas at frequent regular intervals and projecting these as rapidly as taken upon a soft paper sheet or ribbon passing by the gas ejecting nozzle. The instrument must not only take a fair sample of the gas but must show a paper record closely duplicating in appearance the density of the smoke column coming from the breeching or stack. The device manufactured by the Hamler-Eddy Smoke Recorder Company, of Chicago, is the best of its kind and is a very ingenious, accurate, and otherwise reliable instrument.

Coal Weighing Instruments. Coal weighing instruments are in every instance built upon the ordinary platform scale system of lever arms and scale beam and are usually an integral part of a coal larry system delivering coal to stoker hoppers in turn. The value of keeping accurate records of the coal consumed by each

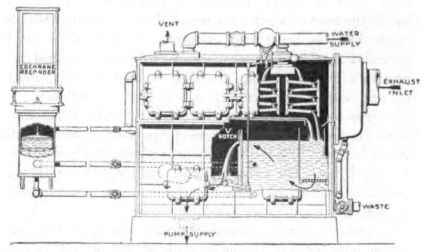

Fig. 32. Cochrane Metering Heater with Outside Chamber for Recorder Float
Courtesy of Harrison Safety Boiler Works, Philadelphia, Pennsylvania

boiler is coming to be better appreciated, and unless by the use of this form of apparatus other operating features are adversely affected, coal weighing is well worth any reasonable expenditure of effort and money, especially when data concerning the water evaporated is also available.

Water Measuring or Weighing Devices. *Integrating Meter.* Water measuring or weighing devices are of several forms, of which the most common is the familiar type of integrating meter placed on water supply lines. For boiler feed, especially when the water is hot, the serviceability, or at least the accuracy, of such meters is open to question, though of course they may always be calibrated. Meters are always, or should be, installed in by-passes to permit removal for repairs.

V-Notch Meter. A second type of meter known as the V-notch is shown in Fig. 32 as a part of a feed-water heater. The principle of operation is to determine by accurate means the height of the water flowing over a V-shaped weir and to apply this water head in a computation based upon other known experimental factors. The resulting quantity of flow is made manifest by indicators, a recording chart, and an integrating meter when connected up with suitable clock and other mechanism, the whole being an accurate and convenient manner of determining feed-water quantities.

Venturi Meter. A liquid flowing through a contracted area of pipe constructed as shown in Fig. 33 will exert varying pressures at two sections A and B, the pressure at B being less than at A because the velocity at the throat is higher than that at the

Fig. 33.   Section of Venturi Meter Tube

inlet section. By properly proportioning the pipe this pressure loss is restored at section C. The loss of pressure at the throat can be accurately measured by a manometer gage and is found to increase approximately as the square of the throat velocity, so that if the velocity at B is doubled the pressure difference becomes about four times as great. The use made of this phenomenon is simply to connect the inlet section to one and the throat section to another of two vertical wells, containing mercury baths, communicating at their bottom end means of a small pipe connection. In each well is a heavy float resting on mercury, a part of which flows from one well to the other in direct proportion to the difference in the two pressures. Consequently, one float rises as the other descends and this movement is transferred through substantial rack and spur gearing to an indicator dial hand shaft.

A typical installation is illustrated in Fig. 34, which shows the connections at the Venturi pipe with two leads of small pipe transmitting the pressures at the inlet and throat sections to the mercury wells in the lower back part of the instrument case. The

Fig. 34. Venturi Meter Installation
Courtesy of Builders Iron Foundry, Providence, Rhode Island

front displays a recording chart on top, an integrating mechanism immediately below it, and a rate-of-flow indicator.

Steam-Flow Meters. To illustrate the principle of action of the Pitot tube as applied to steam-flow meters, an elementary form is shown in Fig. 35. Assume that two small pipes are inserted in the main pipe in such a manner that one opening, called the *leading opening*, faces against the direction of flow and the other opening, called the *trailing opening*, faces in the direction of flow of the steam, water, air, or gas being measured. These two pipes are connected to the two glass legs of a vertical U-tube containing mercury.

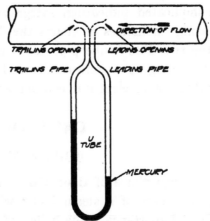

Fig. 35. Diagram Showing Principle of Action of Pitot Tube

It is evident that the steam, water, air, or gas when flowing impinges against the leading opening and sets up a pressure in the leading pipe, which equals the static pressure plus a pressure due to the velocity head. The drag of the gas or fluid over the trailing opening lowers the pressure in the trailing pipe. Owing to the differential pressure the mercury in the U-tube is deflected until the weight of mercury represented by the difference in the two columns exactly balances the differential pressure of the flowing medium. The amount of deflection is indicative of the rate of flow, other conditions remaining the same. Therefore it is feasible to expect a true indication, within reasonable ranges, of the quantities passing through the Pitot tube section of the pipe if the tube is properly combined with suitable indicating and recording mechanisms.

Fig. 36. Indicating Flow Meter
Courtesy of General Electric Company, Schenectady, New York

The General Electric Company manufactures for steam, gas,

air, and water use a number of different types of instruments from the simplest indicating flow meter, shown in Fig. 36, to the most complicated indicating, integrating, and recording types. Translating on indices or charts the differences in pressure exerted by the two Pitot tube pipe leads gives rise to several devices, some depending upon pure mechanical mercury height measurement and others upon electrical contact and resistance variations.

CARE OF BOILERS
BOILER MANAGEMENT

Importance of Good Care. Any amount of time spent in the proper care of a steam boiler will be amply repaid, for this is of great importance. The boiler, of course, should be so designed and constructed that all parts can be readily inspected and cleaned; but this is of little benefit unless proper and rigid inspections are made. All internal fittings, such as fusible plugs, water alarms, feed pipes, and the like, should occasionally be examined to see if they are tight and in good working order. It is especially important that if traces of oil be found the causes should immediately be removed. If due care is not given to the boiler, its life will be materially shortened.

Care of Pressure Apparatus. The following operating rules have been established by the Hartford Steam Boiler Inspection and Insurance Company and should be carefully followed, whether or not the boiler is insured by the above-mentioned company:

Condition of Water. The first duty of an engineer, when he enters his boiler room in the morning, is to ascertain how many gages of water there are in his boilers. Never unbank or replenish the fires until this is done. Accidents have occurred and many boilers have been entirely ruined through neglect of this precaution.

Low Water. In case of low water, cover the fires immediately with ashes; or, if no ashes are at hand, use fresh coal and close the ash-pit doors. Never turn on the feed nor tamper with or open the safety valve. Let the steam outlets remain as they are.

In Case of Foaming. Close the throttle and keep it closed long enough to show the true level of the water. If that level is sufficiently high, feeding and blowing will usually suffice to correct the evil. In case of violent foaming, caused by dirty water or by change from salt to fresh water or *vice versa*, in addition to the above, check the draft and cover the fires with fresh coal.

Leaks. When leaks are discovered, they should be repaired as soon as possible.

Blowing Off. If the feed water contains sediment forming matter, the boilers must be blown down at regular intervals. It will usually suffice to blow down one inch of water each watch. In case the feed water contains foam producing matter, the blowing down must be sufficient to make it possible to observe a fairly steady gage glass indication. When surface blow cocks are used, they should be opened frequently for a few minutes at a time.

Filling Up the Boiler. After blowing down, allow the boiler to become cool before filling again. Cold water pumped into hot boilers is very injurious, on account of the sudden contraction.

Exterior of Boiler. Be careful that no water comes in contact with the boiler exterior, either from leaky joints or from other causes.

Removing Deposit and Sediment. In tubular boilers, the hand-holes should be opened frequently, all collections removed, and fore plates carefully cleaned. Also, when boilers are fed in front and blown off through the same pipe, the collection of mud or sediment in the rear end should be removed frequently.

Safety Valves. Raise safety valves cautiously and frequently to prevent their sticking fast in their seats.

Safety Valve and Pressure Gage. Should the gage ever indicate the limit of pressure allowed, see that the safety valves are blowing off. In case of difference, notify the insurance company's inspector.

Gage Cocks, Glass Gage. Keep the gage cocks clear and in constant use. Glass gages should not be relied on altogether.

Blisters. When a blister appears, immediately have it carefully examined and trimmed or patched, as the case may require.

Clean Sheets. Particular care should be taken to keep sheets and parts of boilers exposed to the fire perfectly clean; also all tubes, flues, and connections well swept. This is particularly necessary where wood or soft coal is used for fuel.

General Care of Boilers and Connections. Under all circumstances, keep the gages, cocks, etc., clean and in good order, and things generally in and about the boiler room in a neat condition.

Getting Up Steam. In preparing to get up steam after the boilers have been open or out of service, great care should be exercised in making the manhole and handhole joints. Safety valves should then be opened and blocked open, and the necessary supply of water run in or pumped into the boilers, until it shows at second gage in tubular and locomotive boilers; a high level is advisable in vertical tubulars as a protection to the top ends of the tubes. After this is done, fuel may be placed on the grate, dampers opened, and fires started. If the chimney or stack is cold and does not draw properly, burn some oily waste or light kindling at the base. Start the fires in ample time, so that it will not be necessary to urge them unduly. When steam issues from the safety valve, lower it carefully to its seat and note the pressure and behavior of the steam gage. If there are other boilers in operation, and stop valves are to be opened to place boilers in connection with others on a steam-pipe line, watch those recently fired up, until pressure is up to that of the other boilers to which they are connected; then open the stop valves slowly and carefully.

The precaution just mentioned is automatically taken care of if all the boilers on the same steam main are equipped with automatic stop-and-check valves and the additional control valve on the boiler being brought up to steam pressure is open, so that the automatic valve can operate as intended.

Care of Setting and Attachments. *Avoiding Air Infiltration.* While the care of the boiler or pressure apparatus is important, it is just as important that the enclosure of the boiler and its furnace receive careful attention. The penalty for not so doing is to sacrifice efficiency in operation. It is impossible to emphasize too strongly the necessity for maintaining brickwork tight, for every bit of air filtered into the setting without taking part in the combustion process represents a direct loss. Close investigation of this subject discloses the fact that engineers and firemen do not appreciate the harm that can result from a failure to attend to boiler settings by not preventing air leakage and radiation losses, though they usually are keen to attend to the *safety* elements of the installation in their charge. It is conservative to say that the money losses that can be avoided by reasonable care of boiler settings greatly exceed the money losses due to boiler failures.

CORROSION

There are several causes which tend to shorten and destroy the life of every boiler. These may be divided into two general classes, chemical and mechanical, and are usually the result of improper feed water or of improper care. Pure water, free from air and carbon dioxide, has no evil effect on the iron; but all natural waters, whether from rain, lake, river, or sea, contain air and a little carbon dioxide in solution, and such water will cause iron to corrode, even though no other impurities are present. Sea water, heated under a steam pressure of 30 pounds, even if it contains no air, will liberate a little hydrochloric acid, which instantly attacks the iron of the boiler unless counteracted by a chemical agent.

EXTERNAL CORROSION

Causes. There are two forms of corrosion, external and internal. External corrosion may be due to faulty setting, to improper care, to moisture from external sources, or from leakage from joints and valves. A large amount of external corrosion is the result of setting boilers in a mass of brickwork, which readily absorbs moisture, and which, when not under fire, is likely to keep the boiler plates damp. The exterior of a boiler encased in brickwork, moreover, is not so easily accessible, and a considerable amount of deterioration may take place without being readily detected.

Prevention. Internally fired boilers are supported on saddles and are easily accessible; and the magnesia or asbestos lagging with which they are usually covered will tend to absorb a certain amount of moisture, which will be given off when hot, thus helping to keep the boiler dry. If a leak of appreciable size occurs, the covering will become softened and its presence will be detected at once and repairs made. The exterior of an internally fired boiler, being at all times accessible, can be properly taken care of, which is not true of a boiler set in brickwork. Rivets and riveted joints should, as far as possible, be kept out of contact with the fire.

Water-tube boilers are for the most part so enclosed that the tubes do not come in direct contact with the brickwork. In this respect the criticism just offered to brick enclosures for boilers does not hold. Even with water-tube boilers brick comes in contact with metal, though some settings are remarkably free in this respect.

INTERNAL CORROSION

Causes. This is the result of the chemical action of impure feed water. It may occur in the form of a general corrosion or wasting away of the boiler plates, or in the form of pitting or grooving, the effects of which are likely to be local. Pitting and general corrosion are entirely the result of chemical action, while grooving is the result of chemical and mechanical action combined.

It is not easy to discover general corrosion, because it acts more or less uniformly over a large surface. Sometimes the rivet heads rust in proportion to the plates, so that the wasting away of the plates is not easily noticeable. A uniform corrosion is the hardest to detect, and can usually be discovered only by drilling the boiler and gaging the thickness of the plate. If the thickness of the plate is found to be materially reduced, the working pressure of the boiler should be lowered in proportion.

Sometimes the water will attack the plates only in the vicinity of the water line, in some instances confining the damage to a belt 6 inches or 8 inches wide. Sometimes a few rivets below water level will be corroded, the remainder being in comparatively good condition. Often the stays are weakened more rapidly than the plates, and the screw threads of a stay may be badly corroded while the shank of the stay remains uninjured.

Pitting. Fatty acids, which are likely to come over in the feed water if vegetable oils are used to lubricate engine cylinders, are especially active in producing small pits throughout the interior of the boiler. Pitting appears in the form of small holes or in patches from $\frac{1}{4}$ inch to 1 inch in diameter, or even as irregularly shaped depressions. If the holes are small and close together, the plate is said to be honeycombed. It is generally believed that this phenomenon, the result of chemical action, is due to a lack of homogeneity in the material of the boiler, although an entirely satisfactory explanation has not yet been given. Pitting may also be caused by galvanic action, which may take place especially if sea water is used. As pitting occurs when there is no cause whatever for galvanic action, this can be only a secondary cause at best. It is reasonable to suppose that acids will attack the most susceptible portions of the plate; and if there is any lack of homogeneity in the iron, it is probable that the places or spots most favorable to chemical attack will suffer first.

Grooving. Grooving is probably the result of straining, springing, or buckling of the plates, aided by local corrosion or by the same forces which cause pitting. Straining of the plates may be due to insufficient or improper staying, thus causing the plates to spring back and forth as the steam pressure varies. This phenomenon is most commonly found in stationary boilers of the Cornish or Lancashire types appearing in the flat end plates around the edge of the angle iron, or in the root of the angle iron. Too rigid staying of the ends by gussets or diagonal stays, or too great a difference in expansion between different parts, is almost sure to produce grooves.

When a sheet of a boiler is flanged to a small radius, as in some forms of boiler construction, like the head of a shell, it is commonly supposed that a "breathing" action takes place (due to variations of internal pressure and heat stresses) which sets up "fatigue" of the metal, concentrating this stress over a small distance in the curve of the flange. A crack or groove may then develop along the line of greatest stress and, if allowed to progress, may result in a disastrous explosion. The best boiler designers recognize this as a most important item to be considered, and overcome the grooving tendency by providing long radius flanges.

Internal grooving may be caused as the direct result of excessive calking, which, by injuring the surface of the metal, exposes it to the corrosive action of the feed water. It is to be expected that if strains which cause the plates to come and go are set up in the boiler —especially if the stresses can be concentrated along a definite line —a weakness will be developed there, and it will be a susceptible point for chemical attack. Sometimes grooving is so fine as to appear to be a mere crack. But the crack, although perhaps only $\frac{1}{64}$ inch in width, may extend into the plate for a considerable depth. Grooves are not readily detected and, if allowed to continue for any length of time, are likely to produce serious results.

Prevention. The best way to prevent internal corrosion is to use water that has no corrosive effect on the plates. If internal corrosion has begun, a change of feed water may prolong the life of the boiler, but in many instances it is cheaper to build a new boiler than to change the water supply frequently. Sometimes the introduction of a thicker plate at places where the water is found to be most active will be advisable; but, as these plates are stronger than the rest of the boiler, the strains will not be uniformly distributed, and stresses are likely to concentrate along the edge of this heavy plate, which will be a susceptible point for the formation of grooves.

The acidity of the feed water may be neutralized by some alkaline substance, such as soda, before it enters the boiler. The amount of soda to be used varies with the acidity of the water; but it should always be used in the smallest possible quantity, as the soda is likely

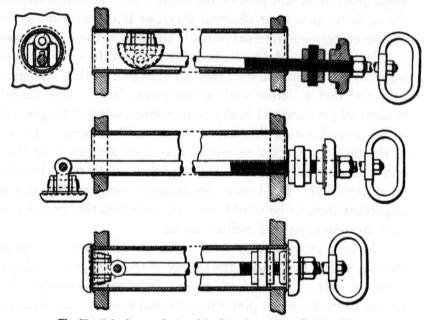

Fig. 37. Tube Stopper Designed for Insertion without Drawing Fire

to produce priming in the boiler and will be injurious if there is much salt present. Vegetable oils should not be used for cylinder lubrication if the condensation is to be fed back to the boiler, as such oils contain acids which will always produce injurious effects. Mineral oils alone should be used.

To allow for a general corrosion, $\frac{1}{16}$ inch to $\frac{2}{16}$ inch extra thickness of shell should be provided. All seams of a boiler should be tight, and no welded tubes should be used, as pitting and grooving are likely to occur in the vicinity of the weld. When not in use, no moist air should be allowed in the boiler. A boiler can be thoroughly dried out either by the application of heat or by putting lime into it, which will readily absorb the moisture.

The water fed to the boiler should be thoroughly filtered to remove as much grease as possible, for, although mineral oil is not likely to cause pitting, it has a serious effect in other ways.

Tube Stoppers. It frequently happens, when fire-tube boilers are under pressure that leaks occur in the tubes through pitting, defective welding, or the development of cracks. Formerly, when this occurred, the fire was drawn and the ends of the tube plugged with hardwood bungs driven hard home, or with iron plugs calked in. With high pressures, such procedure is impossible. Tube

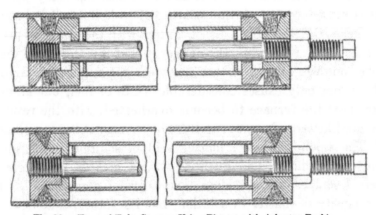

Fig. 38. Type of Tube Stopper Using Pistons with Asbestos Packing

stoppers used for high pressure are joined together by a tie-rod of some sort. They are usually wedge-shaped; and the tie-rod, passing through the stopper at one end, with a plug at the other end, can be screwed tight up.

The simplest form of stopper has to be inserted from the rear, and necessitates drawing the fire; but Fig. 37 illustrates a stopper which can be inserted without drawing the fire. At the end of the rod is hinged a folding bung, which can be passed through the tube and which opens out in the combustion chamber before being pulled into position. At the smoke-box end of the boiler, an india-rubber washer, pressed between two pieces of metal, affords temporary protection while the plug is being put in position. The stopper can then be screwed up tightly with a handle provided for that purpose.

Fig. 38 illustrates another arrangement which can be inserted in the leaky tube without drawing the fire. The ends, being in the form of stuffing glands, press an asbestos packing hard against the side of the tube.

INCRUSTATION OR SCALE FORMATION

Causes in General. The incrustation formed by the accumulation of the deposit of sediment in the feed water is called scale or sludge. The solid matter in the feed water may be precipitated by the rise in temperature, or left behind as the result of the evaporation of the water. Some of these precipitates remain soft and can be blown out, while others deposit as hard scale, especially where the heat is most intense. A thin coating of scale in itself is beneficial, for it keeps the water from direct contact with the iron, and prevents corrosion and pitting; but the danger is that if a thin scale forms, a thicker one will form, and this heavy scale, being a poor conductor of heat, not only causes considerable waste of fuel, but allows the plates next the furnace to become overheated, with the result that they are likely to give way, and the boiler may collapse or bag.

The amount of solid matter held in solution is measured in grains per gallon. The quantity varies greatly in waters from different sources, but is seldom over 40 grains per gallon. It is not the quantity of matter in solution, but its nature, that determines the influence of feed water. With proper attention to the boiler, the presence of a certain amount of carbonate or sulphate of soda would not be injurious; while the same number of grains per gallon of salts of lime would cause serious trouble. Salts of lime (calcium), together with carbonate of magnesia, are the solids most frequently found, and are the most troublesome. Hard water contains considerable quantities of lime. So-called soft water has usually but little solid matter in suspension, but it may contain vegetable or organic impurities that will cause corrosion or pitting.

Oil. The oil used in the engine is likely to get into the boiler through the feed water, if it is not carefully filtered or passed through a *grease extractor* or *oil separator*. The oil is likely to be deposited on the sides and tubes of the boiler, and not only is a poor conductor of heat but, mingling with the sediment which is precipitated from the hot water, produces a mixture which is readily baked on to the boiler plates and is especially obstinate and difficult to remove. Because this oily deposit resists heat transmission, the metal adjacent to it may become overheated and fail to withstand the boiler pressure and give away. These failures are often very costly to both life and property. There are efficient oil separators now on the market, which will remove practically every trace of oil.

Carbonate of Lime. Carbonate of lime is held in solution in water by an excess of carbondioxid. As the water is heated, the excess of carbondioxid, or carbonic acid, is driven off, and the carbonates will be precipitated in the form of a whitish or grayish sediment of the consistency of mud. If these precipitates are not mixed with impurities, they may be washed out of the boiler after it has been allowed to cool; but if there is oil, organic matter, or sulphate of lime, the deposits are likely to become hard. They may readily be drawn off through the bottom blow-out; but if there is much pressure in the boiler, the blow-out valve should be opened only for a very short time. If a considerable amount of water is blown out while the boiler is still very hot, a large part of this precipitation is likely to be baked on to the tubes and interior of the boiler in a manner that defies removal. Short and frequent blowings will accomplish the desired result; for while the boiler is in action these precipitates are more or less in motion, and frequent blowing will keep the boiler clear. Oil and various organic matters rising to the surface can easily be removed by frequently opening the surface blow-out.

Sulphate of Lime. This troublesome salt, like the carbonate of lime, is precipitated with a rise of temperature; and at 280° F. none is left in solution. This sediment is likely to form a hard, adhering scale; but if a little carbonate of soda, or soda ash, is introduced with the feed water, calcium carbonate is precipitated in the form of a white powder which can be readily washed out. The carbonate of soda should be introduced at regular intervals, a portion of it being dissolved in water which can be mixed with the feed in the hot well. As little soda as possible should be used, as it is likely to cause priming and foaming. The hardness of the scale formed by the sulphate of lime depends on the other impurities in the water and on the temperature, and consequently the amount of soda that can safely be used can be determined only by trial. Ammonium chloride, commonly called sal-ammoniac, is sometimes used to break up these lime compounds, but is not always desirable, as it may break up the chlorides if other conditions are right, thus forming free chlorine, which attacks the boiler.

Carbonate of Magnesia. Carbonate of magnesia is seldom found in such large quantities as calcium salts. Like the carbonate of lime, it is precipitated in hot water. If there is any oil or organic matter present, it is likely to form an injurious precipitation.

Iron Salts. Iron salts form a reddish incrustation which is very injurious to boiler plates. Brackish water containing chloride of magnesium is also injurious; for, when heated, the chloride decomposes, forming magnesia and hydrochloric acid, the latter rapidly corroding iron.

A piece of thick scale broken from the plates of the boiler will show a series of layers of various thickness, some of them crystalline and some amorphous. Between these hard layers are frequently found layers of soft or earthy matter.

Nothing definite is known in regard to the loss of heat caused by scale on heating surfaces, for there are too many circumstances to be considered to admit of exact calculation. It has been stated that a layer $\frac{1}{16}$ inch thick in the tubes of multitubular boilers is equivalent to a loss of from 15 to 20 per cent of fuel. The loss increases rapidly with the thickness of the scale. A uniform coating of scale is not nearly so harmful as irregular deposits, for in the latter case the evil effects of overheating are likely to be produced, and overheating will result where it is least suspected.

Prevention. *Chemical Precipitation.* Incrustation may be prevented by precipitating the scale-forming substances before the feed water reaches the boiler, by the introduction of chemical compounds to neutralize the evil effects, or by removing the sediment before it becomes hard.

Removal by Hand. Scale may, of course, be removed by hand from the interior of the boiler, but this is a slow and tedious process. One of the chief objections to removing scale by hand is that the surfaces of the boiler are likely to become abraded by the chipping tools, and this offers excellent opportunity for pitting and local corrosion to set in.

Turbine Tube Cleaners. Scale deposits on the heating surface of boilers give rise to the design and use of many devices for the removal of scale by mechanical means. When dealing with water-tube boilers, as the scale is deposited on the inside of the tube, the device can usually be applied directly on the deposit and the affected surface thoroughly cleaned. The device employed is generally an air-, steam-, or water-driven turbine which, in rotating, swings arms bearing cutters against the scale and interior tube surface. When a fire-tube boiler is to be cleaned of scale, the process is either to scrape it off by hand or to knock it off by inserting a water- or steam-driven rotating turbine hammer on the inside of the tube.

Fig. 39 illustrates a turbine cleaner suitable for water-tube boilers. This cleaner is water driven, the rotating effect being

Fig. 39. "Weinland" Turbine Cleaner
Courtesy of The Lagonda Manufacturing Company, Springfield, Ohio

obtained by the reaction of the blades—shown just within the cylindrical head—when water under pressure is delivered by means of a hose to the opposite end of the head. The cutters are carried on arms which are pivoted on pins carried on the central spindle; thus the cutter arms are thrown outwardly by centrifugal force.

Contraction and Expansion. Scale has sometimes been removed by blowing the boiler off at comparatively high pressure, and then filling it with cold water. This causes a severe contraction of the plates, and is likely to loosen the scale; but it will at the same time cause serious injury to the boiler, and is a practice that should not be tolerated.

Blow-Out Apparatus. After the impurities are deposited in the boiler, the soft precipitates may be removed through the blow-out apparatus. When a boiler is let down it should be cooled slowly, and then the water may be drawn off and the boiler properly washed and scraped. A considerable amount of heat is abstracted from the boiler by frequent blowing off, and this is a matter of direct loss, but the loss is not as great as that caused by the formation of scale.

Boiler Compounds. Water may be purified to a certain extent by passing it through a purifier before allowing it to enter the boiler. The carbonate and sulphate of lime are precipated at the same time that the water is heated. The purifier was referred to under the topic of "Feed-Water Heaters". The use of soda for the neutralization of sulphate of lime has already been spoken of; but various compounds are on the market for overcoming the evil effects of other solids; and it is possible, by an analysis of the feed water, to prescribe a boiler compound that will give satisfactory results. Cheap compounds, sold without reference to the analysis of the feed water, should be avoided. Caustic soda may be used instead of the carbonate but should be used in small quantities. A rapid circulation of the water will prevent the formation of scale, the sediment being swept from the tubes or shell into the mud drum, whence it may be blown off. This is one of the chief advantages claimed for water-tube boilers.

Electrolytic Action. Zinc plates have been used frequently to prevent corrosion and incrustation. The brass fittings are likely to set up a galvanic action with steel plates; but if the zinc is put in, it will be acted upon instead of the iron, which otherwise might be rapidly wasted. It is claimed that this galvanic action prevents the formation of scale by liberating hydrogen at the exposed surfaces. The zinc neutralizes the free acids, by combining with them, and takes the place of iron in causing precipitation of copper salts when present.

BOILER EXPLOSIONS

Safety the First Requisite in Design and Care of Boilers. Safety is one of the first requisites in a steam boiler and must be assured not only by proper design in the beginning but by subsequent care and proper maintenance. Since the explosion of a boiler, especially in a city or a factory, is likely to prove fatal to many people and to cause the destruction of considerable property not only by the explosion itself but also by the fire which almost invariably follows such an occurrence, too great emphasis cannot be laid on the boiler being in proper working condition.

Strictly speaking, failure of a pressure part of a boiler constitutes an explosion, provided the failure is such as to release steam and water from its natural confinement. There are literally hundreds of explosions every year in the United States, the term being used in the sense just given; many of them are of little pecuniary importance though the inconvenience may be considerable. On the other hand, the aggregate of losses sustained by owners during a year by reason of minor explosions is astonishing and quite important. These failures differ in magnitude only from the more serious explosions having the same causes and the same preventives.

Boiler Inspection. All boilers must be carefully tested—land boilers, by the State inspectors; marine boilers, by the United States inspectors. The boilers are carefully examined inside and outside and subjected to a hydraulic pressure test 50 per cent greater than the designed pressure of steam; and if there is the slightest sign of pitting or corrosion, the boiler plates may be drilled and the thickness calipered, the hole being refilled by a proper plug. If a boiler passes inspection, a subsequent explosion will probably be the result of mismanagement, although inspection is not infallible.

The owner of the boiler is usually held liable, in case of explosion, but may protect himself from financial loss by insurance against accident in any of the boiler insurance companies. If so insured, the insurance inspector, as well as the state inspector, examines the boiler; and there is consequently less likelihood of an explosion, for an insurance inspector will naturally be exceedingly careful in the interests of his company.

Nature of Explosions. The damage done by an explosion is due to the energy stored in the hot water, which energy can be calculated by thermodynamic methods. If a boiler contains a large quantity of water at high pressure, and that pressure is suddenly relieved, as would happen in case of rupture, a considerable portion of this large volume of water will be turned instantly into steam and an explosion will result.

When a fracture starts in a boiler plate, the steam escaping through the rent or opening tends to diminish the pressure rapidly within the boiler; and this causes the rapid formation of a large amount of steam. It must be remembered that the water in the boiler at high pressure is held in the form of water only because of the high pressure exerted on it. If this pressure is relieved, large quantities of water will evaporate into steam at once, without the application of further heat. The larger the body of hot water, the greater the disaster. This accounts for the relative safety of water-tube boilers. The division of the water in such a boiler into small masses in different sections, prevents a violent explosion. Should a water tube burn out, probably nothing more serious would happen than the rapid escape of a considerable quantity of steam, which might fill the boiler-room, drive out the attendants, and ultimately cause the destruction of the boiler because of the absence of water and the presence of a hot fire. It would be necessary for several water tubes to burst at once in order to cause serious damage from such an accident. Drums of water-tube boilers may, of course, fail the same as any other shell.

Energy Developed in an Explosion. The available energy in one pound of hot water at 150 pounds absolute pressure and 358° F., is about 42,800 foot-pounds; that is, it is sufficient to move one pound nearly eight miles; and if at 250 pounds pressure, it has sufficient energy to move it nearly twelve miles. This energy may be determined in the following manner: From the table of the properties of saturated steam, given in the back of the book, it is seen that at 150 pounds absolute pressure (approximately 135 gage), the temperature is 358.5° F. The heat above freezing temperature contained in a pound of hot water at this temperature will be 330 B.t.u., equivalent to 330×778, or 256,740 foot-pounds. This represents the total heat energy in one pound of hot water at boiler pressure; but since one pound of steam at atmospheric pressure contains very many more heat units than a pound of water at 150 pounds pressure, it is apparent that only a portion of this water can evaporate into steam, the remaining portion continuing as hot water. About 17 per cent of the total energy will be thus available in vaporizing the water into steam; or, approximately, 42,800 foot-pounds per pound of water will be developed. The remaining heat is contained in the hot water.

A cylindrical boiler 5 feet in diameter and 16 feet long is likely to contain about 6,600 pounds of water and 22 pounds of steam. Neglecting the energy of the steam, which is relatively small, the energy in the water due to its expansion from water at boiler pressure into steam at atmospheric pressure will be approximately $6,600 \times 42,800$ or 282,480,000 foot-pounds, or 141,240 foot-tons.

A marine boiler 13 feet in diameter and 12 feet long would develop approximately twice this energy, which would be about equivalent to the energy developed by the explosion of a ton of gunpowder. The explosion of one boiler on a modern battleship would develop sufficient power to lift the ship completely out of the water. Of course it must be realized that a large part of this energy is not applied to any moving part of the boiler, and considerable is consumed in the destruction of the boiler itself, which leaves but a comparatively small amount to be expended in wrecking the immediate surroundings; but, nevertheless, it is a fact that the energy developed in the explosion of a large boiler is almost beyond the power of comprehension.

Causes of Explosions. *General Discussion of Causes.* Boiler explosions are usually the result of low water, or the presence of grease or scale. The two latter, by preventing the transmission of heat from the water, are likely to cause undue overheating of the furnaces or tubes, which may result in their collapse; these two causes—grease and scale—have been discussed under the subject of "Incrustation".

Low water may be caused by failure of the water glass to indicate properly the amount of water in the boiler, or by failure of the feed pump to work properly.

Safety valves have been known to be rusted to their seats so tightly that they failed to work at the proper time.

It is seldom that a boiler can fail as the result of defective design, for the laws in regard to construction, especially of marine boilers, are very definite. Defective workmanship or material, however, cannot be easily discovered; and it is possible that corrosion or incrustation may take place locally without being readily detected; and, indeed, boiler plates may even be tapped, and their thickness calipered, without discovering small local weaknesses which later may cause disaster. Minute fractures which escaped the inspector's detection have later become serious. Without doubt, however, the majority of explosions can be traced to mismanagement in either care or operation.

Defective Design. If a boiler is improperly set, or if the stays are too small, too few, or cut or bent to clear floats, pipes, etc., danger is likely to result therefrom. All manholes, large handholes, or domes should be strengthened with a reinforcing plate to make up for the material cut out. If the boiler is set too rigidly on its seating, without proper provision for its expansion, trouble will probably follow. A defective water circulation is likely to cause excessive incrustation and unequal expansion of the plating, which is liable to open seams and produce fractures in the plates.

Deterioration. The strength of a boiler is likely to be impaired by fractures, general corrosion, pitting, or grooving, but external corrosion is the cause of many disasters. It proceeds unnoticed in many cases, and rupture may occur when least expected. In the discussion of "Corrosion", it was shown that improper setting of the boiler would cause, or at least aggravate, external corrosion; and that, on account of the close setting of the boiler, it was not easy to get at the plates to examine them. The strength of a boiler originally sufficient to sustain high pressure may become suddenly reduced by overheating or overstressing, either of which weakens the plates. Overheating may be caused by poor circulation, lack of water, or the accumulation of sediment or scale. Overstressing is caused by sudden cooling and contraction, or equally by sudden expansion. In starting the fire in a Scotch boiler—or, in fact, in any boiler with a large quantity of water—care must be taken that the fire is started slowly, or the boiler, becoming overheated locally, will develop excessive stresses.

Defects of Workmanship. Defective workmanship does not occur so frequently under present conditions as formerly, when many defects used to be produced by the careless punching of plates; but for most boilers, and for all marine boilers at present, punching rivet holes to size is prohibited; the holes are drilled in the solid plate, and the plate edges planed and carefully calked; or are punched small, then reamed or drilled with adjacent sheets tacked in position as when assembled. A rigid inspection of material is required, and there seems little danger of unsatisfactory work. Cheap boilers may, of course, be subject to various defects, but a good boiler should be free from such troubles. Defective material may be used and this may not be readily detected; but careful tests reduce these possibilities to a minimum.

Mismanagement. The pressure in a steam boiler may rise above that at which the safety valve has been set to operate, because of corrosion or overloading of the valve. Stop valves are sometimes placed between the boiler and the safety valve; but this practice should be condemned, as it is possible that the stop valve may be closed when the fireman thinks the safety valve is open to the boiler pressure. If the size or lift of the safety valve is too small, steam may be generated faster than it can escape, in which case the pressure will rise in spite of the safety valve. It has been claimed that the blowing off of the safety valve when the boiler is under excessive pressure may be the cause of starting an explosion; but the reason why this should be so does not seem to be especially clear, and it seems to be improbable, if the opening of the safety valve is sufficient to cause a reduction in pressure. Safety valves have sometimes been loaded down temporarily to prevent leakage at working pressure; but such a practice is little short of criminal. If a safety valve leaks, it should be reground, but under no circumstances should the weight on the lever be altered.

Effect of Sudden Influx of Water on Hot Plates. It is a common idea that when the furnace plates become very hot, perhaps heated to redness, due to a lack of water, and the feed is turned on, a violent explosion is sure to follow. Experiments show that when a piece of wrought iron is heated to redness and plunged into a weight of water three or four times greater than that of the iron, a comparatively small quantity of steam is disengaged. There is no reason to believe that this quantity would be greater if the iron were in the form of a boiler than in the form of a plate. If a small quantity of water should be admitted to the hot plates, the danger would be greater; and, while a boiler under this condition might explode, the comparatively small quantity of water in it would make the resulting danger much less than it would if the boiler were under working conditions.

The following experiments illustrate the action of cold water on hot plates. A boiler 25 feet long and 6 feet in diameter was heated red hot and the feed turned on. No explosion occurred; but the sudden contraction of the overheated plates caused the water to pour out in streams at every seam and rivet hole as far as the fire mark extended. In another instance, the water was almost entirely drawn off while the fires were burning briskly. When the remaining water had been converted into steam and all the fusible plugs melted out, water at the rate of 28 gallons per minute in a series of fine jets was played on the hot plates. Such treatment may ruin a boiler for further service, although the boiler may not explode.

That a tough paper or cloth is easily torn when once a tear is started is a well-known fact. Similarly a boiler plate may be ruptured at slight pressure if a fracture·has been started.

Influence of Position of Fracture on Results of Explosion. The position of the fracture or hole has a great influence on the results. In case a large rent occurs at the top of a cylindrical boiler, the steam and hot water may blow out of the hole; and the boiler, if strongly enough seated to stand the reaction, will remain on its seat. The damage to the boiler would be slight. But if the same rent were situated on the under side of the boiler near the ground or floor, the effect would be very different. The reaction of the escaping steam would probably blow the whole boiler through the roof.

Investigation of Explosion. When an explosion occurs, it should be investigated, not only to fix the responsibility where it belongs, but also to provide for and take means to prevent future disasters. It has been customary to attribute all explosions to low water, since it is an easy way to throw the responsibility from the makers or owners upon the fireman, who, even if living, cannot defend himself. In the investigation of an explosion, the weights, shapes, positions, and directions of the scattered pieces should be noted, so that their original places may be known. The original size and shape of the boiler and of the fittings should be ascertained as accurately as possible. The primary rent may be discovered from comparison and from deductions of the directions taken by the heavier pieces. Light pieces will generally take the direction of the escaping steam, while the heavy parts take an opposite direction—that of the reaction. A careful examination of the pieces, noting the age of fractures, thickness of plates, amount of corrosion, condition of plates, etc., will generally show the cause. A test of the plates will in many cases show a softening or yielding to the pressure and excessive thinness caused by bulging.

Preventive Measures. The means taken to prevent boiler explosions from most of the previously mentioned causes have already been given. It is of primary importance that at the start only a well-designed and well-made boiler should be used. The matter of type is not of so much importance; but it is well to use a water-tube boiler in large cities or in buildings where many people are employed. There are many methods, some of which have been discussed, that are taken to prevent deterioration by corrosion, fracture, etc. Proper setting is of great importance in this matter. Mishaps from mismanagement may be greatly lessened by the employment of licensed attendants. A boiler should never be in the hands of a man who is not thoroughly competent to run it. The most effective method to prevent explosions is the law of the State, compelling regular, thorough inspection and licensed firemen. The inspection by the boiler insurance companies is also an efficient method.

During a period of eleven and one-half years, 70,000 boilers were inspected by boiler insurance companies. It was estimated that there were 140,000 in use during that time. Of the inspected boilers, there were 23 explosions and 50 collapses, resulting in 27 deaths from explosions, and 28 deaths from collapses. The accident rate was 1 in 10,000; and the death rate, 1 in 13,000. The uninsured boilers did not make so good a showing, the death rate being 1 in 5,000 boilers, or nearly 3 times as high as among the insured boilers.

SMOKE PREVENTION

Essence of Cure for Smoke. For a detailed explanation of the principles entering into the subject of smoke prevention the student is referred to the Instruction Paper, "Chemistry of Combustion", and to the several other works intended to cover the topic fully. The natural laws pertaining to the subject have been well-known for many years and, while they have been variously stated by different writers, their substance can be expressed briefly in the following words:

"Any fuel can be burned economically without the creation of smoke, provided sufficient air is mixed with the burning gases at a high enough temperature to maintain combustion, and provided time for the progress of the combustion process is afforded while the temperature is sustained."

This simple statement includes every phase of an otherwise perplexing subject. Every device used for the prevention of smoke either assists in fulfilling some feature of the requirements mentioned above, or it can have no useful purpose toward reducing smoke.

Brief Discussion of Preventive Devices. *Mechanical Stokers, Steam Jets, etc.* The uniform charging of fuel is one of the means of making it simpler in other respects to prevent smoke. It is in this way that mechanical stokers offer the greatest assistance in preventing smoke. The construction of fire-brick arches assist by affording mixing facilities, and by creating high-temperature chambers in which the gases can burn before encountering the comparatively cool surfaces of the boiler. Steam jets aid by intimately mixing the air with the gases, performing this function in a purely mechanical way. The introduction of air, either automatically or manually, over freshly charged fuel, as in hand-fired furnaces, makes it more easily possible for the carbon particles, which would otherwise escape as smoke, to seize their required quota of oxygen.

No Single Cure Entirely Successful. To approach the matter of smoke prevention intelligently requires that a full understanding of materials and fuels shall be available. By merely providing one of the necessary elements of success there is the danger that some equally important requirement may be overlooked. To illustrate this point, it is only necessary to say that it is easily possible to arrange for the admission of entirely too much air into the combustion chamber, with the effect that the temperature of the whole space may be reduced below a desirable point, and then the results may be very unsatisfactory. In other words, enough air is quite desirable, but it is easy to exceed the desirable quantity. Even though such means might solve the smoke problem in one particular instance, the result might still be economically bad.

The construction of fire-brick piers and arches may be carried out to such an extent that serious restrictions to the gases are created, and the available chimney will in that case fail to supply the required amount of air through the fuel bed. There is the possibility, also, that the gain from the use of complicated and expensive arches may be more than offset by the cost of keeping them intact.

Effect of Municipal Regulations. The public, in large cities especially, are demanding that smoke shall be avoided, and in several notable instances, especially in Chicago, Milwaukee, Cleveland, and Detroit, the smoke bureaus of the city governments have educated groups of men who have specialized in the art of smoke prevention. Wherever it becomes obligatory to comply with a city regulation aimed against smoke, the means taken in the community to accomplish the desired end can be explained by the officials of that community. It is well to remember that the means which are successful in one locality are not necessarily so in another. The difference arises from the difference in fuels.

FUELS AND FUEL ECONOMY

HEAT VALUE OF FUELS

There are various kinds of fuel used in steam production, location, cost, and the exigencies of the case being the deciding factors. Usually the kind of fuel is determined upon, and the boiler designed for its use. Sometimes, however, the fuel must be adapted to the boiler.

Coal. Coal is not only the most important fuel, but in many localities the only one available. It is of vegetable origin, being the long-decayed product of ancient forests. Frequently it occurs so mixed with earthy matter as to be of little value; but the supply of good coal is still abundant, and likely to be so for many years to come.

The most important elements in coal are hydrogen, producing 62,000 B.t.u. per pound, and carbon, producing 14,500 B.t.u. per pound. Although several coals may have the same total percentage of combustible material and ash, the heat values may not be the same, because heat value depends upon the amounts of available hydrogen and carbon they contain. The heat value of fuel is determined by chemical analysis, or by calorimetric test, and varies for coals from different localities. Table I is compiled from several sources.

In practice, no fuel delivers results up to its theoretical evaporation value. On account of several losses which are inevitably incurred, all of the available heat of the fuel is not converted into

TABLE I

Analyses and Heat Values of Various Coals

KIND OF COAL	PER CENT OF ASH	B.t.u. PER LB. DRY
Penn. Anthracite, Large....................	5.97	13720
Penn. Anthracite, No. 1 Buckwheat.............	11.60	12100
Penn. Semi-Anthracite....................	11.47	13547
W. Va. Semi-Bituminous, Mine Run.............	5.57	14959
Ala. Bituminous, Mine Run.................	10.70	13628
Ill. Bituminous, Franklin Co., Egg.............	11.43	11727
Ill. Bituminous, Macoupin Co., Mine Run........	12.42	10807
Ind. Bituminous, Brazil Co., Block.............	8.00	13375
Ind. Bituminous, Knox Co., Mine Run...........	9.79	12911
Iowa Bituminous, Lucas Co., Mine Run..........	15.94	11963
Kan. Bituminous, Cherokee Co., Lump..........	12.45	13144
Ky. Bituminous, Hopkins Co., Mine Run........	10.77	13036
Colo. Lignite, Boulder Co....................	9.91	10678
N. Dak. Lignite, McLean, Lump..............	12.11	11036
Tex. Lignite, Wood Co.....................	11.63	10600
Wyo. Lignite, Crook Co....................	8.37	12641

energy in the steam. The admission of too much air into the furnace, either through the doors or through cracks in the setting, reduces the actual evaporation. Improper firing causes considerable loss; and errors in design, construction, or setting of furnaces and boilers all contribute to the losses.

The different kinds of coal are too numerous to be easily named, but in general they may be classified as anthracite or bituminous, commonly called hard or soft, respectively, of which there are various subdivisions.

Anthracite. Anthracite coal consists mainly of carbon, with a small amount of hydrocarbon and considerable ash. Good anthracite is lustrous, hard, and flinty, but breaks up easily under high temperature. It burns with very little flame and smoke and gives an intense heat. It does not ignite so readily as the softer varieties of coal but, once started, the fire requires less attention. It is an excellent fuel where the production of smoke is a decided objection.

Semi-Anthracite. This is a coal between pure anthracite and semi-bituminous. It is not so hard as anthracite and burns more freely. It is not so compact as anthracite and burns with a short flame, the anthracite having practically no flame.

Semi-Bituminous. This is the next softer grade of coal. It burns more freely than either anthracite or semi-anthracite, contains more volatile hydrocarbon, and is a valuable coal for steaming purposes. The ash content is low and its heat value high. It is lustrous and has a very granular fracture.

Bituminous. Bituminous coal forms by far the larger portion of steam coal. It contains a large but varying amount of hydrocarbon or bituminous matter. Unless fired with care, it will produce a considerable amount of smoke and clinkers.

Dry Bituminous. This is a black coal with a resinous luster. It burns freely, and kindles with much less difficulty than the anthracites. It is hard, but is easily splintered. When burning, it gives a moderate amount of flame, with but little smoke, and does not cake. It is found chiefly in Maryland and Virginia.

Caking Bituminous. This contains less carbon and more hydrocarbon than the former class. It is not so black; is more resinous; and, under intense heat, readily forms into a solid, pasty mass. Unless frequently broken up, this pasty mass forms a blanket over the grate, and checks the air supply. Caking bituminous is a valuable coal for the manufacture of gas. It is mined chiefly in the Mississippi Valley.

Cannel. Cannel, or long-flame bituminous coal, produces a considerable quantity of smoke. It is mined chiefly in Pennsylvania, Indiana, and Missouri; and is a free-burning coal, with a strong tendency to cake. It is largely used for open-grate purposes.

Lignite. Lignite, or brown coal, is intermediate between coal and peat. It is made up mostly of carbon, with a large percentage of moisture and some mineral matter. Poor varieties are of little value. Good lignite kindles with ease, and burns freely. It is not a very good fuel, but is used in some localities where other varieties are more expensive. It comes largely from Colorado, Texas, Washington, and the Dakotas.

Peat. This is a form of fuel consisting of decayed roots, tree-trunks, etc., and earthy matter. It is found in swamps and bogs, and has been in process of decomposition a much shorter time than any of the coals. It is cut out in blocks and dried. Peat has a specific gravity of .4 to .5, but it can be compressed to a much greater density. It is necessary that peat should be kept in a dry place, for it will readily absorb moisture.

Coke. Coke is made by driving off by heat the hydrocarbon of bituminous or semi-bituminous coals. It may be made in gas retorts, as a by-product of gas production; or it may be made in coking ovens, the gas being the by-product. The latter form of coke is more valuable as a fuel. If the coal is very moist, or if steam is used in the coking process, as in the manufacture of water gas, the sulphur is burned out. Coke burns without flame, and, with a free supply of air, will make an intensely hot fire.

Charcoal. Charcoal is practically never used for steam fuel, its chief use being for household or manufacturing purposes. It is made by evaporating the volatile matter from wood, either by partial combustion or by heating in retorts. About 50 bushels of charcoal can be obtained from a cord of wood.

Culm. This is a name given to refuse dust at the coal mines, sometimes called slack. It can be bought at the mines at a very low rate; but the cost of transportation prohibits its use except in the immediate vicinity of the mines. On account of its fineness, it cannot be burned on an ordinary grate, and is sometimes blown into the furnace with a sufficient quantity of air, where it burns somewhat like a gas. A grate beneath usually contains a moderate fire, which keeps the culm well ignited and prevents the loss of any particles that might otherwise drop out of the furnace.

Wood. There are two principal divisions of wood—hard wood, which is compact and comparatively heavy, such as oak, ash, and hickory; and soft wood, which is of soft and porous texture and of less specific gravity, such as pine, birch, and poplar. Wood contains considerable moisture, even if left to season in a dry place; and after being thoroughly dried, it will absorb and retain from 10 to 20 per cent of moisture. Kiln-dried wood contains nearly 8000 B.t.u. per pound, while the average wood which contains about 25 per cent of moisture, has a heating value of about 6000 B.t.u.

The chemical composition of different woods is nearly the same, and, pound for pound, one class of wood contains about the same heating value as another. Pine weighs about half as much as oak per cubic foot, and a cord of such wood contains about half the heating value that a cord of oak would contain.

Sawdust and shavings are frequently used as fuel in sawmills and planing mills. This kind of fuel is blown into the furnace by air from a fan, and makes an intense heat. A fine grate at the bottom collects the burning embers, which might otherwise drop into the ash pan. In mills where sawdust and shavings are used, they are a by-product.

Straw. Threshing machines through the West use straw almost entirely for fuel. It gives an intense heat, furnishing 5000 to 6000 heat units per pound; and this is a quick and easy way to get rid of it.

Bagasse. Bagasse is the fibrous portion of the sugar cane left after the juice has been extracted. In the modern process of sugar manufacture, the cane is pressed so tightly that it is ready for fuel without further treating. Under favorable conditions it forms an excellent fuel. The pressed cane is a by-product which must in some way be got rid of. It is usually fed into the furnace through an automatic hopper; or it may be dumped in the fireroom and fed into the furnace by hand. The furnace is constructed of brick, independent of the boilers; and when bagasse is consumed at a high temperature, the oxygen contained in it is nearly sufficient to satisfy the carbon and hydrogen, so that little air from the outside is required. Such material, of course, cannot be fed into an ordinary furnace.

Liquid Fuels. These consist of petroleum and its products, and their use has become quite extensive in the last few years. The field would undoubtedly be wider were there less difficulty in obtaining a regular and constant supply. The greatest quantities of petroleum oil are produced in the United States and Russia. Large quantities are found on the Pacific Coast, especially in Southern California; and in that section of the country, oil is used as fuel to a greater extent than in the East, being largely used on tugboats, ferryboats, and locomotives.

The following, approximately, is the composition of petroleum:

Carbon......................82 to 87 per cent
Hydrogen...................11 to 15 per cent
Oxygen......................$\frac{5}{10}$ to 6 per cent

The theoretical heat value of petroleum is approximately 20,000 B.t.u. per pound, which is nearly half as much again as that of good coal. Oil has a further advantage over coal, in that no unburned fuel necessarily passes through the furnace, and there is no ash—an important item in marine work.

TABLE II

Evaporative Power of Gases

Quantity	Natural Gas	Coal Gas	Water Gas	Producer Gas
Cubic feet of gas..................	1000	1000	1000	1000
Pounds of water evaporated........	893	591	262	115

The composition and specific gravity of petroleums vary considerably, many of the lower grades being unsafe on account of their low flash-point.

Gas. Gas has many advantages over any other kind of fuel. There are four different varieties—natural gas, coal gas, water gas, and producer gas. Natural gas is used largely in the vicinity of Pittsburgh, Buffalo, and some parts of Indiana, both for illuminating and for steam purposes. Where natural gas is plentiful, it is by far the cheapest fuel that can be used.

Coal gas, made by the distillation of coal, and water gas, obtained by the decomposition of steam by incandescent carbon, have been used both for lighting and for fuel; but in most cases these gases may be used to greater economy directly in the cylinder of a gas engine than as fuel under a steam boiler. The same may be said of producer gas, which is made by blowing steam and air through incandescent coal.

The relative values of these gases for evaporation are shown in Table II.

Experiments in Pittsburgh have shown that 1000 cubic feet of natural gas equals 80 to 133 pounds of coal. The coal used in the comparison varied from 12,000 to 13,000 B.t.u. per pound.

The Western Society of Engineers has stated that one pound of good coal is equivalent in heating value to $7\frac{1}{2}$ cubic feet of natural gas.

As in the case of petroleum, the economy of burning gaseous fuels depends upon the locality.

Artificial Fuels. Waste charcoal, coal, or wood sawdust are frequently compressed into briquettes in which pitch or other adhesive substances form the binder. When properly made, they can be stored and handled in a very satisfactory manner, often being of better fuel value than the base fuel which enters into the manufacture. Briquetting has not thus far been extensively resorted to because the natural fuels have been plentiful enough to obviate the necessity of employing the reclaiming of waste fuels which affords the best reason for resorting to this form of fuel manufacture. However, it is certain that for domestic use, at least, briquetted fuel will become increasingly familiar. In this field briquettes offer an ideal fuel, being attended by no new burning difficulties while overcoming the customary disadvantages of dust, smoke, soot, and clinkers, where the natural fuels are unsatisfactory in these particulars.

Pulverized Coal. As a result of extensive progress in cement manufacture where pulverized coal found its first successful large application, the general use of pulverized coal has improved to a large extent in other directions so as to displace gas and oil in special metallurgical furnaces and in connection with steam generation. In the field of steam engineering the installations are thus far relatively few, but the art of using coal in this form for that purpose is now understood in all of its main aspects, while the results prove to be economically good enough to warrant the cost of preparation.

It has been known for many years that pulverized coal could be burned in very much the same way that oil is burned, but a few elements were not fully appreciated as to their importance, thus operating against a wider use of this system of fuel burning.

The steps of main importance where pulverized coal is prepared and burned include the following:

(1) A receiving hopper from which the natural coal is conveyed to a crusher and thence moved to a storage bin.

(2) A magnetic metal removing device to take foreign metal parts out of the coal to be pulverized.

(3) Drying crushed coal to less than 1 per cent of moisture preparatory to pulverizing to a fineness of 85 per cent through a 200-mesh screen.

(4) The mechanical conveyance to a pulverized coal bin and from thence as needed in measured quantities to the burner head.

(5) The introduction of fan-driven air of correct quantity carrying the pulverized coal in suspension into a fire-brick combustion chamber.

(6) Facilities for the precipitation of slag and its removal from the furnace chamber.

(7) Contrivances for adjusting the rates of coal and air delivery and varying the furnace draft so as to carry the burning gases out of the furnace and through the boiler setting.

In connection with all these items, it must be considered that pulverized coal is highly inflammable when air quantities are correct for its combustion and carrying more than 1 per cent of moisture cannot easily be screened or moved mechanically.

BOILER PERFORMANCE

HORSEPOWER OF BOILERS

Boiler Horsepower Unit. The unit which we call boiler horsepower is arbitrary. This unit for boilers has been adopted on the assumption that 30 pounds of steam are required per horsepower per hour for an average engine.

One boiler horsepower is the evaporation of 30 pounds of water per hour, from a temperature of 100° F. into steam at 70 pounds gage pressure. This is practically equivalent to the evaporation of 34½ pounds per hour from and at 212° F.

Significance of Boiler Horsepower. Strictly speaking, the term boiler horsepower is a misnomer, for the factor it is usually intended to represent is not power at all. The reader who understands the exact physical significance of the term *energy* will recognize that boiler horsepower is really a term applied to the amount of energy transfer or absorption, the original source being the energy released by the burning of fuel. Common use fixes the meaning of the phrase so no serious difficulty results.

It is also well to distinguish clearly the difference between boiler horsepower and the still more inexact term *size of a boiler*. The former has to do with something that actually occurs, while the latter refers to the probable ability of the boiler to deliver a performance under average conditions. It is best to use the expression boiler horsepower *rating* in the latter case.

As all boilers do not generate steam at the same pressure and from the same temperature of feed water, it is necessary to reduce the actual evaporation to an equivalent evaporation. Unless this is done, the relative performances of boilers cannot be compared.

For this comparison, the actual evaporation is reduced to the equivalent evaporation from and at 212° F., that is, we suppose the water to be fed at 212° F. and evaporated into steam at 212° F.

Let W be the water actually evaporated in pounds; H, the total heat of steam above 32° F., at actual absolute pressure; T, the temperature of feed water; and w, the equivalent evaporation from and at 212° F.

Since 970.4* B.t.u. are necessary to evaporate one pound of water from and at 212° F., the equivalent evaporation may be found from the formula

$$W(H+32-T)=970.4w$$

or

$$w=\frac{W(H+32-T)}{970.4}$$

Then the horsepower of the boiler is

$$\text{h. p. } =\frac{w}{34.5}$$

The above method is considerably shortened by substituting for the quantity $\dfrac{H+32-T}{970.4}$, the number found in Table III, which corresponds to the actual feed-water temperature and steam pressure.

For example, a boiler is required to furnish 2100 pounds of steam per hour. If the gage pressure is 80 pounds, and the feed water enters at 50° F., what is the equivalent evaporation, and what is the horsepower?

From Table III, the factor for 80 pounds pressure and 50° F. is 1.2028. Then the equivalent evaporation would be 1.2028×2100, or 2525.9 pounds; and $\dfrac{2525.9}{34.5}$ equals 73 (approximate) horsepower.

---

*This value is taken from Marks and Davis' "Steam Tables and Diagrams", now commonly accepted (1918).

TABLE III

Factors of Evaporation

Taken with permission from Marks and Davis' "Steam Tables and Diagrams", published by Longmans, Green and Company

Feed Temperature Degrees Fahrenheit	Steam Pressure by Gage															
	50	60	70	80	90	100	110	120	130	140	150	160	170	180	190	200
32	1.2143	1.2170	1.2194	1.2215	1.2233	1.2251	1.2265	1.2280	1.2292	1.2304	1.2314	1.2323	1.2333	1.2342	1.2350	1.2364
40	1.2060	1.2087	1.2111	1.2131	1.2150	1.2168	1.2181	1.2196	1.2209	1.2221	1.2231	1.2241	1.2250	1.2259	1.2267	1.2274
50	1.1957	1.1984	1.2008	1.2028	1.2047	1.2065	1.2079	1.2093	1.2106	1.2117	1.2128	1.2137	1.2147	1.2156	1.2164	1.2171
60	1.1854	1.1881	1.1905	1.1925	1.1944	1.1961	1.1976	1.1990	1.2003	1.2014	1.2025	1.2034	1.2044	1.2053	1.2061	1.2068
70	1.1751	1.1778	1.1802	1.1822	1.1841	1.1859	1.1873	1.1887	1.1900	1.1911	1.1922	1.1931	1.1941	1.1950	1.1958	1.1965
80	1.1648	1.1675	1.1699	1.1720	1.1738	1.1756	1.1770	1.1785	1.1795	1.1809	1.1819	1.1828	1.1838	1.1847	1.1855	1.1863
90	1.1545	1.1572	1.1596	1.1617	1.1636	1.1653	1.1668	1.1682	1.1695	1.1706	1.1717	1.1725	1.1735	1.1744	1.1752	1.1760
100	1.1443	1.1470	1.1493	1.1514	1.1533	1.1550	1.1565	1.1579	1.1592	1.1603	1.1614	1.1623	1.1633	1.1642	1.1650	1.1657
110	1.1340	1.1367	1.1391	1.1411	1.1430	1.1448	1.1462	1.1477	1.1489	1.1500	1.1511	1.1520	1.1530	1.1539	1.1547	1.1554
120	1.1237	1.1264	1.1288	1.1309	1.1327	1.1345	1.1359	1.1374	1.1386	1.1398	1.1408	1.1418	1.1427	1.1436	1.1444	1.1452
130	1.1134	1.1161	1.1185	1.1206	1.1225	1.1242	1.1257	1.1271	1.1284	1.1295	1.1305	1.1315	1.1324	1.1333	1.1341	1.1349
140	1.1031	1.1058	1.1082	1.1103	1.1122	1.1139	1.1154	1.1168	1.1181	1.1192	1.1203	1.1212	1.1221	1.1230	1.1239	1.1246
150	1.0928	1.0955	1.0979	1.1000	1.1019	1.1036	1.1051	1.1065	1.1078	1.1089	1.1099	1.1109	1.1118	1.1127	1.1136	1.1143
160	1.0825	1.0852	1.0876	1.0898	1.0916	1.0933	1.0948	1.0962	1.0975	1.0986	1.0997	1.1006	1.1015	1.1024	1.1033	1.1040
170	1.0722	1.0749	1.0773	1.0794	1.0813	1.0830	1.0845	1.0859	1.0872	1.0883	1.0893	1.0903	1.0912	1.0921	1.0930	1.0937
180	1.0619	1.0646	1.0670	1.0691	1.0709	1.0727	1.0741	1.0756	1.0768	1.0780	1.0790	1.0800	1.0809	1.0818	1.0826	1.0834
190	1.0516	1.0543	1.0567	1.0587	1.0606	1.0624	1.0638	1.0653	1.0665	1.0676	1.0687	1.0696	1.0706	1.0715	1.0723	1.0730
200	1.0412	1.0439	1.0463	1.0484	1.0503	1.0520	1.0535	1.0549	1.0562	1.0573	1.0584	1.0593	1.0602	1.0611	1.0620	1.0627
210	1.0309	1.0336	1.0360	1.0380	1.0399	1.0417	1.0441	1.0446	1.0458	1.0469	1.0480	1.0489	1.0499	1.0508	1.0516	1.0523

Measurement of Moisture in Steam. Steam from a boiler is generally accompanied by more or less moisture. This, being mechanically suspended in the steam, cannot readily be measured without the use of special apparatus. An instrument by means of which the percentage of moisture in steam can be determined is generally called a calorimeter. There are several different types of this instrument, only three of which will be described.

Barrel Calorimeter. This was invented by the distinguished engineer, G. A. Hirn, and is not only one of the earliest of these devices, but is by all means the simplest and most inexpensive form of calorimeter in practical use. It is shown in Fig. 40. The essential apparatus consists simply of a barrel holding about 400 pounds of water, and scales for weighing. A pipe, with suitable connections leading from the boiler or steam main, conveys the sample of steam to be tested. This pipe should be provided with a valve, and on the end should be a piece of rubber hose which can be readily inserted in the barrel or removed. The principle of this calorimeter is extremely simple. As steam flows through the pipe, it is con-

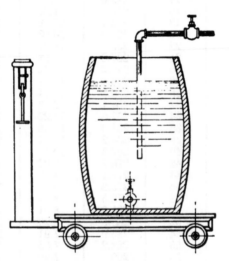

Fig. 40. Barrel Calorimeter

densed by the water in the barrel, and the increase in the weight of the barrel after the test indicates the total amount of moist steam condensed, while the rise in temperature of the water in the barrel is an exact measure of the quantity of heat obtained from this moist steam.

Table IV gives the number of B.t.u. in dry steam and hot water at various temperatures and pressures; and with this data and the previously mentioned observations made in the barrel, the percentage of steam and moisture can be readily determined.

The sampling pipe usually projects into the steam main a few inches, the end being perforated so that the sample will be drawn from a point near the middle of the pipe. An agitator should be

TABLE IV
Properties of Saturated Steam

Taken with permission from Marks and Davis' "Steam Tables and Diagrams", published by Longmans, Green and Company.

Pressure Pounds Absolute	Temperature Degrees F.	Specific Volume Cu. Ft. per Lb.	Heat of the Liquid B. T. U.	Latent Heat of Evap. B. T. U.	Total Heat of Steam B. T. U.	Pressure Pounds Absolute
2	126.15	173.5	94.0	1021.0	1115.0	2
4	153.01	90.5	120.9	1005.7	1126.5	4
6	170.06	61.89	137.9	995.8	1133.7	6
8	182.86	47.27	150.8	988.2	1139.0	8
10	193.22	38.38	161.1	982.0	1143.1	10
12	201.96	32.36	169.9	976.6	1146.5	12
14	209.55	28.02	177.5	971.9	1149.4	14
*14.7	212.0	.....	.....	970.4	......	14.7
16	216.3	24.79	184.4	967.6	1152.0	16
18	222.4	22.16	190.5	963.7	1154.2	18
20	228.0	20.08	196.1	960.0	1156.2	20
22	233.1	18.37	201.3	956.7	1158.0	22
24	237.8	16.93	206.1	953.5	1159.6	24
26	242.2	15.72	210.6	950.6	1161.2	26
28	246.4	14.67	214.8	947.8	1162.6	28
30	250.3	13.74	218.8	945.1	1163.9	30
32	254.1	12.93	222.6	942.5	1165.1	32
34	257.6	12.22	226.2	940.1	1166.3	34
36	261.0	11.58	229.6	937.7	1167.3	36
38	264.2	11.01	232.9	935.5	1168.4	38
40	267.3	10.49	236.1	933.3	1169.4	40
42	270.2	10.02	239.1	931.2	1170.3	42
44	273.1	9.59	242.0	929.2	1171.2	44
46	275.8	9.20	244.8	927.2	1172.0	46
48	278.5	8.84	247.5	925.3	1172.8	48
50	281.0	8.51	250.1	923.5	1173.6	50
52	283.5	8.20	252.6	921.7	1174.3	52
54	285.9	7.91	255.1	919.9	1175.0	54
56	288.2	7.65	257.5	918.2	1175.7	56
58	290.5	7.40	259.8	916.5	1176.4	58
60	292.7	7.17	262.1	914.9	1177.0	60
62	294.9	6.95	264.3	913.3	1177.6	62
64	297.0	6.75	266.4	911.8	1178.2	64
66	299.0	6.56	268.5	910.2	1178.8	66
68	301.0	6.38	270.6	908.7	1179.3	68
70	302.9	6.20	272.6	907.2	1179.8	70
72	304.8	6.04	274.5	905.8	1180.4	72
74	306.7	5.89	276.5	904.4	1180.9	74
76	308.5	5.74	278.3	903.0	1181.4	76
78	310.3	5.60	280.2	901.7	1181.8	78
80	312.0	5.47	282.0	900.3	1182.3	80
82	313.8	5.34	283.8	899.0	1182.8	82
84	315.4	5.22	285.5	897.7	1183.2	84
86	317.1	5.10	287.2	896.4	1183.6	86
88	318.7	5.00	288.9	895.2	1184.0	88
90	320.3	4.89	290.5	893.9	1184.4	90
92	321.8	4.79	292.1	892.7	1184.8	92
94	323.4	4.69	293.7	891.5	1185.2	94

*Atmospheric pressure. The latent heat value of 970 B.t.u. will be sufficiently accurate for use in this paper.

TABLE IV—Continued

Properties of Saturated Steam

Taken with permission from Marks & Davis' "Steam Tables and Diagrams", published
by Longmans, Green and Company.

Pressure Pounds Absolute	Temperature Degrees F.	Specific Volume Cu. Ft. per Lb.	Heat of the Liquid B.T.U.	Latent Heat of Evap. B.T.U.	Total Heat of Steam B.T.U.	Pressure Pounds Absolute
96	324.9	4.60	295.3	890.3	1185.6	96
98	326.4	4.51	296.8	889.2	1186.0	98
100	327.8	4.43	298.3	888.0	1186.3	100
105	331.4	4.23	302.0	885.2	1187.2	105
110	334.8	4.05	305.5	882.5	1188.0	110
115	338.1	3.88	309.0	879.8	1188.8	115
120	341.3	3.73	312.3	877.2	1189.6	120
125	344.4	3.58	315.5	874.7	1190.3	125
130	347.4	3.45	318.6	872.3	1191.0	130
135	350.3	3.33	321.7	869.9	1191.6	135
140	353.1	3.22	324.6	867.6	1192.2	140
145	355.8	3.11	327.4	865.4	1192.8	145
150	358.5	3.01	330.2	863.2	1193.4	150
155	361.0	2.92	332.9	861.0	1194.0	155
160	363.6	2.83	335.6	858.8	1194.5	160
165	366.0	2.75	338.2	856.8	1195.0	165
170	368.5	2.68	340.7	854.7	1195.4	170
175	370.8	2.60	343.2	852.7	1195.9	175
180	373.1	2.53	345.6	850.8	1196.4	180
190	377.6	2.41	350.4	846.9	1197.3	190
200	381.9	2.29	354.9	843.2	1198.1	200

placed in the barrel, so that the water may be thoroughly stirred
and a uniform temperature maintained during the test.

To test a sample of steam by this method, fill the barrel about
two-thirds full of cold water; place it on platform scales, and carefully note its weight and temperature. The weight of the barrel and
fittings, when empty, should of course be known, so that the weight
of the water alone can be determined. With the hose removed from
the barrel, allow steam to blow through the pipe until it has become
thoroughly heated. If the sampling pipe is long, it should be
wrapped with hair felt or some form of lagging, to prevent condensation during the test. As soon as the pipe line has become thoroughly
heated, plunge the hose into the barrel and allow the steam to blow
through the water until it has become well heated. Shut off the
steam, and carefully note the weight and temperature.

Suppose W is final weight of water in barrel; w is weight of cold
condensing water before steam is turned on; t_1 is temperature of the
cold water; t_2 is temperature of the hot water; and P is absolute

pressure of steam in steam pipe (gage pressure+atmospheric pressure).

From Table IV we find that q is the B.t.u. in one pound of the liquid contents of the moist steam; q_1 the B.t.u. in one pound of the cooling water, before the steam was added; q_2 is the B.t.u. in one pound of this water after the steam has been added; and r is the heat of vaporization corresponding to the absolute pressure—*i. e.*, B.t.u. given up by one pound of steam condensed into water.

If x equals the percentage of dry steam contained in the supply pipe, $1-x$ will represent the amount of priming; $x(W-w)$ equals the total amount of dry steam condensed; and $(1-x)(W-w)$ equals the total amount of moisture brought into the barrel by the moist steam.

If q_1 equals the heat in one pound of cooling water, then q_1w will equal the total heat in the barrel at the beginning.

For the same reason q_2W will equal the total heat after the steam has been condensed, and q_2W-q_1w will equal the total amount of heat gained by the water in the barrel.

If r is the heat of vaporization, then $rx(W-w)$ will equal the B.t.u. contained in the dry steam; and if q is the heat of the liquid corresponding to the same pressure, then $q(1-x)(W-w)$ will equal the B.t.u. contained in the moisture brought over by the steam. It is apparent that the sum of these two quantities will be the total number of B.t.u. brought from the steam main to the water barrel, and must be equal to q_2W-q_1w, the heat gained by the water in the barrel. The solution of this equation will result in a formula which will save some mathematical computations.

That the method may be perfectly clear, let us first consider a numerical example in full.

Example. Find the amount of dry steam and the amount of priming in one pound of moist steam.

Let w equal 455 pounds; W equal 495 pounds; t_1 equal 50° F.; t_2 equal 140° F.; P equal 75 pounds; and from Table IV q equals 277.4; q_1 equals 18; and q_2 equals 108. Then the total heat in the barrel after condensation is equal to

$$(495 \times 108) = 53,460 \text{ B.t.u.}$$

The total heat before condensation was equal to

$$455 \times 18 = 8190 \text{ B.t.u.}$$

Therefore, the heat brought over by the moist steam will be

$$53,460 - 8190 = 45,270 \text{ B.t.u.}$$

Now, from Table IV,

$$q = 277.4 \qquad r = 903.7$$

The heat given up by condensation of the dry steam will then be

$$903.7 \times (495 - 455) \, x = 40x \times 903.7 = 36,148x$$

And the heat of the liquid in the moisture and condensed steam will be

$$40 \times 277.4 = 11,096$$

Making the total heat in the moist steam equal $11,096 \times 36,148x$. Therefore,

$$11,096 + 36,148x = 45,270$$
$$36,148x = 34,174$$
$$x = 0.945$$

That is, every pound of moist steam contains .945 pounds dry steam and .055 pounds moisture; or we may say there was 5.5 per cent of priming.

A formula for the above analysis may be derived by the following algebraic work:

Total heat in bbl. after condensation $= W q_2$

Total heat in bbl. before condensation $= w q_1$

Total heat brought over by steam $= W q_2 - w q_1$

Heat of liquid in condensed steam $= (W - w) q$

Latent heat in dry steam $= x (W - w) r$

Total heat in moist steam $= x (W - w) r + (W - w) q$

Therefore

$$x (W - w) r + (W - w) q = W q_2 - w q_1$$
$$x r (W - w) = W q_2 - w q_1 - W q + w q$$

or, transposing to a more convenient form

$$x = \frac{w (q - q_1) - W (q - q_2)}{r (W - w)}$$

The use of barrel calorimeter is not especially to be commended, for it is liable to error, and a slight discrepancy in the weights or the temperatures may cause a large error in the result. In the above calculations, no allowance is made for loss of heat by radiation.

Separating Calorimeter. This instrument, shown in Fig. 41, consists of a chamber A, into which is led a steam pipe D, bringing a sample of steam from the boiler or steam main. This pipe leads into an enlargement perforated with small holes, or into a chamber A as shown in Fig. 41. The calorimeter separates the moisture from the steam just as a steam separator does; and the exhaust, which is dry steam, passes out of the pipe. P, wherein is inserted a diaphragm containing small orifices, by means of which the quantity of steam flowing out can be calculated by thermodynamic methods. The exhaust steam can, of course, be led to some form of condensing apparatus, if desired, and the amount of condensation found by weighing.

As the steam enters the calorimeter, the moisture is drawn toward the bottom of the chamber. The amount of water collected can readily be read from the gage glass at the side, to which a graduated scale should be attached.

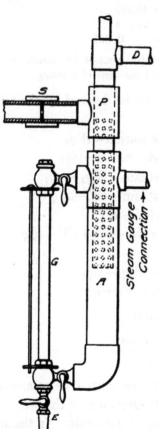

The amount of moisture contained in the steam can be weighed directly by drawing it out of the gage cock E. The amount of dry steam is measured by its flow through the orifices, or by condensation. If W equals weight of steam discharged from the calorimeter, w equals weight of water collected and P equals percentage of priming, then

$$P = \frac{w}{W+w}$$

If only a small quantity of steam is used, an allowance must be made for condensation; but if the instrument is well lagged with hair felt or other suitable material, and a sufficient quantity of steam is used, the error from radiation may be neglected. Steam should be allowed to flow through the instrument until it has become thoroughly heated before beginning the test.

Fig. 41. Separating Calorimeter

Throttling Calorimeter. This was invented by Professor Cecil H. Peabody, and is made with varying constructive details. Fig. 42 shows the general arrangement. The mixture of steam and water from the boiler is taken from the main steam pipe through what is termed a sampling pipe. Various forms of this pipe are made. One arrangement consists of a pipe closed at its inner end, but having numerous holes $\frac{1}{8}$ inch in diameter drilled staggered around the sides. The calorimeter should be placed as close as possible to the main steam pipe, and the gage for indicating the pressure in the main steam pipe should be placed on the latter and near the calorimeter. The gage is sometimes connected to a tee on the pipe leading to the calorimeter; but it is better to have this gage where the velocity of

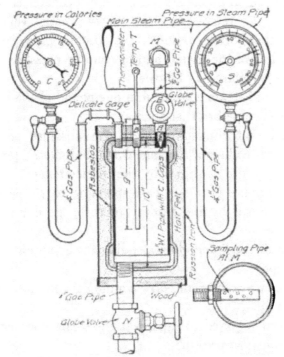

Fig. 42. Diagram of Arrangement of Peabody Throttling Calorimeter

the flowing steam is less. A valve is placed in the pipe to the calorimeter, below which is inserted a nipple A having a small converging orifice D, about 0.2 of an inch in diameter and very carefully made. The object of such an orifice is to determine the weight of steam flowing through the calorimeter, so that an allowance may be made for the loss when testing an engine or boiler, where the net weight used is required. A cup B is screwed into the top, for holding an accurate thermometer. The cup is made of brass, and is filled with oil; but if mercury is used, the cup must be of iron or steel. A delicate gage C, for determining the pressure in the calorimeter, and a pipe and valves at the bottom, complete the apparatus. The valve N is sometimes omitted, and a simple pipe used, as the throttling is best accomplished by use of the valve E or orifice D. All pipes leading to the calorimeter should be well covered with a good nonconductor.

To use the instrument, proceed as follows: Open wide valves E and N, to bring the apparatus to a uniform temperature; then gradually close E until the steam in the calorimeter is superheated; that is, until the temperature as shown by the thermometer is greater than that corresponding to the absolute pressure determined from the reading of the gage C and barometric pressure. The result may now be calculated as follows:

x = weight of steam contained in one pound of the mixture from the main steam pipe or other source;

λ_c = total heat corresponding to the absolute pressure determined from the reading of the gage C and barometric pressure;*

T = temperature as shown by the thermometer;

t_c = temperature of steam corresponding to the absolute pressure as determined by the reading of the gage C and barometric pressure;

q_s = heat of the liquid corresponding to the absolute pressure in the steam pipe;

r_s = heat of evaporation corresponding to the absolute pressure in the steam pipe;

0.48 = heat required to superheat the steam one degree Fahrenheit under constant pressure.

Using the above notations, we find the total heat in one pound superheated steam in calorimeter equals $\lambda_c + 0.48 (T - t_c)$ B.t.u.; and total heat in one pound moist steam in steam main equals $x r_s + q_s$ B.t.u.

These two quantities are equal; and x being the only unknown quantity, the following equation can easily be solved:

$$x = \frac{\lambda_c + 0.48 (T - t_c) - q_s}{r_s}$$

*Some steam tables use H instead of the Greek letter λ (lambda).

Example. Barometric pressure, 14.78 pounds. Absolute pressure in main steam pipe, 87.78 pounds. Absolute pressure in calorimeter, 23.03 pounds. Temperature $(T) = 260°$ F. Then,

$$\lambda_c = 1158.8 \qquad q_s = 288.9$$
$$t_c = 235.45 \qquad r_s = 895.2$$
$$x = \frac{1158.8 + .48\,(260 - 235.45) - 288.9}{895.2} = 0.984 \text{ lb.}$$

Or, in other words, 98.4 per cent of the mixture is steam; or the moisture equals $1 - 0.984$, or 0.016, or 1.6 per cent.

This form of calorimeter is suitable only for cases where the moisture does not exceed three per cent of the mixture. Its principle is based upon the assumption that there is no loss of heat, in which case steam mixed with a small amount of water is superheated when the pressure is reduced by throttling.

BOILER TRIALS

METHOD OF MAKING TEST

Quantities to be Determined. The object of a boiler trial is to determine the quantity and quality of steam the boiler will supply under given conditions, the horsepower of the boiler, the amount of fuel it takes to make the required steam, and the efficiency of operation.

The quantity of steam is taken as the amount of water evaporated, which, of course, is the total amount fed into the boiler during the test, the water level being the same at the beginning and the end less the moisture in the steam.

The quality of the steam can be determined by some form of calorimeter already described; and the efficiency is the ratio of the heat units absorbed by the boiler to the total heat generated in the furnace. The heat utilized in evaporation can be found by multiplying the number of pounds of feed water by the number of heat units required to change the water at the temperature of the feed into steam at gage pressure, making allowance for the moisture in the steam. The heat units supplied can be determined by carefully weighing the fuel used during the test, and deducting the amount of ash and unburned fuel going through the grates, with proper allowance for moisture, multiplying the result by the total heat of combustion of the fuel. The heat of combustion can be obtained by calculation, or by means of a fuel calorimeter.

Conditions Before the Test. Before a test starts, the boiler must be in good working order and fired for some hours before the beginning of the test, so that the brickwork and chimney may be thoroughly heated. Shortly before the test is begun, the fire may be allowed to burn low; and, by reducing the amount of steam taken from the boiler, the pressure can be kept constant. The fire may then be drawn, the grate cleaned, and a new fire quickly started, with wood and fresh coal. Toward the end of the test the fire may be allowed to burn low, and at the close may be drawn and quenched with water, the unburned fuel being allowed for. This method has been supplanted by the "flying" start and stop method, in which beginning and ending conditions are made as nearly alike as possible.

Quantities Which Must be Known. During the boiler trial, observations of temperatures and pressures should be made at the same time, and at about 15-minute intervals. In order to obtain the result of the test, the following must be known:

(1) Amount (in pounds) of coal burned, and number of pounds of ashes left;

(2) Number of pounds of water pumped into boiler;

(3) Temperature of feed water when it enters boiler;

(4) Pressure of steam in boiler;

(5) Quality of steam discharged from boiler—that is, the per cent of moisture in the steam.

(6) The heat value of the fuel.

Weight of Coal. The coal for the furnace can be conveniently weighed in barrels, and may be fired directly from these barrels or dumped on the fireroom floor. The barrels should be carefully weighed when full and empty, and the time recorded, so that there may be no possibility of counting one barrel twice or omitting any. The rate of combustion will be fairly uniform, and the calculations at the times of emptying the barrel will fairly indicate whether or not an error has been made. Any unburned coal should be weighed and the amount subtracted.

Condition of Fire. The condition of the fire should be the same at the beginning and the end. This condition is estimated by the eye; and unless great care is used, an appreciable error is likely to be made. The clinker and ashes should be carefully collected and weighed, and a sample of the ashes analyzed, to obtain the amount of unburned fuel.

Amount of Water Pumped into Boiler. There are several ways of determining the amount of water pumped into the boiler. The best method is to weigh it in tanks or barrels set upon standard scales. There should be two or more barrels of sufficient size, so that the filling and emptying may not be hurried. They should be set high enough to discharge readily into the tank or hot well from which the feed water is drawn. The valves should be large, and should open quickly, so that the emptying may not be delayed. If barrels are used, they should be numbered, and the weight of each accurately noted, so that there may be no mistake in deducting the weight of a barrel from the total weight of barrel and water. When one barrel is being emptied, the other may be filled. The weigher must use care and intelligence; otherwise he may become confused in his records, as in a boiler of considerable size the barrels fill and empty rapidly. At the beginning of the test, the level of the water in the hot well should be recorded, and at the end of the test should be brought to the same mark. If inconvenient to weigh the water, it may be measured by a meter; but if a meter is used, it should be tested and its error determined under like conditions of temperature and pressure. The feed water should be free from air, as otherwise too large a meter reading will be recorded.

The level in the water glass of the boiler should be carefully noted at the beginning and at end of the test. If possible, the level should be constant throughout the test; and if there is any difference between the beginning and the end, due allowance should be made for it.

Temperature of Feed Water. The temperature of the feed water can be taken best by means of a thermometer in a cup filled with oil screwed into the feed pipe near the check valve. If the temperature is nearly constant, readings at 15-minute intervals will suffice; otherwise readings should be taken more frequently.

Steam Pressure. The steam pressure shown by the gage should be as nearly constant as possible throughout the test, and should be practically the same both at the beginning and at the end. Gage readings should be recorded every 15 minutes, and the fireman should see that the pressure is constant. The gage should be tested, and corrected if necessary.

Barometer Readings. Barometric readings should also be taken, two or three being sufficient for a ten-hour run. These readings, in inches, may be made to indicate pounds pressure by multiplying by .491, this being the weight of one cubic inch of mercury. If the trial is on a vertical boiler which furnishes superheated steam because of the heat being in contact with the tubes above the water level, both the pressure gage and the thermometer should be used, so that the amount of superheating can readily be found by subtracting the temperature due to pressure (obtained from the steam tables) from the temperature readings.

Quality of Steam Used. The quality of steam can be readily determined by a calorimeter. If there is sufficient steam space within the boiler, from 1 to 2 per cent priming will generally result. If the steam space is inadequate, there will be more priming. If more than 2 per cent priming is present, the steam will blow white from the gage cocks when opened; if less than 2 per cent, it will appear blue.

Miscellaneous Observations. The above observations are of the more important class, and *must* be taken. In addition to these, it is well to take samples of the flue gas at intervals and from various places in the furnace or chimney, the object being to determine whether there is a sufficient supply of air admitted, or whether there is too much. The draft of the chimney may be measured by means of a U-tube partly filled with water, or by a draft gage.

ABSTRACT OF A. S. M. E. BOILER TEST CODE

It is well to bear in mind that in making the boiler test the utmost care must be used, both in taking observations and in recording them, and in working up the results of the trial. A committee of the American Society of Mechanical Engineers has recommended a code of rules for boiler trials, and the following constitutes an abstract from a voluminous code of rules prepared by this society. The reader is referred to the latest revised code for more complete information on the subject, though it should be remembered that the principles found therein will agree closely with the methods here given.

Preliminaries. 1. In preparing for and conducting trials of steam boilers, the specific object of the proposed trial should be clearly defined and steadily kept in view.

2. Measure and record the dimensions, position, etc., of grate and heating surfaces, flues, and chimneys; proportion of air space in the grate surface; kind of draft, natural or forced.

3. Put the boiler in good condition. Have heating surface clean inside and out; grate bars and sides of furnace free from clinkers; dust and ashes removed from back connections; leaks in masonry stopped; and all obstructions to draft removed. See that the damper will open to full extent, and that it may be closed when desired. Test for leaks in masonry by firing a little smoky fuel and immediately closing damper. The smoke will escape through the leaks if there be any.

4. Have an understanding with the persons in whose interest the test is to be made as to the character of the coal to be used. In all important tests, a sample of coal should be selected for chemical analysis.

5. Establish the correctness of all apparatus used in the test for weighing and measuring. These are: (1) Scales for weighing coal, ashes, and water. (2) Tanks or water meters for measuring water. Water meters, as a rule, should only be used as a check on other measurements. For accurate work the water should be weighed or measured in a tank. (3) Thermometers and pyrometers for taking temperatures of air, steam, feed water, waste gases, etc. (4) Pressure gages, draft gages, etc.

6. Before beginning a test, the boiler and chimney should be thoroughly heated to their usual working temperature. If the boiler is new, it should be in continuous use at least a week before testing in order to dry the mortar thoroughly and heat the walls.

7. Before beginning a test, the boiler and connections should be free from leaks, and all water connections, including blow and extra feed pipes, should be disconnected or stopped with blank flanges, except the particular pipe through which water is to be fed to the boiler during the trial. In locations where the reliability of the power is so important that an extra feed pipe must be kept in position and, in general, when, for any other reason, water pipes other than the feed pipes cannot be disconnected, such pipes may be drilled so as to leave openings in their lower sides, which should be kept open throughout the test as a means

of detecting leaks or accidental or unauthorized opening **of** valves.   During the test the blow-off pipe should remain **exposed**.

If an injector is used, it must receive steam directly from the boiler being tested, and not from a steam pipe or from any other boiler.

See that the steam pipe is so arranged that water of condensation cannot run back into the boiler. If the steam pipe has such an inclination that the water of condensation from any portion of the steam-pipe system may run back into the boiler, it must be trapped so as to prevent this water from getting into the boiler without being measured.

8.   A test should last at least ten hours of continuous running, and twenty-four hours whenever practicable.

9.   The conditions of the boiler and furnace in all respects should be, as nearly as possible, the same at the end as at the beginning of the test.   The steam pressure should be the same, the water level the same, the fire upon the grates should be the same in quantity and condition, and the walls, flues, etc., should be of the same temperature.

Method of Starting and Stopping a Test.   To secure as near an approximation to exact uniformity as possible in conditions of the fire and in temperatures of the walls and flues, the following methods of starting and stopping a test should be adopted.

10. *Standard Method.*   Steam being raised to the working pressure, remove rapidly all the fire from the grate, close the damper, clean the ash pit, and as quickly as possible start a new fire with weighed wood and coal, noting the time of starting the test and the height of the water level while the water is in a quiescent state, just before lighting the fire.

At the end of the test, remove the whole fire, clean the grates and ash pit, and note the water level when the water is in a quiescent state; record the time of hauling the fire as the end of the test.   The water level should be as nearly as possible the same as at the beginning of the test. If it is not the same, a correction should be made by computation, and not by operating pump after test is completed.   It will generally be necessary for a time to regulate the discharge of steam from the boiler tested by means of the stop valve, while fires are being hauled at the beginning and at the end of the test, in order to keep the steam pressure in the boiler at those times up to the average during the test.

11. *Alternate Method.* Instead of the Standard method above described, the following may be employed where local conditions render it necessary.

At the regular time for slicing and cleaning fires, have them burned rather low, as is usual before cleaning, and then thoroughly cleaned; note the amount of coal left on the grate as nearly as it can be estimated; note the pressure of steam and the height of the water level—which should be at the medium height to be carried throughout the test—at the same time; and note this time as the time of starting the test. Fresh coal, which has been weighed, should now be fired. The ash pits should be thoroughly cleaned at once after starting. Before the end of the test the fires should be burned low, just as before the start, and the fires cleaned in such a manner as to leave the same amount of fire, and in the same condition, on the grates as at the start. The water level and steam pressure should be brought to the same point as at the start, and the time of the ending of the test should be noted just before fresh coal is fired.

Keep Conditions Uniform. 12. The boiler should be run continuously, without stopping for mealtimes or for rise or fall of pressure of steam due to change of demand for steam. The draft, being adjusted to the rate of evaporation or combustion desired before the test is begun, should be kept uniform during the test by means of the damper.

If the boiler is not connected to the same steam pipe with other boilers, an extra outlet for steam with valve in same should be provided, so that in case the pressure should rise to that at which the safety valve is set, it may be reduced to the desired point by opening the extra outlet without checking the fires.

If the boiler is connected to a main steam pipe with other boilers, the safety valve on the boiler being tested should be set a few pounds higher than those of the other boilers, so that in case of a rise in pressure the other boilers may blow off and the pressure be reduced by closing their dampers, allowing the damper of the boiler being tested to remain open, and firing as usual.

All conditions, such as force of draft, pressure of steam, and height of water, should be kept as nearly uniform as possible. The time of cleaning the fires will depend upon the character of the fuel, the rapidity of combustion, and the kind of grates. When very good coal is used, and the combustion is not too rapid, a ten-hour test may be run without any cleaning of the grates other than just before the beginning and just before the end of the test. But in case the grates have to be cleaned during the test, the intervals between one cleaning and another should be uniform.

Keeping the Records. 13. The coal should be weighed and delivered to the fireman in equal portions, each sufficient for about one hour's run, and a fresh portion should not be delivered until the previous one has all been fired. The time required to consume each portion should be noted, the time being recorded at the instant of firing the first of each new portion. It is desirable that at the same time the amount of water fed into the boiler be accurately noted and recorded, including the height of the water in the boiler and the average pressure of steam and temperature of feed during the time. By thus recording the amount of water evaporated by successive portions of coal, the record of the test may be divided into several divisions, if desired, at the end of the test, to discover the degree of uniformity of combustion, evaporation, and economy at different stages of the test.

Priming Tests. 14. In all tests in which accuracy of results is important, calorimeter tests should be made of the percentage of moisture in the steam, or of the degree of superheating. At least ten such tests should be made during the trial of the boiler, or as many as may be needed to reduce the probable average error to less than one per cent. The final records of the boiler test should be corrected according to the average results of the calorimeter tests.

On account of the difficulty of securing accuracy in these tests, the greatest care should be taken in the measurements of weights and temperatures. The thermometers should be accurate within a tenth of a degree; and the scales on which the water is weighed, to within one-hundredth of a pound.

Selecting Coal for Analysis. 15. As each fresh portion of coal is taken from the coal pocket, a representative shovelful should be selected from it and placed in a barrel or box, to be kept until the end of the trial, for analysis. The samples should then be thoroughly mixed and broken. This sample should be put in a pile and carefully quartered. One quarter may then be put in another pile, and the process repeated until five or six pounds remain. One portion of this sample is to be used for the determination of the moisture and heating value, the other, for chemical analysis.

Miscellaneous Conditions. 16. The ashes should be weighed dry, and a sample frequently taken to show the amount of combustible material passing through the grate. To get a representative ash sample, the ash pile should be quartered as required for the coal.

17. The quality of the fuel should be determined by analysis.

18. The analysis of the flue gases is an especially valuable method of determining the relative value of different methods of firing or of different kinds of furnaces. Great care should be taken to procure average samples, since the combustion of the gases may vary at different points in the flue; and as the combustion of flue gas is liable to vary from minute to minute, the sample of gas should be drawn through a considerable period of time.

19. It is desirable to have a uniform system of determining and recording the quantity of smoke produced. This is usually expressed in percentages, depending upon the judgment of the observer.

20. In tests for the purpose of scientific research in which the determination of all variables is desirable, certain observations should be made which in general are not necessary—such as the measurement of air supply, the determination of its moisture, the determination of the heat loss by radiation, the infiltration of air through the setting, etc.—but as these determinations are rarely undertaken, no definite instructions are here given.

21. The following two methods of defining and calculating the efficiency of the boiler are recommended:

(1) $\text{Efficiency of boiler} = \dfrac{\text{Heat absorbed per lb. of combustible}}{\text{Calorific value of 1 lb. of combustible}}$

(2) $\text{Efficiency of boiler and grate} = \dfrac{\text{Heat absorbed per lb. of coal}}{\text{Calorific value of 1 lb. of coal}}$

The first of these is the one usually adopted.

22. An approximate statement of the distribution of the heating value of the coal among the several items of heat utilized may be included in the report of a test when analyses of the fuel and chimney gases have been made.

Record of the Test. 23. The data and results of the trial should be recorded in a systematic manner, according either to Table I (see Vol. XXI, Transactions of the American Society of Mechanical Engineers), or according to the following tabular matter (Table II), taken from those "Transactions".

Data and Results of Evaporative Test

Arranged in accordance with the short form advised by the Boiler Test Committee of the American Society of Mechanical Engineers, Code of 1899:

Made by..........................on.............boiler, at.............
    To determine..
Kind of fuel..
Kind of furnace...
Method of starting and stopping the test (*Standard* or *Alternate*, Arts. X and XI, Code)
Grate surface..sq. ft.
Water-heating surface..sq. ft.
Superheating surface...sq. ft.

Total Quantities

1. Date of trial..
2. Duration of trial..hours
3. Weight of coal as fired....................................lb.
4. Percentage of moisture in coal.....:.....................per cent
5. Total weight of dry coal consumed........................lb.
6. Total ash and refuse.....................................lb.
7. Percentage of ash and refuse in dry coal................per cent
8. Total weight of water fed to boiler......................lb.
9. Water actually evaporated, corrected for moisture or super-heat in steam......................................lb.
10. Equivalent water evaporated into dry steam from and at 212° F...lb.

Hourly Quantities

11. Dry coal consumed per hour...............................lb.
12. Dry coal per square foot of grate surface per hour....lb.
13. Water evaporated per hour corrected for quality of steam...lb.
14. Equivalent evaporation per hour from and at 212° F..lb.
15. Equivalent evaporation per hour from and at 212° F. per square foot of water-heating surface...........lb.

Average Pressures, Temperatures, Etc.

16. Steam pressure by gage..........................lb. per sq. in.
17. Temperature of feed water entering boiler..........degrees
18. Temperature of escaping gases from boiler..........degrees
19. Force of draft between damper and boiler..........in. of water
20. Percentage of moisture in steam, or number of degrees superheating................................per cent or degree

Horsepower

21. Horsepower developed (item $14 \div 34\frac{1}{2}$)...................h. p.
22. Builder's rated horsepower...........................h. p.
23. Percentage of builder's rated horsepower developed.......per cent

Economic Results

24. Water apparently evaporated under actual conditions per pound of coal as fired (item $8 \div$ item 3)..................lb.
25. Equivalent evaporation from and at 212° F. per pound of coal as fired (item $10 \div$ item 3).............................lb.
26. Equivalent evaporation from and at 212° F. per pound of dry coal (item $10 \div$ item 5).................................lb.
27. Equivalent evaporation from and at 212° F. per pound of combustible [item $10 \div$ (item 5 − item 6)]...................lb.

If items 25, 26, and 27 are not corrected for quality of steam, the fact should be stated.

Efficiency

28. Calorific value of the dry coal per pound..................B.t.u.
29. Calorific value of the combustible per pound...............B.t.u.
30. Efficiency of boiler (based on combustible)................per cent
31. Efficiency of boiler, including grate (based on dry coal)......per cent

Cost of Evaporation

32. Cost of coal per ton of —— lb. delivered in boiler room.....$
33. Cost of coal required for evaporating 1,000 lb. of water from and at 212° F......................................

A log of the test should be kept on properly prepared blanks containing headings as follows:

Time	Pressures			Temperatures					Fuel		Feed Water		
	Barometer	Steam Gage	Draft Gage	External Air	Boiler Room	Flue	Feed Water	Steam	Time	Pounds	Time	Lb. or cu. ft.	

INDEX

INDEX

F

G

Also From Merchant Books

The Dynamics Of Particles	Webster, Arthur, Gordon
The Recovery Of Volatile Solvents	Robinson, Clark Shove
Iron Bacteria - Organisms And Their Identification	Ellis, David
Protozoa Microbiology And Guide To Microscopic Identification	Minchin, E. A.
Diazo Chemistry - Synthesis and Reactions	Cain, John Cannell
Dielectric Phenomena In High Voltage Engineering	Peek, Jr. F. W.
The Thermionic Vacuum Tube And Its Applications	Van Der Bijl, Hendrik J.
Transient Electric Phenomena and Oscillations	Steinmetz, Charles Proteus
Conduction of Electricity Through Gases	Thomson, J. J.
Modern Toolmaking Methods - A Treatise	Jones, Franklin D.
Model Engineering - A Guide to Model Workshop Practice	Greenly, Henry
Five Hundred And Seven Mechanical Movements	Brown, Henry T.
Nikola Tesla: His Inventions, Researches and Writings	Martin, Thomas, Commerford
Four Lectures On Relativity And Space	Steinmetz, Charles Proteus
Electromagnets: Their Design and Construction	Mansfield, A. N.
American Telegraphy - Encyclopedia of the Telegraph	Maver Jr., William
Radio-Telephony For Everyone	Cockaday, Laurence M
The Complete Practical Machinist	Rose, Joshua
Recovering Precious Metals - A Complete Workshop Treatise	George, Gee E.
The Manufacture of Metallic Alloys	Fesquet, A. A.
Electroplating And Electrorefining Of Metals	Watt, Alexander
The Magnetic Circuit - Electromagnetic Engineering	Karapetoff, Vladimir
Pole And Tower Lines For Electric Power Transmission	Coombs, R. D.
Underground Electric Transmission And Distribution	Meyer, E. B.
Worm And Spiral Gearing	Halsey, Frederick A.
Perfumes And Their Preparation	Askinson, George William
Design And Construction Of Electric Furnaces	Borchers, Wilhelm
Yeasts: Characteristics and Identification	Guilliermond, Alexandre
Limes Hydraulic Cements And Mortars	Gillmore, Quincy A.
Theory And Calculation Of Electric Circuits	Steinmetz, Charles Proteus
Industrial Nitrogen Compounds And Explosives	Martin, Geoffrey
Centrifugal Pumps	Cameron, J. W.
Graphical And Mechanical Computation	Lipka, Joseph
Distillation Principles And Processes	Young, Sydney
Electric Arcs - Between Different Electrodes	Child, Clement D.
Physical Optics – Illustrated	Glazebrook, R. T.
Elements Of Projective Geometry	Cremona, Luigi
Concerning The Nature Of Things – Illustrated	Bragg, William
Engineering Construction - Tunneling, And Road Building	Shields, J. E.
The Emission Of Electricity From Hot Bodies	Richardson, O. W.
A Course In Mathematical Analysis - Volume I	Goursat, Edouard
The Electrical Properties Of Flames And Of Incandescent Solids	Wilson, Harold A.
The Gas Turbine - Theory And Practice	Davey, Norman
A Course Of Pure Mathematics	Hardy, G. H.
Coordinate Geometry	Fine, Henry Burchard
A Sequel To The First Six Books Of The Elements Of Euclid	Casey, John